CIM

PRACTICE & REVISION

New syllabus

Stage 1

Marketing Fundamentals

BPP Publishing
September 2002

First edition September 2002

ISBN 0 7517 4882 X

British Library Cataloguing-in-Publication Data
A catalogue record for this book
is available from the British Library

Published by

BPP Publishing Limited
Aldine House, Aldine Place
London W12 8AW

www.bpp.com

in association with
Nottingham Business School
Nottingham Trent University

Printed in Great Britain by W M Print
45-47 Frederick Street
Walsall, West Midlands
WS2 9NE

We are grateful to the Chartered Institute of Marketing for permission to
reproduce the syllabus, Specimen Paper and past examination questions. The
suggested solutions to past examination questions have been prepared by BPP
Publishing Limited.

Author
Neil Towers

Series editor
Paul Brittain, Senior Lecturer in Marketing and Retailing at Nottingham
Business School, Nottingham Trent University

CONTENTS

BPP PUBLISHING

Introduction

The headings indicate the main topics of questions, but questions often cover several different topics.

Questions marked by * are **key questions** which we think you must attempt in order to pass the exam. Tick them off on this list as you complete them.

BPP PUBLISHING

ABOUT THIS KIT

You're taking your professional CIM exams in December 2002 or June 2003. You're under time pressure to get your exam revision done and you want to pass first time. Could you make better use of your time? Are you sure that your revision is really relevant to the exam you will be facing?

If you use this BPP Practice & Revision Kit you can be sure that the time you spend revising and practising questions is time well spent.

The BPP Practice & Revision Kit: Marketing in Practice

The BPP Practice & Revision Kit, produced in association with Nottingham Trent University Business School, has been specifically written for the new Stage 1 syllabus by an expert in marketing education, Neil Towers.

- We give you a **comprehensive question and answer checklist** so you can see at a glance which are the key questions that we think you should attempt in order to pass the exam, what the mark and time allocations are and when they were set (where this is relevant)

- We offer **vital guidance** on revision, question practice and exam technique

- We show you the new **syllabus** examinable in December 2002 and June 2003. We **analyse papers** set so far, with summaries of the examiner's comments

- We give you a **comprehensive question bank** containing:
  - *Short questions* to jog your memory
  - *Exam-standard questions*
  - *Full suggested answers* - with summaries of the examiner's comments.

- A **Test Paper** consisting of the Specimen Paper, again with full suggested answers, for you to attempt just before the real thing

- A **Topic Index** for ready reference

The Study Text: further help from BPP

The other vital part of BPP's study package is the Study Text. The Study Text features:

- Structured, methodical syllabus coverage

- Lots of case examples from real businesses throughout, to show you how the theory applies in real life

- Action programmes and quizzes so that you can test that you've mastered the theory

- A question and answer bank

- Key concepts and full index

There's an order form at the back of this Kit.

Help us to help you

Your feedback will help us improve our study package. Please complete and return the Review Form at the end of this Kit; you will be entered automatically in a Free Prize Draw.

BPP Publishing
September 2002

To learn more about what BPP has to offer, visit our website: www.bpp.com

---

REVISION

This is a very important time as you approach the exam. You must remember three things.

> Use time sensibly
>
> Set realistic goals
>
> Believe in yourself

Use time sensibly

1   **How much study time do you have**? Remember that you must EAT, SLEEP, and of course, RELAX.

2   **How will you split that available time between each subject?** What are your weaker subjects? They need more time.

3   **What is your learning style?** AM/PM? Little and often/long sessions? Evenings/ weekends?

4   **Are you taking regular breaks?** Most people absorb more if they do not attempt to study for long uninterrupted periods of time. A five minute break every hour (to make coffee, watch the news headlines) can make all the difference.

5   **Do you have quality study time?** Unplug the phone. Let everybody know that you're studying and shouldn't be disturbed.

Set realistic goals

1   Have you set a **clearly defined objective** for each study period?

2   Is the objective **achievable**?

3   Will you **stick to your plan**? Will you make up for any **lost time**?

4   Are you **rewarding yourself** for your hard work?

5   Are you leading a **healthy lifestyle**?

Believe in yourself

Are you cultivating the right attitude of mind? There is absolutely no reason why you should not pass this exam if you adopt the correct approach.

- **Be confident** - you've passed exams before, you can pass them again

- **Be calm** - plenty of adrenaline but no panicking

- **Be focused** - commit yourself to passing the exam

QUESTION PRACTICE

Do not simply open this Kit and, beginning with question 1, start attempting all of the questions. You first need to ask yourself three questions.

> Am I ready to answer questions?
> Do I know which questions to do first?
> How should I use this Kit?

Am I ready to answer questions?

1   Check that you are familiar with the material by attempting the **short questions** for a particular syllabus area.

2   If you are happy, you can go ahead and start answering the questions in the Question Bank. If not, go back to your BPP Study Text and revise first.

How should I use this Kit?

1   Once you are confident with the short questions you should try as many as possible of the exam-standard questions; at the very least you should attempt the **key questions,** which are highlighted in the **question and answer checklist/index** at the front of the Kit.

2   Try to **produce full answers under timed conditions**; you are practising exam technique as much as knowledge recall here. Don't look at the answer, your BPP Study Text or your notes for any help at all.

3   **Mark your answers to the questions as if you were the examiner**. Only give yourself marks for what you have written, not for what you meant to put down, or would have put down if you had had more time. If you did badly, try another question.

4   Take note of the advice given and any **comments by the examiner**.

5   When you have practised the whole syllabus, go back to the areas you had problems with and **practise further questions**.

6   Finally, when you think you really understand the entire subject, **attempt the test paper** at the end of the Kit. Sit the paper under strict exam conditions, so that you gain experience of selecting and sequencing your questions, and managing your time, as well as of writing answers.

EXAM TECHNIQUE

Passing professional examinations is half about having the knowledge, and half about doing yourself full justice in the examination. You must have the right approach to two things.

> The day of the exam
> Your time in the exam hall

The day of the exam

1   Set at least one alarm (or get an alarm call) for a morning exam.

2   Have something to eat but beware of eating too much; you may feel sleepy if your system is digesting a large meal.

3   Allow plenty of time to get to the exam hall; have your route worked out in advance and listen to news bulletins to check for potential travel problems.

4   Don't forget pens, pencils, rulers, erasers.

5   Put new batteries into your calculator and take a spare set (or a spare calculator).

6   Avoid discussion about the exam with other candidates outside the exam hall.

Your time in the exam hall

1   **Read the instructions (the 'rubric') on the front of the exam paper carefully**

    Check that the exam format hasn't changed. It is surprising how often examiners' reports remark on the number of students who attempt too few - or too many - questions, or who attempt the wrong number of questions from different parts of the paper. Make sure that you are planning to answer the right number of questions.

2   **Select questions carefully**

    Read through the paper once, then quickly jot down key points against each question in a second read through. Select those questions where you could latch on to 'what the question is about' - but remember to check carefully that you have got the right end of the stick before putting pen to paper.

3   **Plan your attack carefully**

    Consider the order in which you are going to tackle questions. It is a good idea to start with your best question to boost your morale and get some easy marks 'in the bag'.

4   **Check the time allocation for each question**

    Each mark carries with it a time allocation of 1.6 minutes (including time for selecting and reading questions). A 20 mark question therefore should be completed in 32 minutes. When time is up, you must go on to the next question or part. Going even one minute over the time allowed brings you a lot closer to failure.

5   **Read the question carefully and plan your answer**

    Read through the question again very carefully when you come to answer it. Plan your answer to ensure that you keep to the point. Two minutes of planning plus eight minutes of writing is virtually certain to earn you more marks than ten minutes of writing.

6 **Produce relevant answers**

Particularly with written answers, make sure you answer the question set, and not the question you would have preferred to have been set.

7 **Gain the easy marks**

Include the obvious if it answers the question and don't try to produce the perfect answer.

Don't get bogged down in small parts of questions. If you find a part of a question difficult, get on with the rest of the question. If you are having problems with something, the chances are that everyone else is too.

8 **Produce an answer in the correct format**

The examiner will state in the requirements the format in which the question should be answered, for example in a report or memorandum.

9 **Follow the examiner's instructions**

You will annoy the examiner if you ignore him or her. The examiner will state whether he or she wishes you to 'discuss', 'comment', 'evaluate' or 'recommend'.

10 **Present a tidy paper**

Students are penalised for poor presentation and so you should make sure that you write legibly, label diagrams clearly and lay out your work neatly. Markers of scripts each have hundreds of papers to mark; a badly written scrawl is unlikely to receive the same attention as a neat and well laid out paper.

11 **Stay until the end of the exam**

Use any spare time checking and rechecking your script.

12 **Don't worry if you feel you have performed badly in the exam**

It is more than likely that the other candidates will have found the exam difficult too. Don't forget that there is a competitive element in these exams. As soon as you get up to leave the exam hall, forget that exam and think about the next - or, if it is the last one, celebrate!

13 **Don't discuss an exam with other candidates**

This is particularly the case if you still have other exams to sit. Even if you have finished, you should put it out of your mind until the day of the results. Forget about exams and relax!

THE EXAM PAPER

Format of the exam

The exam is based on a case study describing a business situation.

		Number of marks
Part A:	compulsory question relating to the case study	40
Part B:	Three questions from a choice of six relating to the case study (20marks each)	60
		100

Analysis of past papers

Specimen Paper

Part A (compulsory question worth 40 marks)

1   Battery firm is launching a new range of rechargeable batteries.

   (a)   Segmentation
   (b)   New product development
   (c)   Marketing mix for consumer and business markets

Part B (three questions, 20 marks each)

2   Distribution channels
3   Service marketing mix
4   Marketing to different buyers. Social responsibility
5   Marketing plans and budgets
6   Marketing mix in different life cycle stages
7   Branding, relationship marketing and customer retention

This paper forms the Test Paper at the end of this Kit.

June 2002

Part A

1   PIX cinemas – repositioning the brand
   (a)   Marketing services – the problems
   (b)   Adapting the promotional/communications mix for market penetration
   (c)   buyer behaviour and marketing planning

Part B

2   Product life cycle
3   Relationship marketing
4   Distribution and packaging
5   Marketing planning
6   Customer care
7   Marketing research

December 2001

Part A

1   Botswana Telecoms Corp facing challenges
  (a)   Introducing a marketing orientation
  (b)   Services v products
  (c)   Marketing mix elements

Part B

2   Promotional plan and behaviour
3   Product life cycle
4   Information technology
5   Ansoff matrix and distribution
6   Pricing and methods
7   Market research and databases

Examiner's comments.

It was generally felt that candidates have handled this paper well, as the pass rate was higher than the previous session in June. Failures were mainly due to the fact that candidates have problems with the usual following points:

- Misinterpretation of question requirements

- Understanding how to analyse a question

- Preparation and study skills in terms of in-depth understanding of the syllabus

- Reluctance to comply with the question requirements

- Including everything about the subject

- Format and presentation of material. Candidates will need to make sure that they comply with the format instructions and present their material professionally.

- Lack of practical examples

- Poor time management

June 2001

Part A

1   Moorcroft plc report
  (a)   Market research
  (b)   Customer behaviour
  (c)   Communication/promotional mix

Part B

2   Market penetration strategy
3   Product life cycle/services
4   Relationship marketing
5   Pricing policy
6   Marketing orientation
7   Marketing planning process

Examiner's comments

See December 2001 for a summary of the main weaknesses that consistently appear in scripts.

December 2000

Part A

1 Energy power systems report
   (a) Marketing planning process
   (b) Marketing mix elements, consumer and business to business segments
   (c) Communication/promotional mix

Part B

2 Direct marketing/life cycle
3 Databases/relationship marketing
4 Secondary/primary research
5 Customer care: practical approaches
6 New product development/buyer behaviour
7 Services/products/marketing mix

Examiner's comments

As the Senior Examiner for Marketing Fundamentals it has been pleasing to observe that the number of general problems which seem to occur over most of the CIM papers has improved. This report has been written after consultation with the Examining team and most of the points cited are common to many centres.

It was generally felt that candidates seem to have handled this paper much better than the June examination paper. However, there were still a number of usual problems and tutors and students must ensure that they are able to obtain a copy of the Examiner's Report as this always gives very clear indicators and guides for the next examination paper and content.

There were some very good A grades this year, which was a vast improvement from the previous session. However, there were a number of candidates who gained low marks for this paper which generally resulted from problems with their answers for a number of questions.

The failures were mainly due to the fact that candidates have problems with the same points as made in the June 2000 sitting.

June 2000

Part A

1 Interflora customer service report
   (a) Practical approaches to improving customer care
   (b) Extended marketing mix
   (c) Promotional campaign

Part B

2 SWOT analysis and marketing planning
3 Either   (a)   Customer decision making process
   or   (b)   Marketing research report
4 Product life cycle
5 Pricing decisions

6   Information technology and the management of customer orientated culture
7   Either   (a)   Distribution channels
    or   (b)   Marketing channels and distribution

Examiner's comments

Unfortunately, it was generally felt that candidates seemed not to have handled this basic marketing fundamental paper as well as the December examination paper. There were still a number of usual problems and tutors and students must ensure that they are able to obtain a copy of the Examiner's Report as this always gives very clear indicators and guides for the next examination paper and content. It should be noted that these reports and specimen answers are now also published on the web site, thus this should allow both students and tutors ready access to them.

General problems:

- Misinterpretation of question requirements
- Reluctance to comply with the question requirement
- Including everything about the subject
- Format and presentation of material
- Lack of practical examples
- Poor time management

December 1999

Part A

1   New casual footwear
    (a) New product development process
    (b) Information required for a pricing strategy

Part B

2   Either   (a)   Charity marketing information system – design and role
    or   (b)   Consumer attitudes, buying behaviour and decision process
3   Decline stage and marketing mix strategy
4   Packaging for 'grey' market and push/pull promotional techniques
5   Services marketing characteristics and mix
6   Either   (a)   Ansoff matrix and new distribution channels
    or   (b)   Green marketing
7   Presentation and theme park's customer care standards

Examiner's comments

Students did not handle this paper very well. The results were not as good as in June 1999, even though the examiner's comments for that paper gave 'clear indications' of the areas likely to be examined. The main problems arose in the following areas.

- Misinterpretation of question requirements
- Reluctance to comply with the question requirement
- Including everything about the subject
- Format and presentation of material
- Lack of practical examples
- Poor time management

SYLLABUS

Aim

The Marketing Fundamentals module develops a basic knowledge and understanding of marketing, marketing process and the marketing mix. It aims to provide participants with a framework on which to build marketing knowledge and skills through the modules of this Stage, through modules at later Stages and in the workplace.

Participants will not be expected to have any prior knowledge or experience in a marketing role.

Related statements of practice

Bb.2   Contribute to the production of marketing plans and budgets

Db.1   Contribute to the development of products and services

Eb.1   Contribute to the development of pricing policies

Eb.2   Implement pricing policies

Fb.1   Develop effective channels to market

Fb.2   Provide support to channel members

Hb.1   Contribute to planning and budget preparation

Learning outcomes

Participants will be able to:

■   Explain the development of marketing and the ways it can benefit business and organisations.

■   Identify the main steps in, and barriers to, achieving a marketing orientation within the organisation.

■   Explain the context of, and process for, marketing planning and budgeting including related models.

■   Explain the concept of segmentation and the different bases for effective market segmentation.

■   Identify and describe the individual elements and tools of the marketing mix.

■   Identify the basic differences in application of the marketing mix involved in marketing products and services within different marketing contexts.

Knowledge and skill requirements

Element 1: The development of marketing and market orientation (10%)	
1.1	Explain the development of marketing as an exchange process, a philosophy of business, and a managerial function.
1.2	Recognise the contribution of marketing as a means of creating customer value and as a form of competition.
1.3	Appreciate the importance of a market orientation to organisational performance and identify the factors that promote and impede the adoption of a market orientation.
1.4	Explain the role of marketing in co-ordinating organisational resources both within and outside the marketing function.
1.5	Describe the impacts of marketing actions on society and the need for marketers to act in an ethical and socially responsible manner.
1.6	Examine the significance of buyer-seller relationships in marketing and comprehend the role of relationship marketing in facilitating the retention of customers.

Element 2: Marketing planning & budgeting (20%)	
2.1	Explain the importance of the marketing planning process and where it fits into the corporate or organisational planning framework.
2.2	Explain the models that describe the various stages of the marketing planning process.
2.3	Explain the concept of the marketing audit as an appraisal of the external marketing environment and an organisation's internal marketing operations.
2.4	Describe the role of various analytical tools in the marketing auditing process.
2.5	Explain the value of marketing research and information in developing marketing plans.
2.6	Explain the importance of objectives and the influences on, and processes for setting, objectives.
2.7	Explain the concept of market segmentation and distinguish effective bases for segmenting consumer and business-to-business markets.
2.8	Describe the structure of an outline marketing plan and identify its various components.
2.9	Depict the various management structures available for implementing marketing plans, and understand their advantages and disadvantages.
2.10	Examine the factors that affect the setting of marketing budgets.
2.11	Demonstrate and appreciation of the need to monitor and control marketing activities.

Element 3: The marketing mix and related tools (50%)

3.1	Describe the essential elements of targeting and positioning, and the creation of an integrated and coherent marketing mix.
3.2	Describe the wide range of tools and techniques available to marketers to satisfy customer requirements and compete effectively.
3.3	Explain the development of the extended marketing mix concept to include additional components in appropriate contextual settings: product, price, place (distribution), promotion (communications), people, processes, physical evidence and customer service.
3.4	Demonstrate awareness of products as bundles of benefits that deliver customer value and have different characteristics, features and levels.
3.5	Explain and illustrate the product life cycle concept and recognise its effects on marketing mix decisions.
3.6	Explain and illustrate the principles of product policy: branding, product lines, packaging and service support.
3.7	Explain the importance of introducing new products, and describe the processes involved in their development and launch.
3.8	Explore the range of internal and external factors that influence pricing decisions.
3.9	Identify and illustrate a range of different pricing policies and tactics that are adopted by organisations as effective means of competition.
3.10	Define channels of distribution, intermediaries and logistics, and understand the contribution they make to the marketing effort.
3.11	State and explain the factors that influence channel decisions and the selection of alternative distribution channel options, including the effects of new information and communications technology.
3.12	Describe the extensive range of tools that comprise the marketing communications mix, and examine the factors that contribute to its development and implementation.
3.13	Explain the importance of people in marketing and in particular the contribution of staff to effective service delivery.
3.14	Explain the importance of service in satisfying customer requirements and identify the factors that contribute to the delivery of service quality.
3.15	Examine the effects of information and communication technology on the development and implementation of the marketing mix.
3.16	Explain the importance of measuring the effectiveness of the selected marketing effort and instituting appropriate changes where necessary.

Element 4: Marketing in context (20%)	
4.1	Explain the importance of contextual setting in influencing the selection of and emphasis given to marketing mix tools.
4.2	Explain differences in the characteristics of various types of marketing context: FMCG, business-to-business (supply chain), large or capital project-based, services, voluntary and not-for-profit, sales support (e.g. SMEs), and their impact on marketing mix decisions.
4.3	Compare and contrast the marketing activities of organisations that operate and compete in different contextual settings.
4.4	Explain the global dimension in affecting the nature of marketing undertaken by organisations in an international environmental context.
4.5	Explain the existing and potential impacts of the virtual marketplace on the pattern of marketing activities in given contexts.

Question bank

BPP PUBLISHING

SHORT QUESTIONS – DEVELOPMENT OF MARKETING AND MARKET ORIENTATION

1   Write down the CIM definition of marketing.

2   Marketing orientation focuses on:

   A   Manufacturing goods through an efficient production system
   B   Selling goods to satisfy customer demand
   C   Serving consumer demand within an inclusive offering

3   Value is determined by the seller's perspective.

   ☐   True   ☐   False

4   The main factor influencing a society's attitudes and behaviour is _____

5   Relationship marketing is a short term approach to achieving high sales levels

   ☐   True   ☐   False

6   List 5 external environmental influences in consumer buyer behaviour.

7   For the Finance department list *two* activities that have a marketing emphasis.

8   A societal view of marketing promotes the welfare of society as a whole.

   ☐   True   ☐   False

ANSWERS TO SHORT QUESTIONS

1 Marketing is the management process that identifies, anticipates and supplies customer requirements efficiently and profitably.

2 C

3 False

4 Culture

5 False

6 Cultural
Social class
Groups/family
Situational factors
Marketing efforts

7 Market-orientated pricing
Sales flexed life cycle marketing budgets

8 True

1 Social perspective (12/96)   32 mins

The Chairman of the Students' Section of your local branch of the Chartered Institute of Marketing has read an article that contends that most marketing literature is concerned with the functional activities of marketing management. The article contends that this is because the basic purpose of marketing is to satisfy consumers' needs and wants. The article goes on to say that marketing should be viewed from a wider 'social' perspective and suggests that management responsibilities should involve more than the company/ customer interface.

He has asked you, as an active member of the Students' Section, to lead a seminar that discusses this theme at the next meeting.

Prepare notes for this seminar.   **(20 marks)**

2 Socially responsible marketing (12/97)   32 mins

A local radio station has asked the communications consultancy in which you work for advice in planning a programme on 'green marketing' or, more precisely, a socially responsible concept of marketing. Advise them of some of the issues they should cover in this one hour programme.

(20 marks)

3 Orientation (6/98)   32 mins

You are a marketing assistant for a small college of further education, currently experiencing declining numbers of students. You have been in your position for 12 months and you realise that the college is product orientated.

In an effort to communicate the concept of **marketing orientation** you feel that you must write a report to the principal of the college detailing the following.

(a) The difference between product orientation and market orientation, citing examples of each.   (10 marks)

(b) Give the steps involved in establishing a marketing orientation approach.   (5 marks)

(c) Identify the anticipated benefits to the college of introducing such a marketing approach.

(5 marks)

(20 marks)

4 Consumer attitudes (12/99)   32 mins

(a) Explain why marketers are concerned about consumer attitudes and buying behaviour.

(10 marks)

(b) What are the main influences which impact on the consumer's decision process?

(10 marks)

(20 marks)

5 Green marketing (12/99)   32 mins

(a) Write a brief report defining what is meant by the concept of social responsibility and 'green marketing' practices. Use an example to illustrate your thoughts.   (10 marks)

(b) What are the implications of the above, from a marketing perspective, relating to consumers and the marketing mix?   (10 marks)

(20 marks)

6 Relationship marketing (12/00)   32 mins

You are working for a car dealership and are considering the current database of people who have purchased new cars during the last two years.

(a) Explain how this database could be used to help to build relationships with past customers.   (10 marks)

(b) Explain why it is important to consider relationship marketing management for the retention of customers.   (10 marks)

(20 marks)

7 Relationship marketing and loyalty (6/02)   32 mins

(a) Many organisations are considering the life-long value of their customers and are thus trying to retain their loyal customers. Explain the concept of relationship marketing as a strategy for achieving this goal.   (12 marks)

(b) With reference to an example, explain the role of database marketing in retaining loyal customers.   (8 marks)

(20 marks)

SHORT QUESTIONS – MARKETING PLANNING AND BUDGETING

1   What is the purpose of the marketing planning process?

2   List the 9 steps in the marketing planning process.

3   What do the letters in PEST analysis represent?

4   Complete the following table for a SWOT analysis.

S_____ }   = _____ analysis
W_____ }

O_____ }   = _____ analysis
T_____ }

5   Explain what is meant by market segmentation.

6   List 4 variable used for segmenting industrial markets.

7   Primary research is the collection of data from previously published sources.

    ☐   True   ☐   False

8   Give two examples of qualitative data sources.

9   Complete the following imperatives for evaluation and control.

    A   Setting _____ for performance
    B   Evaluating _____against these _____
    C   Taking _____to correct any deviations from the _____

10 What is meant by SMART objectives?

S	
M	
A	
R	
T	

BPP PUBLISHING

ANSWERS TO SHORT QUESTIONS

1   Organise, direct and control the marketing management activities.

2   Business mission
Marketing audit
SWOT analysis
Business objectives
Marketing objectives
Marketing strategies
Marketing tactics
Implementation
Monitoring & control

3   **P**olitical
Economic
Social
Technological

4

Strengths	Internal analysis
Weaknesses	
Opportunities	External analysis
Threats	

5   Division of market into distinct groups of buyers who are likely to respond favourably to different offerings.

6
- Size of firm
- Type of industry
- Geographical region
- Type of buying organisation

7   False

8   Examples from:

    A   Focus groups
    B   Case studies
    C   Interviews
    D   Survey

9   A   Setting <u>standards</u> for performance
    B   Evaluating <u>performance</u> against these <u>standards</u>
    C   Taking <u>actions</u> to current any deviations from the <u>standards</u>

10

Specific
Measurable
Achievable
Realistic
Time based

8   Market penetration (6/01)   32 mins

A hotel chain has decided to undertake a market penetration strategy with the aim of trying to gain customers from its competitors.

(a)   Explain what is meant by a market penetration strategy and contrast this with a market skimming strategy.   (8 marks)

(b)   Discuss the ways in which this organisation could adapt its marketing mix to implement the market penetration strategy.   (12 marks)

(20 marks)

9   Steps in marketing planning (6/01)   32 mins

You work as a Marketing Assistant for an organisation of your choice and you have been asked to help in the preparation of the marketing plan for the next year.

(a)   Identify the elements of a PEST and SWOT analysis and explain their importance for marketing planning purposes.   (12 marks)

(b)   Briefly explain all the other relevant stages of the marketing planning process.   (8 marks)

(20 marks)

10 Promotional plan and behaviour (12/01)   32 mins

(a)   Referring to a new consumer product or service of your choice, identify and comment upon each stage involved in planning a promotional/communications campaign for the launch.
                                                                              (12 marks)

(b)   Considering buyer behaviour theory, explain why the selection of promotional/ communication tools might differ for a campaign for an industrial product.   (8 marks)

(20 marks)

11 Market research and databases (12/01)   32 mins

A local sports club has recently been experiencing difficulties in getting members to renew their membership subscription.

(a)   Explain and justify the most appropriate research methods which could be used to identify the reasons for this problem.   (10 marks)

(b)   Suggest ways in which the club could use its existing membership database to improve customer loyalty and retention.   (10 marks)

(20 marks)

12 Marketing research I (12/00)   32 mins

(a) Explain what is meant by secondary research and why it is often important to conduct secondary research before primary research is undertaken.   (12 marks)

(b) Identify how the use of information technology could assist in the marketing research process for a product or service of your choice.   (8 marks)

(20 marks)

13 Marketing research II (6/02)   32 mins

You work for a marketing research agency and have been approached by a national electrical goods retailer. They have found that the sales of a new mobile phone are not as high as anticipated. Write a brief report for the retailer that outlines a marketing research programme, and which explains how each element of the research design could contribute to the solution of the problem.

(20 marks)

14 Marketing planning and STP (6/02)   32 mins

A small dairy food manufacturer has asked you to advise them on the development of their marketing plan for next year, which includes the development of a new cheese product.

(a) Explain the benefits of the marketing planning process in this context.   (10 marks)

(b) Explain the concepts of segmentation, targeting and positioning with particular relevance to the proposed new cheese product.   (10 marks)

(20 marks)

15 Systematic research (12/96)   32 mins

You have just been appointed to a post in the marketing department of a company that has not conducted any regular marketing research or systematic information gathering in the past. It has tended to respond to information needs on an ad hoc basis, because the view has been taken that marketing research is for collecting information in order to aid decision making in relation to specific marketing problems.

Your task is to develop a formal marketing research and information gathering system and you have been requested to give a report to your marketing director that outlines the types of tasks and responsibilities that should be undertaken by this new function.

(20 marks)

16 Direct marketing and distribution (12/00)   32 mins

(a) Give reasons, using examples, for the recent growth in direct marketing.   (12 marks)

(b) Explain how distribution decisions may be changed for a consumer product which is entering the mature stage of its life cycle.   (8 marks)

(20 marks)

BPP
PUBLISHING

17 Effective communications (12/98)   32 mins

You have been commissioned by a group of dentists to undertake a marketing research report relating to the effectiveness of their marketing communications to their patients.

(a)   Suggest and justify the most appropriate structure and content of the marketing research **plan** for this report.

(b)   Identify the benefits and limitations of using qualitative data collection techniques such as focus groups and interview for this type of research.

(20 marks)

18 Charity market research (12/99)   32 mins

You work for a charity organisation which is concerned with the welfare of rescued horses. This organisation markets related and seasonal products and giftware, organises fund-raising events and runs adoption schemes. You are currently completing a review of their existing marketing information system and are asked to write a report to the Chief Executive detailing:

(a)   The design of a marketing information system that would be suitable for this organisation.

(8 marks)

(b)   The role of marketing research within the marketing information system.   (12 marks)

(20 marks)

19 Marketing planning process (6/00)   32 mins

(a)   What is a SWOT analysis and how does it lead to an understanding of realistic market opportunities?   (8 marks)

(b)   Explain the importance of marketing planning for a new consumer product to be launched in your country.   (4 marks)

(c)   Using examples, identify the main steps involved in the marketing planning process.

(8 marks)

(20 marks)

SHORT QUESTIONS – THE MARKETING MIX AND RELATED TOOLS

1   Describe the use of targeting in marketing planning.

2   Sketch the typical product life cycle (PLC) chart, including scales.

3   Identify 2 criticisms of the PLC

4   List the 6 stages of New Product Development

5   Give an example of each of the 3 P's of the extended marketing mix for services

Extended 3 P's	Activity
P	
P	
P	

6   Show the marketing implications for two of the Service Characteristics.

7   List 4 functions of packaging

8   Complete the missing words.

    A   Market _____ pricing seeks to introduce products at _____ price levels to maximise revenues

    B   Market _____ pricing seeks to introduce products a _____ price levels to maximise market share

9   Price is the only factor determining the level of demand for a company's product.

    ☐   True   ☐   False

10   An exclusive system of distribution would be selected for a product where the customer requires specialist advice and service facilities

    ☐   True   ☐   False

11   Describe two considerations for distribution channel performance

12   What are the 4 factors that influence a consumer's buying decision?

13   Complete the table below describing the different relationships with a customer or client.

Relationship type	Description
Partner	
Advocate	
Supporter	
Client	
Purchaser	
Prospect	

14 Customer Care emphasises the importance of procedures that encourage responsiveness to customer needs.

☐ True ☐ False

15 What are the differences between the Internet, Extranet and Intranet?

ANSWERS TO SHORT QUESTIONS

1 Positioning is where the marketing mix elements are designed to fit an identified segment

2 In response to your memo relating to the use of the marketing planning tools, I have prepared the following information on the product life cycle.

Stages of the Product Life Cycle

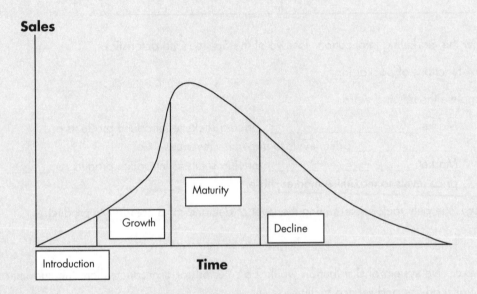

3 A   The time span between stages varies significantly

   B   Products do not proceed to maturity but are substituted at an earlier stage

4

Idea generation
Screening new ideas
Business analysis
Product development
Test marketing
Commercialisation

5

Extended 3 Ps	Activity
People	Employee training
Physical evidence	Company uniform
Process	Billing or admin procedures

6   For any two characteristics:

Intangibility	Judgemental evaluation
Inseparability	Provider and client impact on quality of service
Variability	Consistency based on delivery process
Perishability	Instantaneous consumption that Cannot be stored
Non ownership	Services are used and not owned

7
- Protection
- Promotional message
- Ease of handling and storage
- Product instruction information

8   Market *skimming* pricing seeks to introduce products at *high* price levels to maximise revenues

Market *penetration* pricing seeks to introduce products a *low* price levels to maximise market share

9   False

10   True

11   Any 2 of the following examples:

Order fulfilment
Order cycle time
Information on order status
Response to unplanned orders
No of admin errors
Quality of delivered products

12

Psychological factors
Lifestyle variables
Demographic variables
The economic situation

BPP PUBLISHING

13

Relationship	Description
Partner	The most loyal business associate
Advocate	Active recommendation for business
Supporter	Some tacit approval for offering
Client	Some repeat activity
Purchaser	Completed at least one transaction
Prospect	Likely source of potential business

14 True

15

Internet	Generic world wide global ICT media
Extranet	A secure and restricted ICT link between external supplier and client
Intranet	Secure internal ICT link within an organisation

20 Using the product life cycle (6/01)   32 mins

(a) The product life cycle concept has often been criticised as not being a useful marketing planning tool. Discuss your views on the usefulness of the product life cycle concept for product managers in the financial services sector.   (8 marks)

(b) With reference to a service of your choice, explain how the marketing mix could be adapted for the introduction and growth stages of the product life cycle.   (12 marks)

(20 marks)

21 Customer relationships (6/01)   32 mins

(a) Identify the reasons for developments in the use of relationship marketing techniques in the fast moving consumer goods industry. From your own experience, identify some of the key problems which marketers face when trying to build long term relationships with customers.

(10 marks)

(b) Considering the use of information technology, identify suitable marketing strategies to build customer relationships and maintain customer loyalty.   (10 marks)

(20 marks)

22 Price policy (6/01)   32 mins

(a) Identify the type of information that is required by a small organisation such as an independent fashion retailer before a pricing policy can be agreed.   (10 marks)

(b) Explain two types of price adjustment policies which such an organisation could adopt.

(10 marks)

(20 marks)

23 Pet product life cycle (12/01)   32 mins

You work for a pet food manufacturer of cat food and you have been asked to send a memo to the Marketing Planning Manager to include:

(a) An explanation of the usefulness of the product life cycle concept for decision making for the current cat food products.   (10 marks)

(b) A discussion of how you would adapt the marketing mix for a cat food product which appears to be moving into the decline stage.   (10 marks)

(20 marks)

24 Product life cycle (6/02)   32 mins

(a) Discuss the usefulness of the product life cycle concept as a marketing planning tool for product managers.   (10 marks)

(b) With reference to a consumer product of your choice, explain how the marketing mix could be adapted for the introduction and growth stages of the product life cycle.   (10 marks)

(20 marks)

25 Use of IT (12/01)   32 mins

Explain what is meant by the following terms, and state how each might be used by marketers working at a tactical level within an organisation of your choice.

(a)   Internet
(b)   Intranet
(c)   Extranet

(20 marks)

26 Ansoff matrix and distribution (12/01)   32 mins

For a product or service of your choice, explain the following to the Marketing Assistant who is working with you:

(a)   The Ansoff matrix and the growth strategies which could be adopted.   (8 marks)

(b)   The key issues which the marketing department will need to take into account when considering alternative or new distribution channels.   (12 marks)

(20 marks)

27 Distribution and packaging (6/02)   32 mins

(a)   Specifically considering the role of technology, explain and evaluate the changing nature of the distribution channels within the marketing mix.   (12 marks)

(b)   Using an example, explain the role of packaging and the way it has had to develop within organisations that have adopted direct distribution channels.   (8 marks)

(20 marks)

28 Pricing and methods (12/01)   32 mins

The Managing Director of a small manufacturing company, specialising in industrial packaging tape, is worried that the cost-plus pricing method currently used is not necessarily the most appropriate. She asks you to:

(a)   Explain the role and importance of pricing in marketing terms.   (10 marks)

(b)   Suggest and explain the differences in both competitor-based methods and demand/market-based methods which could be considered as alternatives.   (10 marks)

(20 marks)

29 Life cycle hindrance (6/97)   32 mins

The students' section of your local branch of The Chartered Institute of Marketing has asked you to participate in a debate that proposes the motion:

'This house believes that the concept of the product life cycle is a hindrance to marketing planners'.

You have been given the opportunity to agree or disagree with the motion. Select one or the other. Prepare notes for this debate to assist your presentation.

(20 marks)

30 Development of new products (12/98)   32 mins

Innovation is the life blood of a successful organisation and the management of innovation is central to this success.

(a)   Comment on the importance of the development of new products within organisations.

(b)   Identify and comment on the stages of new product development for a product of your choice.

(20 marks)

31 New product development and buyer behaviour (12/00)   32 mins

Your organisation is planning to develop a new shrink packaging system for food manufacturers.

(a)   Explain each stage of the new product development process.   (10 marks)

(b)   Discuss the potential problems of trying to identify the buying behaviour of organisations which may be interested in this new product.   (10 marks)

(20 marks)

32 Decline stage marketing (12/99)   32 mins

A publisher identifies that one of their products – a special interest photography magazine – is in the decline stage of its product life cycle after enjoying many years with high sales in a growth market. You have been asked to submit a report that:

(a)   Discusses the likely characteristics of the magazine during the decline stage.   (8 marks)

(b)   Advises the company on the marketing mix strategy to be adopted for the magazine.   (12 marks)

(20 marks)

33 New product pricing policy (6/99)   32 mins

You are working in a team of marketers and are planning the launch of a new range of flavoured milk, targeted at children in your own country. Prior to the launch you are to run a pilot in a test market and need to consider the pricing policy for the range.

(a)   What are the main factors to consider when setting the price of these products? Give examples to illustrate where possible.   (12 marks)

(b)   Identify and justify one pricing policy which you feel might be the most appropriate for the launch of this new range.   (8 marks)

(20 marks)

BPP PUBLISHING

34 Pricing (6/00)   32 mins

(a) Identify and explain the key factors, based on financial and economic issues, which may affect the marketer's pricing decisions for a consumer product of your own choice.

(12 marks)

(b) Using specific examples, explain ways in which other marketing mix variables affect pricing decisions.
(8 marks)

(20 marks)

35 Customer care (12/00)   32 mins

You work for an airline company and you have just been approached by a business traveller who has a complaint about the level of service which she has just experienced. The customer was delayed by one hour on an outward domestic flight and also by one hour on the return journey later that day. The main emphasis of her complaint was the lack of information about these delays.

(a) What are the practical approaches which could be undertaken by **this** organisation to improve its standard of customer care?
(8 marks)

(b) Explain the practical steps in establishing an effective customer-care programme.

(12 marks)

(20 marks)

36 New distribution channels (12/99)   32 mins

The forecast marketing plan of an industrial organisation, which manufactures and sells small electronic components to the computer industry, details increased targets for the growth of sales within the next 1-3 years. You have been requested to explain:

(a) The relevance of the Ansoff matrix in achieving the sales growth target.
(8 marks)

(b) The key issues which the Marketing Department will need to take into account when considering alternative or new distribution channels.
(12 marks)

(20 marks)

37 Distribution (6/00)   32 mins

(a) (i) What are the key issues which a Marketing Manager will need to take into account when considering alternative distribution channels?
(10 marks)

(ii) Explain, with examples, the reasons for the recent growth in the use of direct marketing channels.
(10 marks)

(20 marks)

or:

(b) (i) Explain the role of the following **three** different marketing channels for the distribution of consumer products:

(1) Cash and carry warehouses

(2) Superstores

(3) Catalogue showrooms   (10 marks)

(ii) Giving specific examples, distinguish between intensive, selective and exclusive methods of distribution.   (10 marks)

(20 marks)

38 Service industry (6/99)   32 mins

The service industry is a growing part of the economy, mainly due to economic prosperity.

(a) Identify the characteristics of services. What problems do these characteristics present to the marketer?   (8 marks)

(b) For a small service organisation of your choice (for example a dental practice), identify the tactical issues which should be considered relating to the extended marketing mix.

(12 marks)

(20 marks)

39 Grey market promotion (12/99)   32 mins

You are working on the new packaging and promotions for a range of biscuits that is to be repositioned to target the affluent, mature or 'grey' market.

(a) Outline the key considerations which will need to be taken into account when determining the packaging for this product range, to be sold in a country of your choice.   (8 marks)

(b) Your manager has asked you to list the strengths and weaknesses of 'push' promotional techniques, and 'pull' promotional techniques, which could be used for this repositioned product range.   (12 marks)

(20 marks)

40 Services marketing (12/00)   32 mins

(a) Using a financial service of your choice, identify four differences between services and products and discuss the problems that these differences present to the marketer.   (8 marks)

(b) Identify the extended marketing mix which a small service company (such as a management consultancy), would need to consider when marketing its services. (12 marks)

(20 marks)

41 Packaging (6/99)   32 mins

Packaging for the toys and games sectors is one of the marketers' most creative areas. CD-ROM games for personal computers have been packaged for years using conventional boxes. One of the manufacturers, Segge, is now considering new packaging systems for these products.

(a) Write a memo to Segge's product manager identifying the role of packaging for these products.   (8 marks)

(b) Suggest the key issues for new packaging, which must be considered in relation to the marketing mix.   (12 marks)

(20 marks)

42 Services marketing mix (12/99)   32 mins

(a) You have been asked to identify the marketing characteristics for services and discuss the associated implications for marketers.   (10 marks)

(b) You are to advise the Marketing Manager about the use of the extended services marketing mix, as the traditional four Ps are not sufficient for many ranges of service products. Give examples relating to your own country.   (10 marks)

(20 marks)

43 Customer care (6/02)   32 mins

You have been appointed as customer relations manager for a hotel chain which has recently suffered poor levels of repeat business. Senior management has invited you to submit a report that:

(a) Identifies the relevance of customer care to the hotel sector.   (10 marks)
(b) Proposes a new customer care programme for the company.   (10 marks)

(20 marks)

44 Customer care process (6/98)   32 mins

One of your colleagues who is studying for a marketing qualification has read that customer care should be a central focus of marketing policy, which should unite the four traditional elements of the marketing mix with three further elements which have a strong effect on customer care. You have been asked what these further elements are and what their significance is in relation to customer care. Advise your colleague.

(20 marks)

SHORT QUESTIONS – MARKETING IN CONTEXT

1 For small and medium sized enterprises (SMEs) and Not-for-Profit organisations list 2 differences in approaches to marketing

2 Identify 4 modes of international logistics

3 What are the additional issues to be considered in pricing a product for overseas markets?

4 Complete the Ansoff Matrix

5 Give two examples of the use of virtual technology to support marketing activities

ANSWERS TO SHORT QUESTIONS

1

SME	Resource availability Financial considerations
NFP organisations	Virtual monopolies for service provision Political interference

2 Ship/maritime
Canal
Air freight
Road train haulage

3 Examples from:

Currency fluctuations
Product cost structures
Basis of delivery
Involvement of intermediaries

4

		Product	
		Present	New
Market	Present	Market penetration	Product development
	New	Market development	Diversification

5 Examples from:

Video conferencing
Mobile phone technology
Internet & email use
PC communications

BPP PUBLISHING

45 Target markets (6/99)   32 mins

Research is becoming more important in business-to-business marketing, especially in selecting and analysing **target markets**. For an industrial product **and** a consumer product of your choice, identify, describe and justify the major categories of variables which could be used to segment the markets for each product. You should refer to examples to illustrate your answer.

(20 marks)

46 Marketing concept (6/00)   32 mins

(a) Explain and identify both:

(i)   A business to business organisation
(ii)   A non-profit organisation

which, in your opinion, have been successful in the adoption of the marketing concept. Give specific reasons to justify your choices.   (12 marks)

(b) Explain how the use of Information Technology could assist in the management of a customer oriented culture within one of the above organisations.   (8 marks)

(20 marks)

47 International distribution channels (12/98)   32 mins

A UK based manufacturer of branded clothing targeted at a mountaineering and sports people, has an objective of expanding the business into new international markets. The marketing director is considering three different distribution channels.

(a)   Franchise operations
(b)   Mail order direct to potential customers
(c)   Agents in selected countries

You have been asked to identify and explain the advantages and disadvantages of each option to help the Marketing Director.

(20 marks)

48 Relevant marketing mix (6/96)   32 mins

Indicate the main characteristics of marketing mixes which would be appropriate for any **two** of the following.

(a)   A large banking group
(b)   A company that manufactures electronic components for computer manufacturers
(c)   A car manufacturer
(d)   A road haulage company

Include in your answer the relevant justification.

(20 marks)

49 Theme park customer care (12/99)   32 mins

You are applying for a position as a Marketing Assistant at a top European theme park. As part of the application process you are required to give a presentation to senior management that explains:

(a) The strategic implications of customer orientation and how it should relate to the successful marketing of the theme park.   (8 marks)

(b) The importance of customer care and the practical approaches for improving customer care standards within a theme park.   (12 marks)

(20 marks)

Mini-cases

50 North Wales food (6/98)   64 mins

Read the following scenario which was adapted from the Western mail and then answer all parts of the question that follows.

Food and drink exhibitions

Exhibitions are one of the methods which brings the buyers, sellers and competitors together for a number of days. Products can be demonstrated and personal contact can be made with a large number of relevant decision-makers in a short time period. They can be a powerful marketing communication tool but require detailed planned and co-ordination.

The world's biggest food and drink exhibition is being held in London this year. The exhibition attracts companies from around the world with a number of local producers also taking part. There are many different organisations who will be exhibiting.

A consortium of four companies located in Wales will be taking a stand at the exhibition. These food producers: Welsh Creameries, the Welsh Mountain Garden and two Welsh manufacturers of sweets/candy are not in direct competition with each other and so can benefit from a co-operative approach to their marketing.

Another organisation who will be at the exhibition is the Welsh Development Agency (WDA). Across the United Kingdom, the Government has supported the creation of a number of Development Agencies. A Development Agency is charged with helping to attract jobs and inwards investment to an area. The WDA has links with two local councils in Wales to target international food processing companies, with a view to attracting them to relocate or expand their operation in the region. The WDA and councils have formed an alliance to achieve these goals and, therefore, are taking a stand at this exhibition in London.

'We will go to London with a clear message for food processing companies that North West Wales should be their preferred location if they have to expand or relocate their actuates,' says Brian Rees Jones, of the WDA. 'We will tell them that we can provide an ideal strategic location from which they can serve their UK, Irish and European markets, that we have developed sites specifically for food processing companies and that we have a workforce which has a natural understanding for the food industry.'

Required

(a) Bearing in mind the background of the scenario, provide a report that clearly identifies appropriate objectives for attending this exhibition for:

- The consortium of four North Wales food producers.
- The Welsh Development Agency (WDA).   (20 marks)

(b) Within the report, identify methods which could be used by these organisations to evaluate or measure their performance at the exhibition.   (10 marks)

(c) Having evaluated the contracts which were made during the exhibition, one of the Welsh manufacturers of sweets/candy feels that there could be different bases for segmenting the consumer market which this organisation could consider.   (10 marks)

(40 marks)

51 Battle of the brands (12/99)   64 mins

The 1998 football World Cup, which was held in France, was global stage for the biggest and the best. As might be expected all the top football teams were at France '98. However, the competition was the one taking place behind the relatively insignificant struggle between the likes of England and Argentina – this was between the two sportswear brands – Nike and Adidas.

Even the most fleeting trip to Paris firmly brought home the point that football is increasingly the plaything of the huge sportswear corporations. At stake is the small matter of being the biggest sportswear company in the world. The terrain on which this battle will increasingly be fought in football. In the last three years the market for endorsements and advertising deals has exploded. The reasons for this are many and varied – after all, football has never been this big, and just keeps on getting bigger – but they can be boiled down to one key factor: the emergence of Nike as a major player.

'We are very new to football, but we see that as an advantage. We can bring product innovation to the sport, be inventive, take a whole new perspective to football. Already the game is very important to Nike'. So says Debbie Cox, PR Manager of Nike UK. Nike is rumoured to have spent £35 million on the World Cup '98 alone. It booked up strategic poster sites around France more than two years before the event.

The deployment of this bottomless war chest has quickly brought Nike access to the most exclusive centres of the football world. 'We have been able to cultivate our relationship with some of the key players,' enthuses Cox. 'For example Ronaldo (one of Brazil's top players) was actively involved in the design and testing of our latest boot, the Mercurial'.

'Nike is very much the new kid on the block,' says Martin Cannon of the Institute of Sports Sponsorship and head of Cannon Communications. 'It is brash, pushy, a bit of a rebel, while Adidas is very official, a stable, established sports brand for people who are very serious about their football. Nike can call on huge resources to fund their marketing campaigns, and they can also justify the amount of money spent, because in advertising terms the 'reach' is so high. The vast majority of people watching a football match are going to be interested in buying sportswear'.

This is the key. When compared to the sums spent on development and promoting football boots, the market for them in Britain is pretty small. Each year just over a million pairs are sold, at a combined cost of approximately £60 million.

Now, after the latest boom, the market place looks rather crowded. Even Adidas, who remain leaders of the British sportswear sector after several strong years, admit there is likely to be a shakedown. However, unless the world of fashion says different, no one in their right mind is going to go 'down the pub' in a pair of football boots. But when Nike pay Ian Wright (a top British football player) to play in their boots, or when Umbro sign up Alan Shearer (the England captain in the World Cup) for £25,000 a year, they are primarily concerned with promoting the brand not the boot. This is where the real money lies. Put the right logo on a pair of trainers, T-shirt or bag and it will sell well.

Market research company Mintel estimate that the British sportswear market is worth £1.7 billion, which includes 20 million trainers sold every year. Nike have built up a $9 billion-a-year global business on the basis of trainers that can be sold for £80 a pair, but probably cost as little as £1.20 to actually make in a factory in Thailand.

A leading London marketing consultant stages 'It's reached saturation point. A few years ago everyone bought Nike, no one bought Adidas. But the trendsetters have moved on. Those 16 to

BPP PUBLISHING

20 year olds who lead the market won't be seen dead in the same trainers as their parents. To be honest the trainer is starting to look rather tired'.

This passage has been adapted from an article featured in BBC MOTD (Match Of The Day) Magazine, August/September, 1998, and has been reproduced with kind permission from BBC Worldwide Ltd. The statement and questions which follow are fictitious and do not represent in any way the strategies of Nike UK.

You are working as a Marketing Assistant at Nike UK. The research and development department has come up with a new product idea – casual footwear for the youth market, which is quite revolutionary in terms of style and comfort, and they feel that the time is right to explore this new product. They are now seeking your advice as to what to do next. For a country of your choice, write a report that:

Required

(a) Explains **all** the stages and actions involved in the **new product development process** to ensure successful launch and commercialisation of this new product. (25 marks)

(b) Identifies the types of information required for the formulation of a pricing strategy, and that also stages, which reasons, the most appropriate pricing strategy for the new casual footwear. (15 marks)

(40 marks)

52 Interflora Worldwide flower deliveries (6/00)64 mins

Interflora is a non-profit making Trade Association owned by its members who are independent floristry businesses located throughout the world. These members are able to vote on issues at regional meetings and an Annual General Meeting. The aims of the Interflora organisation are encompassed in the mission statement:

'Our mission is to ensure that Interflora will always be the consumer's first choice for flowers and appropriate gifts. This means: recognising and responding to our customers' changing needs; providing a seamless service to our customers; leading our industry in innovation and design; continual improvement in quality, service, processes and costs and enabling our employees and associates to give their best.'

The Interflora organisation consists of 58,000 florists worldwide delivering flowers to 146 countries – each and every one maintaining the stringent standards that Interflora demands. From China to Russia, the USA to Europe, Interflora is able to deliver 'an expression of your thoughts through the most beautiful flowers imaginable.'

Starting with a fresh and original idea, Interflora grew into the world's largest and most popular flower delivery network. Today, the organisation boasts that no one can compete with its combination of creativity, experience and guaranteed quality.

The wide product range includes bouquets, hand-tied flowers, planted arrangements, floral arrangements, cut flowers, and unusual tailor-made floral gifts. Customers purchase their products for a variety of special occasions such as tokens of love, sympathy tributes, birthdays, new births, anniversaries and many others.

A customer selects and pays for a flower order in one of the participating florists who are members of Interflora. The order is then communicated electronically to the nearest convenient Interflora member who makes it up and delivers it to the destination required by the customer (which may be to any place in the world). Interflora uses only floristry businesses that meet stringent criteria such as good shop image, qualified staff, good variety and quality of stocks.

Interflora's trademark depicting the Roman God Mercury, is one of the most recognised trademarks and symbols of quality and service in the world, and which forms a common bond between the worldwide network of florists. The Interflora service is known by different trading names in some parts of the world, such as 'Fleurop' in parts of Europe and 'FTD' in America, Canada and Japan. The name 'Interflora' is used in the UK, Ireland and some other countries.

Source: Adapted from the Interflora web site

Required

The Directors of Interflora have approached your marketing agency and require specific advice for improving levels of customer service. They realise that customer retention and sound customer care are crucial in today's marketplace and that a more targeted promotional campaign may help to achieve increased awareness throughout the world.

Therefore, you are to write a report which:

(a) Explains the practical approaches which the organisation should consider to improve the standards of customer care and customer satisfaction across the participating florists.

(15 marks)

(b) Comments on how the three elements of the extended marketing mix, relating specifically to people, process and physical evidence, could be developed for this service. (15 marks)

(c) Identifies and briefly describes the major promotional methods that could be included within a campaign to raise the awareness of Interflora's products and service within your own country. (10 marks)

(40 marks)

53 Energy Power Systems launches a new battery system (12/00) 64 mins

Energy Power Systems is a division of the Ecco Battery Company (EBC) and manufacture rechargeable batteries. Ecco are the world's largest producer of battery and flashlight products, with twenty production facilities, supplying over 500 products into 165 countries worldwide. The key corporate objectives are to increase profitability by 5% within the next two years and for the battery division, to be positioned as the number one supplier of state of the art technology in batteries.

Energy Power Systems (EPS) manufacture rechargeable Nickel Cadmium, Nickel Metal Hydride and Lithium Ion Cells and Battery Packs for equipment manufacturers and for the consumer market. The cells are produced at the company's Headquarters in Florida, and then either sold directly to the equipment manufactures or assembled into battery packs by one of three assembly facilities in Mexico, Newcastle (UK) or Hong Kong.

Energy Power Systems Rechargeable Battery Product Range

EPS produce a particular range of rechargeable batteries, most of which are used in either cordless power tools, emergency lighting or mobile communications. However, the relatively inexpensive technology employed in current manufacture is being replaced by a new technology. A European directive has been issued to ban all this type of batteries by the year

2008 due to the negative impact that the cadmium electrode within the cell has on the environment when consumers dispose of these cells.

Core Markets

Energy Power Systems employ a differentiated segmentation strategy, modifying the marketing mix for each of its targeted segments. This allows the company to concentrate on markets that offer high returns and opportunities for growth, which is consistent with the corporate objectives of its parent company, EBC.

EPS segments the market into an industrial segment and a consumer segment, and further segments each of these as follows:

Industrial Segment

- Mobile communications manufacturers such as Ericsson, Motorola etc
- Cordless power tool manufacturers
- Computer manufacturers

Consumer Segments

- Audio visual equipment – eg Sony Walkman
- Personal care – such as cordless toothbrush
- Photo – eg camera batteries
- Toys and novelties
- Hand held equipment – such as cordless car vacuums

New Product Range – 'Smart' Batteries

The company is about to launch a new range of 'smart' batteries, using a relatively new type of technology. These batteries have the ability to control their own charging when fitted into a compatible charger. They also have the ability to report back information to the user of the battery, information such as the time left to empty, manufacturers name, age, etc.

EPS are one of the only battery manufacturers that offer in-house design and manufacture of these smart batteries. For the core industrial markets, a completely 'customer-smart' battery can go from conception to production in as little as five months.

The brand name 'Energy' is the name used for all batteries produced by the company. Recently commissioned marketing research has shown that within the consumer segments, the brand is known worldwide. However, this is less important to industrial users, who usually prefer to display their own logo on the batteries. This research has also highlighted the fact that consumers are mainly interested in the length of the battery life and reliability. The company is aiming to secure the market as being the first entrant with this 'smart' technology.

Required

The launch of these new batteries is due to take place within the next year. You are to prepare a report to be used as the basis for discussion within the organisation's Marketing Department, which considers:

(a) The **basic stages** involved in the marketing planning process. (15 marks)

(b) How **each element** of the marketing mix (excluding promotions) should be developed for this product launch, giving careful thought for both the consumer and business to business segments which are to be targeted. (15 marks)

(c) Specific proposals for the **communication/promotional mix** for the launch of the new 'smart' batteries within your own country. (10 marks)

(40 marks)

54 W Moorcroft plc – Art Pottery (6/01)   64 mins

W. Moorcroft plc is an internationally renowned company that produces handcrafted pieces of art pottery such as plates etc. It is located in Stoke on Trent, which is the traditional centre for pottery in the UK. William Moorcroft, the founder of the company, designed the first pieces of Moorcroft pottery in 1897 at the age of 24.

The company won 'Gold Awards' for the quality of its products at international exhibitions in 1904, 1910 and 1925. In 1928, Queen Mary awarded the company the desirable status of official suppliers to Her Majesty the Queen. Its reputation as an award winning company continued over the years, culminating in 1996 when the company was awarded the 'Gold Award for Excellence' at the International Light Show. Examples of its designs, from the 1890s to the present day, are to be found in museums throughout the world, including the Victoria and Albert Museum in London. The organisation is now a medium sized company, but in the past few years it has had problems with its once very successful corporate brand.

The Product Range

The recent implementation of a dynamic marketing plan ensured that there is now a full range of hand crafted products: Moorcroft pottery giftware and table lamps, Moorcroft enamels (decorated enamel boxes or other shaped items), and Cobridge Stoneware (which is a different type of decorated pottery). Attention to detail and ultimate quality is paramount, as each piece is hand-made and decorated using a mixture of traditional and technologically advanced methods. A range of limited and numbered editions is processed as well as the standard lines. Design is of paramount importance and therefore, the company uses new, young and very talented designers to produce new ranges on a regular basis. The prices per piece range from over £36 to £2,000 with many pieces within the £200-£400 range. Each piece of pottery is still turned on the lathe and after this, 'MOORCROFT' and 'MADE IN ENGLAND' are impressed into the clay together with symbols, which denotes the year of manufacture and decorator' marks. These markings are a clear requirement for the collector market to enable them to collect particular decorator's marks and designer's work – adding to the uniqueness of each piece.

Moorcroft Brand objectives

To achieve the marketing objectives, the (re)positioning of the corporate brand (Moorcroft) needs to be developed. The organisation has decided to undertake the following strategy to strengthen the brand:

- Focus the perception of the brand on the uniqueness of quality craftsmanship and innovative new designs

- Reposition the brand to appeal to the core customer base of collectors which is segmented by age and disposable income, (especially the younger market)

- Build a range of sub-brands in the 'Moorcroft Studio'. This relates to the development of a Studio of Designers, where the designers' names and design names would become sub-brands of the Moorcroft corporate brand.

Customer Base

Obviously it was important to ensure that both the trade and end customer are included within the marketing plan. Therefore, the target audiences have been identified as follows:

Trade Customers

- Major trade buyers and decision makers, such as major department stores – e.g. Liberty of London

- International dealerships e.g. Tokyo, New York, New Zealand

End Customers

- Moorcroft collectors segmented by age and disposable income
- Moorcroft collectors segmented by country
- General pottery collectors
- Antique pottery collectors
- Customers looking for giftware or special occasion purchases

Marketing research has identified that the individual collector (or customer) demonstrates high involvement behaviour when purchasing collectable items. Thus it is important that customers feel that they own a unique piece of art. Part of the communications strategy is to develop and maintain a dynamic collectors club of current and potential customers.

W Moorcroft plc has recently purchased a company which produces art glass and collectable pieces under the brand name of 'Okra'. This means that Moorcroft will also become responsible for marketing this range of glass products. The designs of the Okra glass range are now being developed by the Moorcroft designers – which means that these glass products now look more like Moorcroft products and may appeal to Moorcroft's pottery customers.

This case is based on a live organisation, with kind permission from Moorcroft Plc, however, the questions which follow do not represent in any way the strategies of this organisation.

Required

The Chairman at Moorcroft has decided that further marketing research needs to be undertaken to identify the perceptions of the Okra range.

(a) You work for a marketing research agency and have been asked to suggest and justify the most appropriate structure and content of the marketing research proposal for your client at Moorcroft. The proposal should be designed to consider the current awareness, attitudes and perceptions relating to the Okra glass range and other competitor's products for both the end customer and trade target segments in your own country or a country of your choice. *(NB You must **not** include a questionnaire)* (15 marks)

(b) Briefly, explain why it is important that the marketers and sales staff at Moorcroft understand behaviour and perceptions in its trade and customer target markets. (10 marks)

(c) The research has now been completed and having presented the findings to the Chairman of Moorcroft plc, it is clear that the organisation must devise a new promotions/communications plan for the Okra glass and Moorcroft pottery range. You are to prepare a **brief** report that identifies and justifies the most appropriate communication/ promotional mix for this plan, within your own country or a country of your choice. (15 marks)

(40 marks)

55 Botswana Telecommunications Corporation (BTC) (12/01) 64 mins

The telecommunications sector in Botswana, Africa, is characterised by a growing, unsatisfied demand for telecommunications services in both urban and rural areas and among businesses as well as households.

Botswana Telecommunications Corporation (BTC) is a state-owned enterprise incorporated under the BTC Act of 1980 to provide public telecommunications services in Botswana. Currently it has over 100,000 customer access lines in service.

BTC has a telecommunications infrastructure that is one of the most modern in Africa. Its network, composed of an all-digital microwave and fibre optic system with digital exchanges at the main centres, provides a reasonable level of service.

Current services provided include national and international telephony, managed and data networks, leased circuits, toll-free services, Internet, paging, public telephones, voice messaging, telex, telegraph and customer premises equipment. International access is provided from Botswana to almost every country in the world.

Since the introduction of cellular networks in the country through two other companies, BTC has also supplied the backbone networks to facilitate cellular communications throughout the country.

During the past two years, access lines to customers have increased by 19% to exceed 102,000. This has significantly reduced the waiting period for services which had been observed in most parts of Botswana. This increased penetration of the market means that there are now 6.4 telephones for every 100 people in the population.

The Corporation's commitment to bringing telecommunications services to rural areas continues with the implementation of programmes in Barolong and the northern Tuli areas. These were undertaken with Government financial assistance.

The telecommunications industry in Botswana is expected to experience massive growth during the next five years. The mobile telecommunications industry represents a major challenge to BTC. The Corporation knows that it will need to consider this challenge from a market orientation perspective, as previously it has been more product oriented.

Indeed, BTC anticipates that the main challenges facing it are as follows:

- Large investment in networks and development of new services

- Introduction, development and support of new products and services

- Customer care and responsiveness at all levels within the organisation

- Streamlining of processes and work procedures to address customer concerns

- Competing resources in balancing rural and urban telecommunications requirements nationwide.

In Botswana, BTC intends to maintain its position as the primary network provider of choice. BTC is confident that introducing a new customer care policy and billing system will help to attain corporate targets. The company states that it is dedicated to meeting customer and investor expectations.

This case had been adapted from the BTC Annual Report and BTC Position Paper, 2000, with kind permission and co-operation with Mogomotsi Kaboeamodimo, BTC Public Relations Manager.

Required

You have been asked to help BTC in meeting the challenges which face it. Write a report to the Marketing Manager of BTC which:

(a) Identifies, with reasons, the steps for introducing a marketing orientation within BTC and explains how the effective use of information technology may contribute to this aim.

(15 marks)

(b) Explains the key differences between services and products and discusses the problems that these differences may present to the company. (10 marks)

(c) Discusses the elements of the marketing mix which BTC will need to consider when marketing its services. (15 marks)

(40 marks)

56 PIX Cinemas (6/02)   64 mins

PIX Cinemas is Europe's leading cinema chain, with 30 years' experience in the cinema industry. It first entered the UK in 1999 when it bought full control of an existing cinema chain in an outright purchase. In Europe, PIX Cinemas has 84 cinemas and enjoys 13.8% market share.

However, once the acquisition had taken place, PIX Cinemas wanted to position themselves as being serious about films. Film was their number one priority, although the concession areas (including snacks and drinks) in the foyers were considered to be important.

Research conducted by Mintel (2000) found that household penetration of satellite and cable TV increased significantly during the past four years; that more people were renting videos to watch at home and more people were subscribing to movie channels. However, it appears that this growth in home entertainment has not affected cinemas, for it is actually the heaviest cinema-goers who are also more likely to rent videos to watch at home and to subscribe to satellite/cable TV and movie channels. This suggests that the view these forms of entertainment as complements to, rather than substitutes for, going to the cinema. Ultimately, the experience of the big screen is something that cannot be truly replicated in the home and it seems that this will always give cinemas the advantage.

In July 2000, PIX Cinemas launched the first subscription card – 'Unlimited Pass', which is a subscription-based card whereby members sign up for a minimum of 12 months at the rate of £9.99 per month. They can then visit a PIX Cinema as often as they wish. The card is a magnetic card with a digital photo, and it also provides PIX Cinemas with valuable information about the cinema-going habits of their most frequent visitors. This was designed to increase market penetration and encourage people to see films that they would never normally have considered. The subscribers to the 'Unlimited Pass' number 42,500 in the UK. The target is to achieve 85,000 subscribers by 2005.

The activities undertaken by PIX Cinemas to promote the 'Unlimited Pass' have included internal point of sales and an internal sales team who were taken from the 'front of house' team. The sales team was mainly trained in the practical skills of selling the 'pass'. Feedback from the selling team suggests that customers seem to associate a 'risk' with the commitment to a 12 month contract for the 'pass'.

In order to increase awareness among less frequent cinema-goers, PIX Cinemas have recognised that they should be developing plans to market the 'pass' further. As yet, external marketing of the card has relied on word-of-mouth from customers who have already invested in the pass, or who have seen the point of sale material in the cinemas.

While the cinema chain which PIX Cinemas purchased has a strong brand image and distinct market position, the PIX Cinemas brand has no values associated with it in the minds of the target audiences. As a consequence, PIX Cinemas are able to choose how to position themselves, but a great deal of work is needed to create awareness of the brand and its values.

A further area which PIX Cinemas needs to consider is the practice of customers' advance booking and gathering information. Advanced bookings now account for around 20% of all UK ticket sales, thanks largely to centralised telephone booking facilities offered by the majority of cinema chains. Mintel's research (2000) showed that a very small proportion of cinema consumers book tickets on the Internet. This is a reflection of the fact that only two of the six major cinema chains in the UK offered such a service. However, it plays a far more important role in providing information to consumers about films being shown, screening times, admission prices, how to find the cinema and facilities in and around the cinema. All of the major competitors now have a website; however, PIX Cinemas currently does not. In the future, it is likely that the Internet will become a more important channel for booking tickets, and this is an area which needs to be developed by PIX Cinemas.

This information is broadly fictitious and does not reflect the policies of any cinema chains.

Required

You have been employed by PIX Cinemas in a newly created marketing post. PIX Cinemas are looking to reposition their brand and you have been made responsible for the development of a number of areas. Based on a brief presented to you by your manager, write a report that:

(a)   Explains the key characteristics of services and the main problems which face PIX Cinemas' marketing team when trying to reposition the service and market a cinema experience.

(15 marks)

(b)   Discuss the ways in which this organisation could adapt its promotion/communications mix to respond to the changing environment and to implement further the market penetration strategy. (15 marks)

(c)   Explain, in the context of the social environment, how an understanding of buyer behaviour could help in the effective planning of the marketing effort for this organisation.   (10 marks)

(40 marks)

Answer bank

1 Social perspective

Examiner's comments. An unpopular question, badly answered. Some interpreted the question in terms of PEST rather than ecological factors and few mentioned consumerism.

Notes on the importance of a social marketing perspective

Marketing has traditionally been defined as a function or a philosophy engaged in the activity of matching customer needs with the provision of goods and services through an exchange process. In recent years there has been a rapid growth in awareness and interest in the activities of organisations beyond what they simply produce. This trend can best be described as a growing social awareness.

Social awareness is concerned with evaluating the practises of an organisation and assessing to what extent they are behaving in a socially responsible manner. In effect a new range of customer needs have evolved that offer new opportunities or threats to an organisation.

Social marketing takes into account the consumers need for wider satisfaction beyond just the satisfaction of consuming the product. Whilst no complete definition of social marketing is currently agreed, the following areas are generally agreed to be of concern to social marketers.

(a) Green and caring image
(b) Animal welfare
(c) Charitable
(d) Care for employees

Each of these areas comes under the broad banner of 'quality of life'.

Corporate responsibility now requires organisations to consider both the economic costs and benefits and the social costs and benefits of decisions. A balance is now required that might result in lower returns in terms of profitability but increased benefits in terms of customer retention and franchise. It is also possible that an organisation can gain a competitive edge through being seen as socially responsible. Equally an organisation's corporate image can be damaged severely if it becomes public knowledge that it is acting in a socially irresponsible manner.

Many examples exist.

(a) The Body Shop is one of the most successful organisations to position itself as an environmentally friendly organisation.

(b) Shell has recently received extensive bad publicity for its activities in Uganda, a country with a poor human rights record.

(c) Politicians see the environment and socially responsible behaviour as being a potential vote catcher with the electorate.

(d) Many organisations now sponsor one or two charities which gains them national publicity.

(e) Socially responsible employers can gain awards and publicity for good practise. Those employers that have little regard for the safety and welfare of their employees are increasingly coming under the scrutiny of the media.

Social responsibility covers a wider field than the traditionally market focus of marketing. However, the principles of marketing are equally applicable in terms of how organisations respond to this environmental trend and position themselves to best effect to exploit the opportunities that societal markets now offer by becoming genuinely socially responsible organisations.

2   Socially responsible marketing

> Examiner's comment. This popular question enabled a wide range of answers. You might have considered Kennedy's 'rights' to flesh out the answer.

'Green marketing' is a term which reflects society's growing concern with the environment. Products and services are now being designed to reflect a growing consciousness and concern with the damage that is being done to the natural environment through pollution, building/civil engineering projects etc.

The issues that I would advise you to cover in this one hour programme are as follows.

(a)   Evidence to support the need for increased environmental concern. This can be done with a series of summary case histories from recent headline news stories. A clear definition of the meaning of the term and the boundaries it covers.

(b)   The market for green products and services. The programme should recognise that consumers and organisations wear different shades of green from highly committed to occasional concern. Examples include the Shell Brent Spar disposal. It is also the case that some consumers are cynical about green claims made by businesses, as they are confused about 'health issues'.

(c)   Evidence of the growth of green marketing can be given through examples of products/services that represent good practice and the fact that some organisations have been listed on the stock exchange based upon their green credentials. Examples include lower emission vehicles and recyclable packaging.

(d)   The concerns of consumers and consumer organisations/pressure groups with the claims made by some organisation for green credentials when much of their practice is harmful to the natural environment. The programme can make this a 'banner issue'. Again, the example of the oil companies comes to mind.

(e)   Some consideration as to the scale of the green movement and its future momentum and the implications for marketers in how they respond. It might be helpful to bring in guests for part of the programme to debate this issue, from pressure groups such as Friends of the Earth.

(f)   Recognition that green marketing occurs throughout the supply chain from raw material extraction through to consumption and that both consumers and organisations play an important part in its future. Government action and policy will also play an influential part in this process.

(g)   Understanding that green issues are very much concerned with lifestyles. People may be worried about global warming - but are they prepared to abandon their petrol-using cars? How much more will they pay?

(h)   'Green consumers' are a market segment in their own right.

We can tie up the programme, linking 'green' activities to the wider issue of consumer **rights**. Green activism can affect consumers, if it means higher prices, but it also promises a better environment.

3 Orientation

Examiner's comment. This question was answered well. Many candidates were able to relate the theory directly to the scenario, unlike in other questions.

To: College Principal
From: A N Student
Date: 11th June 1998
Subject: Market orientation

Contents

(a) The difference between product and market orientation
(b) The steps involved in establishing a marketing orientated approach
(c) The anticipated benefits to the college of introducing such an approach

(a) Difference between product and market orientation

The college will be product orientated if it displays the following characteristics.

(i)   Courses designed and delivered without reference to market trends and customer needs.

(ii) Limited use / adoption of MKIS systems.

(iii) Short-term, reactive view to changes in the marketing environment.

(iv) Lack of customer-focused systems and processes.

(v)   Organisation structure focused upon courses and not customer and market issues.

The college will be marketing orientated if it displays the following characteristics.

(i)   Course design and development clearly focused upon market trends and evolving customer needs.

(ii) Flexible modes of course delivery and opening hours.

(iii) Organisation structure and systems designed with a customer focus and not an internal organisation focus.

(iv) Empowerment of staff to deliver excellent service.

(v)   Culture of change with limited bureaucracy.

(b) The steps to establish a marketing orientated approach

(i)   The philosophy that lies behind marketing orientation must be embraced with a genuine belief and commitment by the senior management of the college.

(ii) The college will need substantially to upgrade its current student information system to provide more than just name, address and course records. Company and other key stakeholder information should also be accessible within the system.

(iii) The college structure will need to be revised, if it is to achieve increased levels of market and customer orientation. The structure should include customer related functions and roles and not those just satisfy internal organisation needs.

(iv) The college culture must be adapted to suit the more customer focused environment. The organisation and its employees will need to redefine current practice and functions, towards increased co-operation, autonomy and flexibility.

(v) Improved internal communication systems need to be designed to ensure all employees are kept informed of college activity and plans. Communications systems should facilitate feedback.

(vi) A programme of customer care training should be planned for all members of staff and targets agreed. This training should be provided on an ongoing basis.

(vii) An agreed system of monitoring and control should be implemented to ensure that any deviations or shortfalls from the desired standards can be actioned.

(c) **Benefits**

Several benefits will emerge as a result of the college changing from a product to marketing orientation. Some of these will not occur in the short term but will have a significant impact on the colleges performance and competitiveness longer term.

(i) The college will develop a sharper competitive edge clearly focused on the market and customers' needs.

(ii) Its perceived image in the local community will be changed from being seen as fairly staid to being more dynamic and modern.

(iii) Increased revenue will be generated from courses positioned in growing markets.

(iv) The college will be seen to be more responsive to local education needs.

(v) Courses and programmes will be tailored and targeted and thus be seen as having more relevance.

(vi) Recruitment will become more effective through better targeting. As a direct result the college should retain more students to completion of programmes and continuing with further programmes.

(vii) New course developments can be developed in closer line with market needs and evaluated more effectively in terms of the colleges mission and goals.

Whilst this change from product to marketing orientation will involve significant commitment in terms of time and resource, the long term benefits will be considerable.

4 Consumer attitudes

Examiner's comments. This was a new area on the syllabus (and) a popular question. Some of the answers were well argued and applied to the context. There was evidence that some candidates only seemed to guess at the answer. Many candidates did not understand this area judging by the wide-ranging, general answers which were evident.

The second part of the question seemed to be more problematic as some candidates failed to recognise that they were required to consider the decision process as being the reference point for the various influencing factors.

(a) Marketers are concerned with consumer attitudes and buying behaviour because they wish to meet the needs of the consumer with the good or service that they are offering. People are affected by many things: politics, religion, national identity, fashion and music, for example, and these things influence their attitudes and opinions.

Attitude describes a person's view of how they think or feel about an object or issue fairly consistently. Attitude will influence perceptions, likes and dislikes and will therefore strongly influence behaviour.

Marketers need to monitor and understand consumer attitudes if they are to successfully position their offer in consumers' minds. A charity can reinforce or strengthen its position by appealing to a consumer's specific set of attitudes to surrounding a particular social issue.

Attitudes are difficult to change. A person's attitude will often fit into a pattern and therefore an organisation is best advised to fit its offer into existing attitudes rather than trying to change attitudes. Several recent government campaigns have tried to change people's attitudes towards issues such as speeding, drink driving or safe sex. These campaigns have various degrees of success

If an organisation can position and deliver its offer in a way that is consistent with the attitudes held by its target group then it is likely that the consumer will be satisfied with the offer. Satisfaction is an important factor in terms of loyalty to a product or service and therefore repeat purchase. Marketing activity can help to reinforce the position of the product through marketing communications and branding.

Strong promotional messages and visual images can have a significant impact on an individual's attitude and behaviour. The Body Shop effectively utilises its marketing activity to reinforce its position as a leading environmentally friendly cosmetics retailer. This positioning and behaviour are consistent with the attitudes of a large number of consumers who buy Body Shop products.

(b) The main influences which impact on the consumer's decision making process are shown in the diagram below.

Cultural	**Social**	**Personal**	**Psychological**	
Culture	Reference groups	Age and life-cycle stage	Motivation	
		Occupation	Perception	**Buyer**
Sub culture	Family	Economic circumstance	Learning	
		Lifestyle	Beliefs and attitude	

This **combination** of cultural, social, personal and psychological factors which for the most part marketers cannot control will influence the consumer's decision making process and behaviour. It is critical for marketers to understand these influences when developing and implementing marketing strategy.

Cultural and social factors can significantly influence attitudes, values and the decision making process. Basic values and norms are learnt from growing up in a certain place or society. Individuals develop perceptions or the world and set expectations which are socially and culturally constructed. Consumer attitudes to health, careers, holidays and individual lifestyles will be strongly influenced by these factors.

Similarly, **social factors** such as family and reference groups will similarly influence behaviour. Marketers need to understand the roles and influence of parent and children on purchase decisions and behaviour within the family unit. Husband and wife involvement varies widely by product and significant changes in society such as working mothers have led to traditional buying roles being reversed.

Personal circumstances will also influence the purchase decision. Age and stage in the family life cycle will create new needs as will current economic circumstance particularly on the level of disposable income. Lifestyle changes will significantly influence purchase decisions. Lifestyle changes will significantly influence purchase decisions. Lifestyle is a person's pattern of living which is expressed in their activities, interests and opinions. A person's purchase choice is often a reflection of their lifestyle.

Finally, **psychological factors** will influence an individual's purchase decision. How people perceive the world or objects and their motivations for acting are important determinants of how they think and behave. Their attitudes and beliefs will influence their likes or dislikes, interests and disinterests.

This summary of influences which impact on the consumer demonstrates the complexity of the task facing marketers as they attempt to understand and influence the decision making process. Only through investing in consumer research activity will they begin to develop understanding of consumers' decision making processes and utilise this information in their marketing planning and activities.

5   Green marketing

> Examiner's comments. This seemed to be a popular question which was tackled reasonably well. The requirement for a report was often not noted but there seemed to be a good understanding of terms and examples in the main were appropriate.
>
> Part (b) was not answered as well. Weaker answers failed to address it in the context of the marketing mix.

(a)   **Report**

Subject: Green Marketing

Date: December 1999

Social responsibility and green marketing

Organisations are increasingly aware that stakeholders and society are interested in their activities beyond the product that they offer. Organisations are finding the need to demonstrate a 'social conscience' and behave in a socially responsible manner. A new range of needs has evolved around care for society. These represent both opportunities and threats to the organisation.

Green marketing reflects society's growing concern for the environment. Products and services are now being designed to in response to a growing consciousness and concern with the damage that is being done to the natural environment through pollution, large construction projects. There is also a trend to use organic or 'natural' products and to recycle waste.

Increasingly customers are concerned about the moral and ethical responsibility of organisations to their environment. Consumer watchdog, the media and pressure groups are providing wider publicity and channels for consumer concerns. In the future, boards of directors will need to demonstrate through actions and not only words that social responsibility and green marketing are central aspects of their strategy.

Examples of organisations adopting a social responsibility

The Body Shop is a good example of an organisation that is both socially responsible and which adopts green marketing policies. The Body Shop engages in many socially responsible activities outside of its retailing operations. These activities are frequently headed by Anita Roddick to maximise publicity and are consistent with Body Shop values and culture.

The Body Shop policy of not selling products tested on animals and using recyclable and minimal packaging has also positioned this organisation as the leading proponent of green marketing issues.

Organisations such as multiple retailers who currently only pay lip service to green issues through the stocking of organic products on their shelves will in future face considerable pressure to demonstrate greater concern for the green environment. This will be particularly true in relation to their treatment of farmers and rural communities. Simply recognising a market trend for organic food is not a strong support for green issues.

(b) **The implications of these issues from a marketing perspective relating to consumers and the marketing mix**

Ethical behaviour

Organisations should ensure that their actions are those that stakeholders perceive to be ethical. Fir the Co operative bank, this underpins their brand position as the ethical bank. They deliver a series of promises to their target audience to behave ethically and responsibly in their banking activities. The marketing strategy of the bank is governed by this policy. Ethical behaviour also underpins the Body Shop brand with their concern for the natural environment and for animals.

Marketing communications messages

It is key for a socially responsible organisation to ensure that the communications message to consumers and key stakeholders is appropriate and supports the brand's position. In particular, public relations activity should be central to the communications activity, promoting and reinforcing the brand communications. Advertising messages and sales promotions can also be utilised incorporating the socially responsible message.

Recyclable ingredients/packaging

The use of materials and ingredients in products or packaging is also important. Paper, glass and plastics that can be recycled provide an important method of environment protection, particularly in terms of managing scarce resources, waste disposal and energy consumption.

Green distribution methods

Utilising vehicles that minimise the vehicle exhaust pollution or utilise alternative methods of distribution are provide an opportunity to reduce pollution and congestion. Similarly, utilising energy efficient forms of warehouse storage and stock handling can provide benefits to the environment.

Organisation and employee responsibility for the environment

Ensuring that the organisation has a clearly communicated policy of social responsibility and that this is reflected in the organisation's and in its employees' behaviour. It is important that this behaviour is consistent with the positioning of the brand to avoid any possibility of bad publicity.

Transparent pricing and selling

An important implication that arises from adopting a socially responsible position is to ensure that the pricing strategy and selling techniques used by the organisation do not confuse the consumer. In the car industry in the UK, there is currently a widely held belief that the customer is paying more than a fair price. Prices in the rest of Europe are considerably cheaper and more transparent in comparison. In the UK it is the responsibility of the consumer to negotiate the best purchase deal. Daewoo entered the UK car market with a promise of openness and fairness to customers after research indicated that the consumer did not trust car dealers.

6   Relationship marketing

Tutorial note. This is a reasonable attempt at the first part of the question and this is backed up with examples, which are related to the scenario given. There is evidence of a clear understanding of database marketing and has considered the elements of relationship marketing quite well. It has been related to the scenario given and there is an attempt to consider the buyer behaviour model and evaluate the stages in terms of opportunities for building relationships

Examiner's comments. This was a very popular question. Most answers really entered into the spirit of this part of the question with some good ideas for the use of a database applied to the context of car dealership. There were some very innovative suggestions which illustrated a good understanding of the theory and illustrated specific application. The second part was less well answered, since there was a tendency to discuss examples of customer relationships without establishing the benefits to customers and firms.

(a)
MEMORANDUM

To: Mr N Shani, Managing Director, Signature Cars

From: Stuart Ford, Marketing Assistant

Date: 7th December 2001

Subject: Database and Relationship Management

I should like to draw your attention to a number of issues which I believe we should be considering in building loyalty and customer relations from our current database.

Database Marketing

As a car dealership for Fords motorcars, we have developed a database of customers who have purchased cars from this dealership in the last two years. This includes information relating to:

- Age, name, address,
- Date of purchase,
- Finance requirements,
- Type of car, colour, model, accessories,

- Customer service requirements, aftersales requi

- Employee who dealt with the customers

This information allows us to have a clearer understan
underpins the relationship with them. It also allows
understand the contributing factors to their defection tc

We will need to consider how we can use this datab
and decision making. Therefore, we will need to cons
targeted for our special events. We will also be abl
promotions, such as free valeting for the first 12 m
consider the introduction of loyalty schemes such a
purchase a new car from us, where the customer can re

We can use the data in a predicative manner to anti
and respond in an appropriate way, for example, a c...... who has a history of
purchasing a vehicle every two years should be contacted after 20 months to initiate the
relationship during this complex decision process.

The data from this database will allow us to contact our customer directly and reassure
them that they have made the right decision when buying a Ford car from us, creating
loyalty through customer magazines, competition . This should help to reduce post purchase
dissonance which customers often face after buying a new car which is a high involvement
decision.

Databases will make it easier to contact customer for feedback therefore allowing us to
discover satisfaction levels and set about delighting customers. Whenever a past customer
contacts their dealership their records will be to hand, speeding up the processes and
avoiding more paperwork.

(b) **Relationship Marketing**

For any organisation it saves on resources to keep customers rather than finding new ones,
thus relationship marketing is important in developing beneficial longer-term relationships.
Therefore, RM focuses on servicing repeat purchasers rather than delivering short-term
profit.

Under a relationship marketing approach, all the activities of an organisation are used to
build, maintain and develop customer relationships, the objective being to build customer
loyalty, thereby leading the customer retention. Relationship management is concerned with
getting and keeping customers by ensuring that an appropriate combination of marketing,
customer service and quality is provided. In order for relationship marketing to work, it is
important to recognise that both parties must feel that they can benefit from long-term
relationships rather than one-off transactions. A key element of relationship marketing is that
development of such mutually beneficial long-term relationships between customers and
suppliers. Relationship marketing also widens the concept of exchange to consider all of the
parties involved. To ensure successful relationship marketing there needs to be an
appropriate supportive organisational culture and everyone in the business must be
concerned with generating customer satisfaction.

It is important to recognise that consumers have become more sophisticated and therefore,
the purchasing buying behaviour has become more complex. Customers require a more
customised offering and therefore require individual treatment. Customers are becoming
more susceptible to switching behaviour between suppliers and competition has increase in
the marketplace. Focus on trust and loyalty have become key elements of the marketing
activity.

dealership, relationship marketing can be applied through such service ... as test drives, delivery of the purchase, subsequent servicing of the car and ...g issues related to the purchase.

Conclusion

Relationship marketing is a technique that accommodates the broader perspective of building loyal customers in an ever increasingly competitive market place dominated by mobile customers with a wide variety of needs.

7 Relationship marketing and loyalty

Examiner's comments. The first part of the question required candidates to explain the concept of relationship marketing as a strategy for achieving loyal customers. The answer should have included a definition of the relationship marketing concept and the concept of life-long value in relation to customers. Thus, the candidate's answer should have offered reasons for relationship marketing which could have included issues relating to the more sophisticated consumer, increased marketing efforts by competitors, the growth of consumer switching behaviour for FMCGs.

The second part of the question required candidates to explain the role of database marketing for retaining loyal customers. The answer should have first explained the reasons for database marketing and then gone on to discuss the use of a database - for example to identify behaviour, for targeted promotions, etc.

REPORT

Prepared for:	D Beckham, Sales Manager
Prepared for:	M Owen, Marketing Manager
Date:	13 June 2002
Ref:	CRM01
Title:	Relationship Marketing

(a)

1.0 Introduction

Customer relationship marketing is becoming more and more important. This is due to increased customer education and expectations. Many large firms now have reflective policies and I believe that it is now time for use to follow suit.

2.0 Customer Life-time Value

With the recent implementation of a customer orientation, we should now be considering the life time value of our customers. The sale should not be considered the end of the relationship but instead the beginning. The lifetime value of the customer and how it costs more to recruit a new customer (between 3 to 7 times more) than to retain an existing one. It is more beneficial and cost effective therefore to increase the amount of their custom than to attract new customers.

For any organisation it is more efficient to keep customers rather than finding new ones, thus relationship marketing is important. A happy customer will come back for more. Over two thirds of people will go elsewhere if they received an indifferent service. This clearly indicates that there is room for improvement in this area for most companies.

3.0 **Relationship Marketing**

Relationship marketing is a long-term approach to creating, maintaining and enhancing strong relationships with customers and other stakeholders. Organisations need to view any transaction as part of a long-term goal since if the customer is satisfied with the product/service they have received for the price they have paid they are more likely to return. A short-term outlook will consider a quick profit but not consider repeat purchases.

There are five different distinguishable levels or relationships that can be formed with customers who have purchased a company's product. They are:

- Basic – Selling a product without any follow up

- Reactive – Selling a product with follow up encouraged on the part of the customer

- Accountable – Having sold a product the follow up occurs a short afterwards to confirm the customer's expectations have been met

- Proactive – The sales person contact the customer from time to time with suggestions regarding improved products

- Partnership – The Company work continuously with the customer to deliver improved levels of value

Relationship marketing can contribute to an organisation in a number of ways:

- Establish a rapport with customers, creating trust and confidence

- Allows an opportunity to interact and thereby communicate the organisation's commitment to satisfy customers and help improve their experience

- Adds that personal touch, which then associates emotion of both parties, creating a bond.

- As one of its objectives, relationship marketing strives to achieve a sense of belonging, thereby making the customer feel part of the business

- Attempts to tailor products and services to cater for specific needs of customers, hence reducing the need to switch behaviour.

4.0 **Benefits of Relationship Marketing**

Benefits that could be reaped from using such a strategy:

- Significant cost savings – it is 3-7 times more expensive to find a new customer than retaining an existing one

- Entice new customers away from competitors – relationship marketing will make it more difficult for your customers to switch, but make it more desirable for competitors' customers to switch their loyalty to your company.

(b)

MEMORANDUM

Royal Insurance Company

To: Percy Stuart, Marketing Manager

From: Alex Bath, Marketing Assistant

Date: 13 June 2002

Subject: Database Marketing and the Retention of Loyal Customers

I am unable to attend the meeting next week with regards to database marketing, so I would like you to go in my place. I have jotted down a few points for you, so you are fully briefed on this topic.

The role of database marketing in retaining loyal customers:

- Enables us to have strong collaboration of records with full details of our clients

- This enables us to profile our clients into segments. We can also mirror this information and use it for targeting outside the existing list, in terms of demographics and psychographics

- It allows us to direct mail customers about particular products, new products or to upgrade the insurance cover they already have with us.

- It allows us to have better communication with our clients, calling them by their correct title and using the correct full address

- We can monitor the customers' buying behaviour and particular buying habits. Again this is useful for segmentation and the identification of particular types of customers for new products. It also helps us to predict their needs in advance and thus target them with promotions to help them make the decision to stay with our insurance policies.

- We can monitor problems with our service and also the insurance package we offer, if people stop taking our car insurance for instance we can find out why.

- We can survey our customers to help us improve aspects of their concerns.

- We can build a loyalty scheme for our customers who are customers who are ready to renew their insurance. We can have different grades of loyal customers such as gold, platinum and silver which offers different levels of incentives for the customers.

I hope this helps you at the meeting. Please do not hesitate to contact me should you require any further clarification.

8   Market penetration

MEMORANDUM

TO: Managing Directory, Happy Hotel Chain

FROM: Sheila Hope, Marketing Executive, Strategy Systems

DATE: 14 June 2001

SUBJECT: Marketing Penetration Vs Marketing Skimming

In preparing this memorandum for the Happy Hotel chain, Strategy Systems hope to provide sufficient information on market penetration and skimming strategies as well as an appropriate marketing mix breakdown for a penetration option.

Marketing Penetration and the Ansoff Matrix

Market Penetration Strategy – Increase market share in existing markets with current product. This would involve penetration pricing policies, perhaps cutting your existing prices to compete with competitors. Increased promotion including personal selling, sales promotion and advertising in the trade press.

Ansoff Matrix

	Current Products	*New Products*
Current Markets	*Market penetration Strategy* • *Gain customers from competitors* • *Retain loyal customers* • *Ensure customers buy more frequently*	*Product development strategy*
New Markets	*Market development Strategy*	*Diversification strategy*

Market Penetration Strategy Vs Marketing Skimming

Commonly discussed within a pricing context, the concept behind this penetration strategy is to penetrate a market with a pricing policy which will stimulate large levels of demand. The price option is often low when penetrating. It is chosen when economies of scale can be made and the seller faces a market with elastic demand. Japanese motor cycle manufacturers opted for this strategy when launching product in the UK market. Such was their success that they dominated the market in a very short time. A possible barrier to adopting this type of strategy might be branding. It is important to ask how branding might impact upon demand.

In contrast a market skimming strategy is often linked to a new product launch, not necessarily gaining customers from the competition. It involves bringing the product into the market place with a high price tag – such as digital cameras currently. The revenue gained from innovator

BPP PUBLISHING

purchase at this stage can be used to pay for high research and develop, including pre-launch costs, (despite the fact that innovators tend to only represent 2.5% of the buying market). Market skimming can also be chosen when supply is limited and a high level of quality and prestige needs to be attached to that product. Therefore, we need to consider where the Happy Hotel chain sits in terms of brand perceptions when compared to its competitors.

Comparisons Between Penetration and Skimming

Market Penetration	*Market Skimming*
Price of the service is low	Price of the service is very high
This is applied when the product already exists in the market	This is mainly used when it is a new product (new innovation)
Market share captured will be very high	Marketing share captured initially would be low

Market Penetration	*Market Skimming*
Quantity demanded will be high since the price is low	Quantity demanded will be low since the price is high
Used to attract customers from the competitors	Used to attract customers who feel price is an indication of prestige
Promotional spend will be very high and message concentrates on awareness of price and value	Promotion messages will concentrate on prestige of service

(b)

Adaptation of the Marketing Mix for the Hotel Chain Adopting Penetration Strategy

The hotel chain could adopt its marketing mix to achieve penetration by the following:

Price

The price should be low, therefore we need to reduce the price or introduce special weekend breaks, two for one offers, free additional night, offer discount off meals or offer free accommodation but payment for meals (if the restaurant has a good reputation). Need to consider the competitors' pricing strategy and price just below or at the same level but add extra services (see product). A number of hotel chains in the UK has adopted this strategy – eg Travel Inns charge £49.00 per night for the room, regardless of the number of people staying (up to four can stay in the room).

Place/Physical Evidence

Advertise the beauty of the hotels; a unique location, seaside etc. Since the price is low the number of guests would be very high. Therefore the hotel chain should ensure that they have the capacity to cope with this. The hotel rooms, restaurant, reception and linen needs to be always clean.

Product/Service

The hotel should be able to cater for large numbers of guests. The service should be of a reasonable quality which is acceptable for the pricing strategy. There may need to be some consideration of extra services to be added such as a free breakfast however many people staying in the room (up to 4). Again, this needs to be considered in relation to the competitor's offering.

Promotions

Need to increase promotions to ensure that the target market is aware of the pricing and service levels. The use of mass publicity such as advertisements in travel supplements, local advertising, radio, TV, website (which could include a virtual tour). There should be some effort in retaining current customers and ensuring that they stay more regularly. This could be achieved by the database of customers and clients and direct mailshots. A loyalty scheme could be introduced – eg Regular Guest Club with incentives being offered during off peak seasons.

People

A good customer care programme offering a very friendly service to ensure loyalty should be implemented. Therefore staff need to be trained, skilled, motivated resources and committed.

Process

The transaction process is also fundamental. If available the customer will need to have an 'easy time' of making any enquiries or bookings. Therefore, the chain needs to consider its booking in system – perhaps on line, it needs to consider any potential bottlenecks such as waiting times for checking out in the mornings.

Conclusion

I hope that this has helped you consider the implementation of the marketing mix to ensure that the market penetration strategy is successful. Please do not hesitate to contact me should you require any further information.

9 Steps in marketing planning

MEMORANDUM

To: Marketing Manager

From: Kieran Ashford, Marketing Partner

Date: 14 June 2001

Subject: The Importance of PEST and SWOT in Marketing Planning

(a) **PEST Analysis**

PEST stands for Political, Economic, Social/cultural and Technological factors. These should all be considered when formulating a marketing plan. It is essential to undertake an audit to determine where the company is now and we can achieve this by looking at the PEST factors and how they affect the company.

BPP PUBLISHING

The Elements of a PEST and SWOT Analysis

It is important that marketing managers are able to understand the macro environment in which they are operating. This means that a systematic PEST analysis will need to be undertaken on a regular basis. The PEST analysis includes:

- **Political** factors such as a changes in government and the ramifications of their strategies such as tax levels, pollution policies, education issues, increased regulation, etc.

- **Economic** factors such as the impact of the trade cycle, disposable income distribution and changes in purchasing power, inflation, changing consumer spending, etc

- **Social/cultural** issues such as the ageing consumer, increases in one parent families, changing values, attitudes and beliefs to smoking for example, the changing family sizes, role of women, education of people etc.

- **Technological** factors such as the increased rate of computer capability, production methods, etc. This may have an impact on the way customers shop.

The environmental scanning or PEST analysis should help to identify the opportunities and strengths of an organisation and its products/services. In the external audit we may also need to consider Porter's 5 forces which consider further external factors such as the power of the buyer and suppliers, competitors, barriers to entry, etc.

SWOT Analysis

It is also important that a SWOT analysis is undertaken to help plan the marketing mix. SWOT stands for internal strengths and weaknesses and the external opportunities and threats and this is another part of the audit stage of the marketing planning process.

Strengths and weaknesses are internal factors and form part of the internal marketing audit. We should look at all departments here such as finance, sales, research and development.

Opportunities and threats are external factors over which we have no control.

- **Strengths** of the product/ service/ organisation
- **Weaknesses** of the organisation
- **Opportunities** available to the organisation (external factors)
- **Threats** which may come from the competitions or other external factors.

We can use the PEST factors here, as the diagram below illustrates, we should aim to turn our weaknesses into strengths and threats into opportunities. For example the recent foot and mouth crisis in the UK was a major threat to the tourism industry but some attractions turned it into an opportunity by promoting themselves as somewhere to go while the country footpaths were all closed.

SWOT ANALYSIS

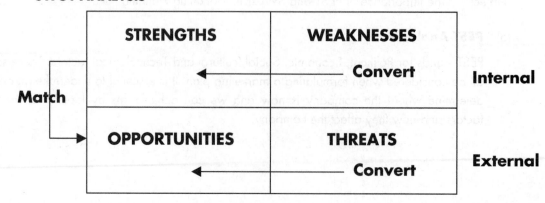

5.0 **Select the Media/ Promotional Tools**

The best method of creating awareness is through advertising through the media, be it television, radio or newspaper, etc. With reference to Relaxing Holidays, I suggest advertising through television will create the most awareness for the new holiday range. Therefore, we will need to consider the most appropriate television stations – i.e. UK Gold on Satellite television or some other niche channels which are consumed by our target audience. We will need to also consider some sales promotions such as an early booking discount to stimulate action.

6.0 **Schedule Media**

I recommend that Relaxing Holidays go with a 'burst' campaign. It is the right time of year (December/January) for the holiday adverts to start. With the burst approach you will have lots of short, sharp adverts in a small space of time to create awareness.

For the elderly clients you wish to attract, you will be looking for television slots from early evening to approximately 9.00 p.m. to coincide with their behaviour.

7.0 **Set Budget**

I can give you an estimate now that for four weeks of advertising at the times I have suggested, it will cost you approximately £50,000 for the air time as we are using niche television channels. You highlighted to me that £60,000 was the limit, so we are within that.

8.0 **Evaluate Effectiveness**

Obviously, the adverts have not gone out yet, so we cannot evaluate at this stage. However, you will be able to evaluate simply by the number of holidays people book with you. If you use promotional discounts these can also be monitored easily. You could also commission some market research for testing awareness.

(b)

MEMORANDUM

TO: Department of Advertising

FROM: Tom Carter – Advertising Manager

DATE: 6 December 2001

SUBJECT: Why Promotional Campaigns will Differ for Industrial Products

1.0 **Industrial Buyers Characteristics**

The following characteristics can be found when considering industrial buyers:

- highly skilled at buying – professionally trained purchasers
- usually large numbers of people involved in the decision making
- goods are purchased for specific reasons within the organisation
- organisational objectives have to be considered when purchasing items for the organisation
- purchases are usually made in bulk, therefore, there are more risks and costs involved than for consumer purchases.

This analysis helps the marketer understand the environment in which the organisation is operating and thus the marketing plan can be devised taking account of the issues identified.

(b) **The Steps Involved in the Marketing Planning Process**

In order to plan the marketing mix effectively, a systematic marketing planning process must be undertaken on a regular basis. The steps involved are as follows:

Corporate objectives

- Decide on a mission statement
- Set the corporate objectives within this

Marketing Audit Analysis:

PEST analysis - marketing opportunities/trends; customers' needs and perceptions; the marketing environment and trends; competition and competitors strategies.

SWOT analysis

As discussed above.

Marketing Objectives set

- What do we want to achieve?
- Should be SMART – specific, measurable, achievable, real and timed

Marketing strategy:

Need to identify the broad perspective and consider the following:

- **Ansoff matrix** to identify the strategy to adopt ie penetration, market development, product development, diversification
- **Segmentation** – what are the key variables?
- **Targeting** – who are our targets?
- **Positioning** for the brand or the product

Tactics - plan marketing mix

- **Pricing policy**
- **Product policy and brand**
- **Place or distribution (logistics and channel management)**
- **Promotion** (mix of advertising, sales promotion, public relations, direct marketing, personal selling, sponsorship etc)

Services mix

- **People** –staff development, motivation, etc
- **Processes** – customer friendly systems, customer care, etc
- **Physical evidence** – uniforms, corporate logo, etc

Implementation of the plan

Monitoring and Control

- Methods to monitor via achievement of objectives on a regular basis
- Readapt the marketing mix to achieve objectives when there is a shortfall

Conclusions

I trust that this is the information which you required. Please let me know if I can help in any other way. I very much look forward to hearing from you.

10 Promotional plan and behaviour

Examiner's comments. The first part of the question relates to the planning of a promotions campaign for the launch of a product of the candidate's choice. Therefore, it was expected that candidates should identify the key stages of planning a promotional campaign and relate it to the launch of a new product. The answer should have considered the promotional objectives, target audience, promotional message, selection of media and promotional tools, budget and some methods of evaluation. Unfortunately, a number of candidates did not fully read the question and in some answers candidates detailed new product development stages and others just wrote about the promotions mix. Clearly, these answers did not gain many marks.

The second part of the question related to the change in promotions mix for an industrial product and this should have been linked to the understanding of the complex B2B behaviour theory. Therefore the answer should have considered the B2B buyer behaviour detailing how this informs the selection of promotional tools. The answer should have considered different objectives, different target audiences and DMU characteristics, smaller budgets, and the appropriateness of the media and reach. The answer would also justify the methods such as personal selling, etc. There should have been some reference to a buyer behaviour model.

(a)

Report to: Amanda Davies – Marketing Manager

From: Tom Carter – Advertising Manager – Relaxing Holidays Plc

Date: 6 December 2001

Subject: Recommended Promotional Campaign for Relaxing Holidays Aimed   at   the Elderly

1.0   Introduction

With reference to Relaxing Holidays Plc, I will discuss the process for devising a campaign for elderly holidays in 2002, which relates to the following model:

Steps for Planning a Promotional Campe

Set promotional objectives

(relating to AIDA)

↓

Identify target audience

↓

Select promotional message

↓

Select media

↓

Schedule media

↓

Set budget

↓

Evaluate effectiveness of promotional campaign

2.0   Set Promotional Objectives

The promotional objectives need to be set. These are usu marketing objectives. Often they relate to the AIDA model, the raising of awareness, stimulating interest, ensuring desir that the target audience takes action. In the case of these important to raise awareness very quickly as the decis holidays is quite complex and lengthy – especially with audience.

3.0   Select Target Audience

As specified in your last memo, the holidays are specificall Therefore, we need to ensure that this segment of the pop we can identify their characteristics and consumption of t once we understand the target audience and their beha specific in the media which we use to ensure that the ta receive the messages.

4.0   Select the Promotional Message

In this case, this is a new range of holidays being offered so the message is all about creating awareness about the holidays.

2.0 **Promotional Tools**

Due to the fact that the characteristics of professional buyers are more specific and the purchase decision is more complex for industrial products the promotional tools used for industrial campaigns are usually different than those for consumer campaigns.

2.1 **Personal Selling** – i.e. trained sales representatives to travel between organisations looking after their needs are more appropriate for industrial products. This is because often the products are more complex and the message can be tailored specifically for that organisation. Therefore, the organisation becomes familiar with the sales team and builds a relationship with them. Therefore, this tool is very important for communications for industrial products – whereas for consumer products this is quite different as there is a mass market usually.

2.2 **Trade Advertising** – advertising in trade magazines (e.g.) manufacturers or car components are more likely to be found in the Auto Trader magazine than they are in House and County magazine. Advertising for industrial products is usually undertaken at a lower level than a campaign for a consumer product, although trade advertising does have a role.

2.3 **Exhibitions** – organised events such as these enable large organisations to get together and promote each other.

2.4 **Public Relations** – corporate hospitality is used to build relationships with the organisation's buyers. Press releases for trade and specific press is also very important as it considered more reliable or believable than advertising by the purchaser – however, the message is not as controlled.

2.5 **Trade Promotions** – the use of promotions such as bulk purchase discount, extended credit, etc can be very helpful in securing some action by the organisation's buyer. These promotions are usually quite different from consumer promotions but do achieve similar objectives i.e. to stimulate action or purchase.

3.0 **Conclusion**

Promotions to industrial buyers are very different to consumer buyers. It would not be worthwhile advertising manufacturers of industrial products of daytime television, as the wrong target audience would view the adverts.

Expertise and knowledge of the products is requires, so that more specific and specialised promotional tools are used.

11 Market research and databases

> Examiner's comments. Candidates should have started their answer by explaining the role of marketing research. The answer should then have detailed the different qualitative methods of research which could have been used such as focus groups, interviews etc. Each method should have been explained and justified for the scenario given. The second part of the answer should have given an introduction to databases and relationship marketing. The answer should then have gone on to explain the sophisticated use of customer databases to improve loyalty and retention for the sports club. Answers could have included identifying customer behaviour, use of mail shots, targets for special events, targeted sales promotion, the introduction of loyalty schemes for past customers etc.

(a)

MEMORANDUM

TO: Chris Broomfield, Manager, Sports Club

FROM: A C Brindley, Trainee Marketing Assistant, Sports Club

DATE: 6 December 2001

SUBJECT: Maximising Membership Renewals

1.0 Introduction

We have recently been experiencing difficulties in getting members to renew their membership subscription. To gain an understanding of why this is happening and what we can do to reverse the situation, we need to conduct some research and come up with solutions to any perceived problems our customers have with us.

2.0 Research

There are a number of research techniques which could be used. The first thing to look at though is whether any secondary research is available, before going on to commission primary research, which will be conducted, to meet our exact needs. We also need to consider internal and external sources of information, and also consider whether we need to use quantitative or qualitative research.

The local council recently carried out research into leisure facilities in the local area. This will give us information our potential customer base and also what options they have – who are our competitors and what they are offering?

Primary research also needs to be undertaken. The most effective research would be by asking our current customers what they think of us, our service, our opening hours, our facilities, etc. This would be qualitative research with an emphasis on open questions to allow the customers to express their views and opinions. Quality of their response is more important than the number of people we research.

This can be done in a number of ways:

2.1 Customer Service Questionnaires – we could make these freely available at reception or sent out to a sample of our customers. It may be worth producing a specific "why did you not review your membership?" questionnaire and mailing it out to customers who do not renew.

2.2 Focus Groups – we could invite customers to come along to an open evening and get them talking about what they like and don't like about the club and

what influences them at renewal time. This is quite an expensive methods but should yield in-depth qualitative data for analysis.

2.3 **Customer Interaction** – our staff can very easily gauge how happy or satisfied our customers are by just asking them when they come in for a visit. Personalise the service to each customer so that they trust us, and they will be more inclined to tell us what we are doing wrong.

2.4 **Customer Suggestion box** – we can provide a suggestion or feedback box for our customers to suggest areas which could be improved.

2.5 **Telephone survey** - this would allow us to discuss more details with respondents but we would need to talk to these people at home. A typical telephone interview would only last a maximum of 15 minutes.

(b)

3.0 **Using the Existing Membership Database**

We already store personal information about our existing customers, as well as when they visit the club, what their fitness programmes are, etc. We need to utilise this information effectively to improve customer loyalty and retention as it costs five times more to attract a new customer as it does to retain an existing one.

Therefore, we could consider the following:

3.1 **Segmenting the Database** – by segmenting the database into times when people use the centre you could offer cut price use of facilities at quieter times to improve football and usage during the day.

3.2 **Incentives** – an incentive for members to introduce new members would be a useful way to grow membership and retain loyalty from the existing members by rewarding them with additional facilities or two months free membership, sports equipment etc.

3.3 **Constant communication** – we could give customers a courtesy call or send a letter or Club newsletter if they haven't been into the club for over three weeks.

3.4 **Promotions** - we could offer to produce a new gym assessment and programme for all customers who haven't visited the gym in the last three months.

3.5 **Social Events** - we could organise some social events at the club, with personal invitations, so that customers associate the club with fun rather than just fitness.

3.6 **Loyalty bonuses** - loyalty bonuses could be offered such as buying 10 sessions with a personal trainer and giving the customer or client 2 free ones.

3.7 **Gold members** - we could provide facilities and services for 'gold' members, such as free towels, use of the crèche, etc for members who visit the club most often. This information would be available from the database.

3.8 **Competitions** – we could run competitions, with prizes of a month or a year's free membership to the winners.

3.9 **Targeting age groups** – we could target certain age groups to come along to different events which might appeal to them. We would get the age profiles from the database.

3.10 **Email communication** – further analysis of the database may show a number of email addressees which could be used for specific communication for these clients. The latest developments and new promotions could be emailed on a very regular basis.

4.0 Conclusion

I hope that some of these suggestions help you. Please do not hesitate to contact me should you require any further information.

12 Marketing research I

Tutor's Note. This answer identifies the concept of secondary research and goes on to discuss actual different sources of information, both internal and external. The reference to the Internet sites was an added bonus. To answer the question fully, the answer then goes on to relate to the reasons why secondary data is collected before primary data. Many other answers related to primary data in some depth, although clearly this was not required. The answer was well presented and also gained marks for this. Many candidates struggled with the second part of this question, but it should be remembered that the uses of IT is going to be a common area on the examination paper in the future.

Examiner's comments: summary/extracts. A popular question, possibly because candidates are relating that some aspect of marketing research is likely to be on the paper.

INTERNAL MEMORANDUM

To: Mr R Hudson-Davies, Marketing Manager
From: R H Roper, Marketing Executive
Date: 7th December 2000
Subject: Marketing Research- The Importance of Secondary Research and the Role of IT in the Marketing Research Process

(a) As you are aware we are currently planning our next phase of research for our newly developed casual shoe which we plan to bring to the market within the next year. Therefore, I feel it is important that we look at the role of secondary research and more specifically the use of information technology in the process of collecting, analysing and presenting the data collected.

However, before we can consider the primary phase of the research it will be necessary to consider the role of secondary research and why we should conduct this type of research before we embark on the more expensive primary phase.

Secondary Research

This is the collection of information which has been already gathered for a particular purpose and has been previously published.

There are two types of **secondary research** sources – internal and external to the organisation.

Internal sources of data could be used to consider the current market place. Internal databases can be used to assess the current sales figures for our existing casual shoe sales from our intermediaries. Information about market needs and trends is usually held within our organisation's marketing intelligence system supported by our sales teams.

External sources relates to collection of information from outside the organisation. Information which has been gathered by the Government such as social trends gives information about lifestyles and leisure activities. The state of the economy can be gathered from the Office of National Statistics which will be important for us to consider in relation to disposable income etc. The Census and population figures will allow us to identify the demographics of the country and identify the size of the potential market.

Market reports which have been researched by agencies, such as Mintel and Keynote, usually provide excellent market intelligence and are now available on the Internet. Journals and newspapers also offer a good range of information about certain issues at the industry and company level.

Secondary Research is important to complete prior to devising the primary stage of the research. This is due to that fact that it may provide all the answers required and therefore negate the need to undertake primary research. Secondary research can be more economical than primary research due to the ease of collection and analysis. It also helps in the design of the research instrument and may identify areas which need to be presented by field research.

(b) **Use of Information Technology in Marketing Research**

The use of developed information technology can now be considered for collecting Secondary data because most governments publish their reports on the Internet, business reports are also available on-line and often via CD Roms. Competitors' websites can be interrogated with the use of search engines to collate information in a format determined by the user.

Primary data can be collected via observational scanning equipment at the retail outlet and home for panel members of a marketing research agency. Interactive digital television will also allow the researcher to gather additional information directly from respondents. These types of data collection methods are known at **quantitative** as they usually be statistically analysed.

However, IT can also be employed in collecting **qualitative** information. Examples of this approach could involve the use of chat rooms and on-line focus groups with webcams etc. There are now also a number of computer packages which can analyse qualitative data (NUDIST).

Analysis of information is another important area where IT can help the researcher. The use of computer software to analyse data with such packages as Windows packages (ie SPSS, Excel), can be used to statistically evaluate quantitative data. Indeed, on-line questionnaires are often set up with a database for responses which can be immediately analysed as soon as the respondents reply.

The **presentation of data** can be vastly enhanced with the use of quite sophisticated IT packages that are linked to the databases used for analysis

Therefore, it can be seen that IT is able to vastly assist in the market research process, from the collection of data, analysis of data to the presentation of data. The use of IT can ensure a high degree of accuracy and credibility of the completed market research report.

13 Marketing research II

Examiner's comments. The question required the candidate to write a report, which outlined a marketing research programme, explaining how each element of the research design could contribute to the slump in sales for a new mobile telephone.

The answer should have defined the problem/objectives of the research; identified the design of research, including secondary sources and primary sources; considered sampling issue - defined the target population; considered the data collection methods including quantitative and qualitative methods; considered the analysis of data: methods to be used, the timing of stages, the personnel to be used. A selection and justification of marketing research methods should have been discussed and the answer should have been realistic in relation to the context set.

REPORT

TO: Saskia Waters, Manager, Singer Electronics

FROM: Gresha Schilling, Research Executive

DATE: 13 June 2002

SUBJECT: Marketing Research Programme for Mobile Telephone

1.0 Introduction

Marketing research has become a key part of ensuring survival of a product and a company. Knowing your market and environment is an integral step on communicating with them effectively.

This report aims to outline such a programme and its design and suggests how this may contribute in showing your problem.

The main steps of the marketing research process are detailed below:

- **Definition of Problem (or objectives setting)**
- **Design of the Research**

    - secondary research from internal and external sources
    - primary research decisions
    - sampling Issues

        - random or non-random
        - size of sample

- **Data Collection and Pilot Phase**

    - qualitative methods (e.g. in-depth interviews or focus groups)
    - quantitative methods (e.g. survey by postal questionnaire)

- **Data Analysis**
- **Findings Related to the Interpretation and Completion of Report**

The manager of this process will also need to consider the staffing skills and budget issues before such research can be undertaken, for example can the organisation afford to commission a research agency to undertake the research.

These steps should lead to the implementation of the findings for quality management decisions.

2.0 Research Programme

2.1 **Clearly identify your problem** – this needs to be done so that all parties involved have a clear knowledge that the sale of the mobile telephones was anticipated to be high, but sales have not met that expectation. A problem cannot be solved if there is confusion as to where the problem lies.

2.2 **Set research objectives for the programme** - this is done to focus all personnel who will be involved in designing, gathering and evaluating information. Clear objectives will also help in evaluating the success of the programme when comparing it with results.

2.3 **Gather Secondary Data** - this includes research collected by your company for previous problems, as well as those published by other institutions:

- Libraries will have trade magazines addressing customer needs, specifications, helping you to see what the problems in design may be.

- Newspapers may have opinion polls on technology. It may provide valuable feedback on your product

- Competitor publications and websites will show how competitors are doing and the various models and features offered by them

- Government publications addressing the political and economic situation in the country, indicating consumer confidence levels and buying patterns

- Market reports such as Mintel and Keynote will have specifically commissioned reports on the usage of mobile telephones.

2.4 **Design of Data Collection** – primary phase. The design of the primary data collection phase must be considered fully in terms of the methods to be used and the sample frames. For this type of research there should be an emphasis on qualitative research methods so that depth information about buying behaviour and perceptions can be identified.

The methods of data collection should be considered:

	Advantages	Limitations
Qualitative Methods Eg interviews, focus groups	More in-depth attitudinal information can be gathered. Observation of NVC can also be gathered. The interviewers can probe and give guidance.	High level skills required by conductors of research. Lengthy process Possibility of bias introduced by interviewers. Analysis of results is more difficult and time consuming Sample size is usually smaller
Quantitative Methods: E.g. surveys, questionnaires	Statistical analysis can be undertaken. Usually easier to analyse the data collected via computer software. Larger sample can be used. Often more economic than other methods.	Inflexible as the questionnaire will need to be short and easy for the respondent. Often low level of response Difficult to use to identify in-depth consumer attitudes and values. Possibility of interpretation of questions by respondents

BPP PUBLISHING

2.5 **Random and Non-Random Samples**

For quantitative research, it is essential that the sample used must be representative of the population from which they are chosen. Random samples are items chosen at random, in a manner which gives all members of the population an equal chance of being chosen.

Non-random sampling methods are quota sampling, stratified sampling, multistage sampling, and cluster sampling. These methods are not as scientific in their approach as not all members of the population have the equal chance of being chosen. However, these methods are usually more economical and less time consuming for most organisations and the results are usually acceptable.

2.6 **Pilot Phase** - a pilot study must be undertaken before the launch of a major piece of research. This type of study will use the same type of respondents from the population although. Usually if it is a questionnaire, which is being piloted, a small number will be sent out and the respondents' responses will be analysed to ensure that the questions are being interpreted correctly.

It is important that a pilot study is undertaken for both qualitative and/or quantitative data collection methods. This will serve to ensure that the instruments and methods used will be effective before the major study is undertaken. If a pilot is not completed, then the organisation runs the risk of not achieving valid data from the research project.

2.7 **Data Analysis** – the methods used for analysing the data should be considered fully. It is more difficult to analyse qualitative data effectively, although there are a number of statistical packages which can help with this such as NUDIST. For quantitative data analysis statistical packages such as SPSS could be used.

A pilot study must be undertaken before the launch of a major piece of research. This type of study will use the same type of respondents from the population although. Usually if it is a questionnaire, which is being piloted, a small number will be sent out and the respondents' responses will be analysed to ensure that the questions are being interpreted correctly.

It is important that a pilot study is undertaken for both qualitative and/or quantitative data collection methods. This will serve to ensure that the instruments and methods used will be effective before the major study is undertaken. If a pilot is not completed, then the organisation runs the risk of not achieving valid data from the research project.

2.8 **Findings Related to the Interpretation and Completion of Report -** the analysis of the data should be interpreted and a comprehensive report which covers the findings from the primary and secondary data collection stages.

3.0 **Conclusion**

To have a comprehensive ongoing research which is recommended a marketing information system should be adopted within the organisation. Thus information could be collected and stored on a regular basis.

Please do not hesitate to contact me should you require any further information about this.

14 Marketing planning and STP

MARKETING PLAN

FOR: R Jenkins, Marketing Director, Golden Vale

FROM: S Ford, Marketing Manager, Golden Vale

DATE: 13 June 2002

TITLE: Benefits of Marketing Planning and STP

(a)

CONTENTS

The following are the factors involved in a marketing plan and will be covered in this report:

1.0   Mission Statement/Corporate Objectives
2.0   Marketing Audit – PEST Factors
3.0   SWOT Analysis – strength, weaknesses, opportunities and threats
4.0   Business Objectives
5.0   Marketing Objectives
6.0   Marketing Strategies – Ansoff Matrix
7.0   Marketing Tactics – Marketing Mix
8.0   Implementation
9.0   Monitoring and Control

There are benefits to using this plan for the development of UK Lush Cheese. The following benefits for each stage are detailed as below:

1.0 Mission Statement/Corporate Objectives

This involves your statement to your customers about your promise to your consumers and objectives as a company. This could involve 'Best fresh dairy products' or 'value for money'. This communicates to your customers that you are committed to these issues as a philosophy for the company.

2.0 Marketing Audit

This involves looking at the changes in the macro environment, Political, Economic, Social and Technological issues. This is beneficial for developing a marketing strategy for your new product and seeing how trends are changing to help target new markets. Porter's 5 forces analysis also allows you to identify competitor information or intelligence. The marketing audit also requires a company not only to research externally but also internally – thus an internal audit of the current marketing practices is required and is beneficial as it requires companies be brutal about what is working and what is not internally.

3.0 SWOT Analysis

This involves considering your company internal strengths and weaknesses, and the external opportunities and threats. It is like a prioritised summary of the marketing audit. The benefits of this would be that you could identify where you need to improve internally and identify opportunities in the future. For example you may need to consider some new competitors like Farming Products Plc who have just launched a children's cheese product. You can also see how to market your new products using your strengths as a basis.

4.0 Business Objectives

These include your objectives for the future e.g. leading brand to have lowest production costs. The benefit here is that this will encourage you to monitor and achieve these objectives as a company and it will make you be more forward thinking.

5.0 Marketing Objectives

These include your marketing objectives such as objectives relating to your share of the market, profit factors and sales targets. The new development of a product such as UK Lush cheese may have a target to achieve a certain market share such as 5% within 3 years. The benefit here is that this objective can be evaluated on an annual basis and this will help in terms of deciding or changing where necessary the strategy and tactics to achieve this.

6.0 Marketing Strategies

The Ansoff Matrix is used to help determine the most appropriate strategy for growth.

	Existing Products	New Products
Existing Markets	**Market Penetration Strategy**	**Product Development Strategy**
New Markets	**Market Development Strategy**	**Diversification Strategy**

The Ansoff Growth Matrix

It is beneficial to see which strategy can be used to consider the strategic options available to market your new product or any existing products effectively.

7.0 Marketing Tactics

This involves the application of the marketing mix to determine the strategy you are going to use. Consideration therefore of price, product, place, promotion, people, physical evidence and processes is important.

It is beneficial to consider each of these to achieve the overall strategy required and this process makes the marketing and sales people think about the overall marketing of the product rather than just their own area.

8.0 Implementation

This involves testing the strategy either for our new UK Lush product or other products.

9.0 Monitoring and Control

This involves feedback and control of the new strategy to ensure it is effective and targeted to the correct market.

(b)

There are concepts of segmentation, targeting and product positioning which are also important for planning your new UK Lush cheese.

10.0 Segmentation of Markets

The growth of specialised segments in a market has resulted in firms producing goods and services that are more closely related to the requirements of particular kinds of customers. Instead of treating our customers as the same, we have identified sub-groups of customers whose precise needs can be more effectively met with a targeted approach. There are three stages of target marketing, which are:

Market Segmentation

Identify basis for segmentation

Determine important characteristics of each market segment

↓

Market Targeting

Select one or more segments

↓

Product Positioning

Develop detailed product positioning for selected segments

Develop a marketing mix for each selected segment

We need to consider the variables for segmenting the market as below:

- **Demographic**; Age, gender, family size, social class and disposable income, and education

- **Perceived benefit**; different people buy the same or similar products for quite different reasons such as considering our new cheese product as a children's lunch item, sandwich filler or healthy option.

- **Loyalty;** analysis of brand loyalty can tell us much about our customers attitude to our current brand and thus we could stretch an existing brand name to include our new cheese product.

- **Lifestyle and cultural considerations**; understanding how consumer groups spend their time and money, reflecting their cultural attitudes and beliefs will be seen in the take up and targeting of products incorporating our new cheese product.

11.0 Targeting

There are three main concepts involving the adaptation of the marketing mix (price, product, place and promotion) when targeting each segment. They are:

- *Undifferentiated targeting* – using one marketing mix to target all segments of the market. This is not a very customer orientated method.

- *Differentiated targeting* – use a few different marketing mixes for a couple of main segments of the market

- *Concentrated targeting* – use one specific marketing mix for each segment of the market – e.g. specific marketing mix for the health market for our UK Lush product.

12.0 Market Positioning for UK Lush Cheese

Having designed the new cheese we will need to adopt a marketing mix to fit a given place in our customer or consumer's mind. Using marketing research we should establish the position of our competitor's products in any given market segment and then determine how to position our products in the most favourable way.

The following perceptual map should help us to do determine the positioning of the UK Lush cheese.

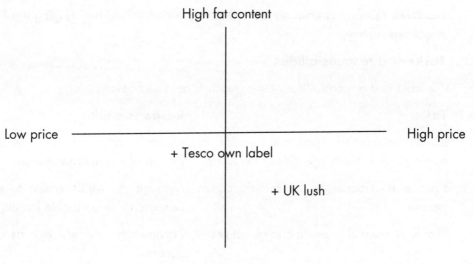

High fat content

Low price ——————————————————— High price

+ Tesco own label

+ UK lush

Low fat content

This determines how each segment of the market will perceive the product.

13.0 **Conclusion**

It is important to use a variety of methods and adapt the marketing mix to target each segment of the market required. A marketing plan is essential when developing such strategies for each product to achieve a competitive advantage.

15 Systematic research

> Examiner's comments: summary/extracts. Many answers discussed the difference between primary and secondary research rather than the need to have an MkIS.

To: Marketing Director
From: Marketing information function
Date: 5th December 1996
Subject: **Tasks and responsibilities a marketing research and marketing information system**

Introduction

The marketing research function is an integral part of a wider marketing information system. In this report I will outline the nature of such a system and the roles and responsibilities that should be undertaken.

Marketing research encompasses a broad range of research activities ranging from market surveys and customer surveys through to measuring the effectiveness of advertising, sales force activity and distributors.

Such information provides useful data upon which to develop marketing strategy and assess the performance of our marketing activities.

The marketing information system requires a broader range of information to be collected and analysed.

The marketing research function is one part of such a system. Marketing decisions should not be made without considering the organisation's marketing environment and internal information such as financial data and quality. The MkIS system should also provide a system whereby such information can be processed and then disseminated to appropriate decision makers.

Marketing research is often outsourced to external suppliers, but bringing it in-house can involve major expenditure.

Tasks and responsibilities

The tasks and responsibilities of such function are listed below.

Tasks	Responsibilities
Identify and advise upon the selection of appropriate research agencies or personnel	Maintain database of agencies or key personnel within organisation
Liase with departments as to information needs	Manage the MKIS system to ensure data produced is in a useable format
Clarify purpose of research and objectives	Provide advisory service to assist marketing personnel
Assist in the design of research programmes and collection/analysis of data	Provide advisory service
Set up and manage environmental scanning system	Collect and collate both macro and micro environment information
Set up and manage internal audit system	Collect and collate internal data
Supply useful and useable information to key decision makers	Set up databases and statistical analysis software

The MKIS will aim to provide a continuous flow of useable and appropriate information throughout the organisation to aid decision making in relation to specific marketing problems. The implementation of such a system with a clear understanding of its roles and responsibilities will reduce the need for making key decisions with ad hoc data.

16 Direct marketing and distribution

Tutorial note. The answer is presented well, even though, this was not specifically asked for in the question, therefore, the candidate picked up marks for this. It is quite a comprehensive answer that covers most of the elements required, but in some areas tends to go off at a tangent. The answer uses some good examples to back up their statements and this should be encouraged.

Examiner's comments. A common fault was to identify types of direct marketing with good examples, but to omit reasons for the growth of direct marketing. The second part of the question was not answered as well. Many candidates were not specific enough.

(a)   INTERNAL MEMORANDUM

To: Supply Chain Director
From: Marketing Director
Date: 7 December 2000
Subject: Report on the growth in direct marketing

Following our recent discussions I have outlined some issues relating to the recent growth in direct marketing.

Direct marketing has become an increasingly popular method of marketing and reaching the consumer. A key reason for this is the increased use and availability of technology which is now a vital tool for the market. The following points explain further the growth of this marketing method:

(i) **Marketing Orientation**

Organisations need to focus on customers in order to achieve long term profitability. They need to be aware of their range of needs and how to satisfy them. This knowledge gives competitive advantage.

Customers are exposed to increasing forms of media – from traditional TV, press and radio through to interactive television (DRTV) and the Internet. Consequently, marketers need to find news ways to access the consumer and direct marketing is one of the key issues. It appeals to customers' needs for speed and convenience.

(ii) **Databases**

Competitive organisations need an efficient marketing information system which stores a variety of data about business and market intelligence, including sales figures, customer buying habits, slow moving lines and recurring faults. The system should be continuously updated and cleaned regularly to ensure integrity and accuracy of the data. It should also be easy to extract information from the data.

The database aids direct marketing because:

- It stores customers' addresses
- It holds information about buying patterns
- It enables us to segment customers requirements
- It enables us to target more accurately our customer base

For example, the information gleaned from the Tesco loyalty card is stored on their database. This enables Tesco to target consumers with direct marketing: offering discounts on product that they regularly buy in order to attract them into the store.

(iii) **The Internet**

The Internet offer another form of data collection. For example, if you access the Virgin record store site you will be required to fill in a registration form which provides Virgin with a host of information about buying habits and enables them to target more precisely their offering. Directing traffic to the website is an important consequence of direct marketing. The website gives vast amounts of information about a company and is a source of revenue through the e-commerce channel.

(iv) **Segmentation and Targeting**

This is increasingly competitive tool as by segmenting their customer base marketers can target customers more efficiently. All customers in a segment (based on geographic, demographic or psychographic criterion) will respond to the same stimuli, and so we can maximise sales in each segment. Direct marketing is a means of exploiting the profitablity of segmentation and targeting.

(v) **Relationship Marketing**

This is another competitive tool which involves building up a long term relationships with the customers in order to establish trust and loyalty. Direct marketing can make customers feel special – for example, J Sainsburys has a reward scheme that is orientated individual customer needs.

(vi) **Cost and Reach**

Direct marketing cuts the cost of intermediaries which may reduce the overheads of our business. It should enable our company to reach a wide audience relatively more economically.

(vii) **Customer Convenience**

Customers may be encouraged to buy via direct marketing because it is convenient – they do not have to go to the shops and they can often buy on credit.

(b) **Introduction - Product Life Cycle**

(i) The product life cycle is a tool for measuring the life of a product and the characteristics of each phase is as follows:

Development	Introduction	Growth	Maturity	Decline
No sales High R&D costs Test market	Low sales Negative profits Innovator customers Few competitors	Rapidly rising sales Rising profits Early adopters More competitors	High sales High profits Middle majority customers Competitors start to decline	Declining sales Declining profits Lagard customers Smaller number of competitors

During the maturity phase, distribution may be changed for the following reasons:

- The product has become well-established and consumers will begin to be drawn to more innovative products. Consequently demand will begin to wane.

- Retails will become less inclined to give the product prime shelf space. Therefore, the company must begin to look for new distribution channels, eg mail order and direct mail. These target customers directly and can be less expensive for the business as it excludes intermediaries in the supply chain. Conversely, those channels which are now proving to be costly to sustain should be rationalised in favour of the more profitable channels.

- Revenue from the product will begin to decline, and there will be less resources available for sales promotions – particularly point of sales displays instore. Direct marketing may represent a way of reducing promotional spend – yet sill getting the product to the customer.

- New markets – the organisations may need to penetrate new markets in order to extend the life of the product. E-business would be a good avenue to explore. By setting up a website and selling on-one, the business could target new customers and potentially save on distribution costs.

Therefore, it is essential that an organisation considers the distribution decisions for a consumer product entering the maturity stage of the PLC and exploits the opportunities advanced from technological innovation in distribution.

17 Effective communications

Marketing research report to investigate the effectiveness of the dentists' marketing communications to their patients.

(a) **Structure and content of the marketing research plan**

(i) **Defining the problem**

The marketing communications problem that the dentists wish to resolve must be properly defined. This will require careful consultation with the group of dentists to clarify the nature of the problem and decide the information needed.

(ii) **Setting research objectives**

Clear objectives for the research project should be stated at the outset. All parties should agree that if these objectives are met the research brief will have been met. Objectives should be explicit and realistic to achieve bearing in mind the time scales and resources available.

(iii) **Design of the research**

The research project should be designed to ensure that the research methods adopted are methodologically sound in terms of the quality, validity and relevance of the data collected. A combination of market research techniques may be adopted to obtain the necessary data.

Qualitative and quantitative techniques can be considered.

Qualitative studies	Quantitative studies
Awareness and recall tests	Tracking studies
Customer perception studies	Questionnaires
Attitudinal studies	Pre and post tests
Behavioural studies	

Qualitative research can be conducted with individuals or in focus groups, with on small sample size. **Quantitative techniques** will be used with an individual but will require larger sample size.

(iv) **Collection of data**

Appropriate data collection methods with good questionnaire design, correct sample sizes and appropriate interview techniques etc are crucial to ensure no bias or incorrect information is obtained from the research. Correct procedures at this stage make data analysis easier at the next stage. Patients should feel comfortable with answering the questions and that for such data collection methods as interviews or focus groups, the environment is conducive to generating discussion.

(v) **Data analysis.** A range of statistical techniques can be used to analyse quantitative data ranging from simple regression and correlation, to testing for statistical significance. Qualitative data analysis is more interpretative of behaviour patterns or attitudes / motives which whilst not quantifiable can provide a richer insight into consumer behaviour. The quality of the findings from this data analysis depends upon the rigour and quality of the research methodology and techniques adopted.

(vi) **Timescale.** The marketing research plan should include a timescale by which the various stages of the research process will be carried out and completed. Regular meetings should be scheduled to monitor progress.

(vii) **Budget.** An indication of cost should be given for each stage of the research project with a clear indication of what is covered. At our next meeting we can discuss areas and levels of required expenditure.

The above represent the most appropriate structure and content of the marketing research plan. I look forward to receiving your comments in due course.

(b) The benefits and limitations of using qualitative data collection techniques such as focus groups and interviews for this type of research are as follows.

Benefits	Limitations
Flexible and can gather large quantity of information.	Small sample sizes therefore difficulty in minimising bias within responses.
Useful for gaining insight into attitudes and behaviour.	Time consuming and relatively more expensive.
Difficult questions can be explained therefore minimising misinterpretation of question.	Difficulty of interpreting non quantifiable data.
Difficult issues can be more readily explored.	Group or individual may not be open and honest with interviewer or peers.
Visual observation of behaviour is possible.	Bias may creep in if participants are aware of being observed or recorded.
Allows interviewer to probe, guide and explore issues as they arise.	Danger of interviewer bias.

18 Charity market research

Examiner's comments: summary/extracts. This was not a popular question, however, those that did attempt it seemed to handle it reasonably well. Good answers identified the components of the MkIS and employed examples in the context of the question. Poorer answers did not apply the MkIS to the example. The second part of the question was often answered in a general way – not addressing the context of the question.

Report

To: Chief Executive
From: Marketing department
Date: 9 September 1999
Re: Marketing information system

(a) **Market information system design**

1.1 The marketing information system that I recommend as suitable for this charity organisation is illustrated in the following diagram.

Marketing planning	Developing information		Marketing environment
Analysis	Assessing information needs	Internal records	Target markets
Planning	Distributing information	Marketing intelligence	Marketing channels
Implementation	Information analysis	Marketing research	Competitors
Organisation			Publics

1.2 The Marketing Information System (MKIS) represents a systematic attempt to supply continuous, useful and useable marketing information to decision makers in an organisation. The information must be gathered from the market place and the market environment and assessed, evaluated and disseminated to the relevant people.

1.3 The MKIS requires a commitment from all the people in an organisation. It also requires resources to be directed at it and formalised procedures for information to be passed on and used.

1.4 The information is fed into the marketing planning process from analysis through to implementation and control.

Sources of information

2.1 The information needed by marketing managers comes from internal company records, marketing intelligence and marketing research. The information analysis system processes this information to make it more useful for managers.

2.2 For this charity, numerous sources of information can be accessed. It is possible to hold information about the contributors to the charity and their level of loyalty on a database. The database can be used to assess frequency and value of donations, identification of lapsed donors, and degree of support.

2.3 The information kept on the database can be used to evaluate the effectiveness of various promotional and direct marketing campaigns. Key trends in charity donations and the impact of external factors such as the lottery can be monitored from secondary data sources.

2.4 Gathering and assessing data about attitudes and motivation can provide useful insights into the behaviour of potential donors and possible new segments to target campaigns towards.

(b) **The role of marketing research within the MKIS**

3.1 Marketing research is a more structured and organised process than the gathering of marketing information. It also provides important information to the marketing decision maker. While market intelligence is fed into the organisation in a piecemeal

BPP PUBLISHING

manner from information gleaned from customers, suppliers, employees and trade publications, marketing research requires more studies or purchase of market information.

3.2 Marketing research provides more structured and detailed information with clear objectives and reason for it being collected. For instance, this information can be used to identify new opportunities, assess the attractiveness of these opportunities, assess donor satisfaction and evaluate effectiveness of marketing activity, Even a small charity such as this can carry out low cost forms of research to aid decision making.

3.3 Marketing research can be sourced from secondary data or collected as primary data. It can be quantitative or qualitative in nature depending on the objectives of the research. Secondary data sources include internal records but also government or market statistics and reports. Primary sources can be collected through questionnaires or interviews and focus groups.

3.4 The important issue is why the charity needs the information and what resources it can commit to both collecting and assessing the data. The marketing data gathered should be used to enable decisions to be made which will improve the charity's marketing effectiveness and its market position.

3.5 Investment in marketing research will assist the charity in understanding its market position, donor behaviour, and the effectiveness of its marketing activity. This information is an important part of the overall MKIS. It is strongly recommended that such an investment is made to support the charity in its marketing planning process.

19 Marketing planning process

Examiner's comments. The first part of the question was often rather bland. Often there was no consideration of where this process fits in marketing planning … little evidence of understanding. Candidates should remember to consider the marks available in relation to what they write.

(a) A SWOT analysis identifies the strengths and weaknesses of the organisation relative to the opportunities and threats it faces in its marketing environment. The SWOT analysis leads to an understanding of realistic market opportunities through the process of a detailed marketing audit, covering market and environment analysis, competitor and supplier analysis, customer analysis and internal analysis.

This analysis will highlight potential market gaps, new customer needs, marketing channel developments, competitor strategies and their strengths and weaknesses. The organisation can evaluate market opportunities against its strengths and weaknesses and identified threats and determine what actions to take to exploit the opportunity.

(b) To successfully launch a new customer product into the UK market the organisation needs to have clear and realistic objectives and identification and understanding of its target market segment. Its channel of distribution, branding, packaging and communications activity need to be in place to support the launch. Forecasts of future demand, and return on investment need to be assessed and projected.

A formalised marketing planning system that involves all departments, customers, agents and suppliers, the complexity and timing of activities is required to support the launch to prevent lack of coordination, resource and ultimate failure. A monitoring system is also required to evaluate the effectiveness of the launch and take actions as required. A successful launch requires a planning process that pulls all the people and activities together, coordinates what is done, by who, when and with what resource.

(c) Marketing planning involves a five stage process

```
┌─────────────────────────────┐
│      Market analysis        │
└─────────────────────────────┘

┌─────────────────────────────┐
│      Objective setting      │
└─────────────────────────────┘

┌─────────────────────────────┐
│    Strategy development      │
└─────────────────────────────┘

┌─────────────────────────────┐
│      Implementation         │
└─────────────────────────────┘

┌─────────────────────────────┐
│    Evaluation and control    │
└─────────────────────────────┘
```

(i)   **Market analysis**. This phase involves establishing an audit process that assesses the macro and micro market environment, market segment analysis, customers, competitors and development strategy. Without a clear understanding of these issues it is difficult to set objectives and develop strategy.

(ii) **Objective setting.** Once the issues arising from market analysis have been understood, objectives can be set. Objectives should be consistent with the overall mission of the organisation and goals, and they must be realistic.

(iii) **Strategy development.** This phase can begin once the objectives have been agreed. In this process alternative strategic options will be evaluated to determine the best way forward for the organisation. Strategy evaluation should consider the organisation's current strengths and weaknesses, market attractiveness, resource requirements, and profitability.

(iv) **Implementation.** This is frequently the hardest part of the marketing planning process. Effective implementation requires co ordination between different organisations, people and departments. An organisation structure and culture that supports this co ordination, good communication and access to information and appropriate levels of resources. In reality, many issues, conflicts and trade offs occur within organisations that act as barriers to effective implementation.

(v)   **Evaluation and control.** The final phase of the process involves setting an effective system of monitoring and control to measure and evaluate performance.

20 Using the product life cycle

REPORT

**PRODUCT LIFE CYCLE FOR
THE FOOTBALL AFFINITY CARD**

TO: James Hogg, Financial Director
FROM: Maelia Gentil – Marketing Assistant
DATE: 14th June 2001

CONTENTS

1.0 Introduction

2.0 Usefulness of the Product Life Cycle

3.0 The Marketing Mix Strategy Introduction and Growth

4.0 Recommendations

(a)

1.0 Introduction

In response to your memo relating to the use of the marketing planning tools, I have prepared the following information on the product life cycle.

Stages of the Product Life Cycle

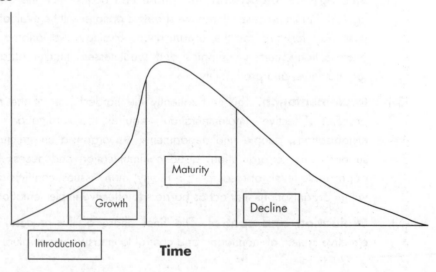

Introduction Phase

A product has just been introduced into a market, awareness is low, promotional costs are high and consumption is low. Profit is low and there are often low or few competitors. Innovators usually want the product at this stage.

Growth Phase

The product is gaining market share, awareness is building, and money is still being spent on promotion. Profits increase and early adopters want the product. There are more competitors entering the market.

Maturity phase

The product is at the peak of its lifecycle, revenue is high, costs may have fallen due to economies of scale and awareness is high. Branding should be strong now.

Decline Phase

The product is now often out of date or unwanted. Substitutes many have been introduced onto the marketing place. Discounts may be given or the product could be relaunched.

Usefulness of the PLC Concept

The product life cycle is of use in planning a balanced portfolio of services to offer our customers and determining the correct marketing mix, but there are many limitations:

- The PLC concept is most suited to FMCG sectors where products tend to enter all phases

- Strategic efforts can influence the cycle or it the case of TESSAs the UK government has intervened and this has resulted in an early decline stage for TESSAs.

- The length of the cycle varies enormously - for our products the length of the cycle illustrated here is deceptive, as the maturity phase may be much longer.

- Not all products or services follow the standard pattern as products may have a very short introduction or be revived as illustrated below:

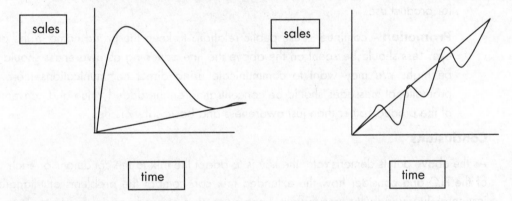

Therefore, although the PLC is of some use in planning, it is perhaps better to combine it with other strategic tools such as the BCG or GE Business Matrix.

(b) **The Marketing Mix Strategy Introduction and Growth**

I have now considered the marketing mix for both the introduction and growth stage. I have chosen to discuss the financial service sector and how the marketing mix can be adapted.

Introduction Stage

- **Price** – I would opt for market penetration in order to become an established player in this highly competitive field. Therefore the cost to the customer would be set at a very low rate of interest.

- **Place** – distribution channels should be used on the Internet to establish the brand image. A good example of this is Egg, the Prudential's Internet brand. It has a snappy, easily identifiable brand name and is accessible for the target market, on-line.

- **Product** – the product should be aimed at the target market. This is a difficult area, however, the product should be of value to the customer and good general services offered.

- **Promotion** – the key here is to raise awareness by ensuring the card is in our promotional literature, advertising in the local press and promoting the product via other interpersonal sources. As the product is intangible, we need to emphasise the security and benefits of using it.

Growth Stage

At this stage our product brand has established itself to a certain degree and effort must be made to continue to differentiate it from the competition.

- **Price** – Profits will have increased but we should charge what the market will bear. Established brands will be able to charge more at this stage as they have brand loyalty.

- **Place** – continue to develop the Internet elements. Make sure that our service is available where and when our customers want it.

- **Product** - continue to ask the customers what they want and do not become complacent. For example Abbey National has recently introduced Inscape, an investment facility for people with over £50,000. They found that customers valued personal contact above all and thus appointed people with a personal financial advisor. We may want to add more services or benefits to the product during this phase, that is, make the offer more sophisticated. For example, we may which to ask our customers if they wish to extend their credit with us, or offer them loyalty points for product use.

- **Promotion** – continue to use public relations to keep the brand name in the public eye. Less should be spent on the above the line adverting as awareness should now be high. We may want to communicate using direct communications more. The promotional messages should be concentrating on the added value and convenience of the product rather than just awareness and basic safety issues.

Conclusions

As the above points demonstrate, the key is to adapt the mix to the conditions of each stage of the PLC and consider how the extended mix can combat the problems of intangibility, insuperability, variability, perishability, non-ownership of our financial products. Therefore, we may which to also consider the people, process and physical evidence elements also for each stage, however, as this was not specifically requested this has not been included. However, please do not hesitate to contact me should require this further information.

21 Customer relationships

REPORT

RELATIONSHIP MARKETING

TO: **CEO, FMCG'S 'R' US**

FROM: **Casey Cruiter, Marketing Executive, CRM Group Inc.**

DATE: **14 June 2001**

CONTENTS:

1.0   **Key reasons for the use of RM in FMCG industry**

2.0   **Problems with building effective long-term relationships**

3.0   **ICT and relationship marketing**

4.0   **Conclusion**

(a) **Relationship Marketing & the Key Reasons for the Use of RM in FMCG Industry**

For any organisation it is more efficient to keep customers rather than finding new ones, thus relationship marketing is important. A happy customer will come back for more. However, it has been proven that 68% of people will go elsewhere if they received an indifferent service. This clearly indicates that there is room for improvement in this area for most companies.

- **Long term** – organisations need to view any transaction as part of a long-term goal. If the customer is satisfied with the product/service they have received for the price they have paid they are more likely to return.

- **A short-term** outlook will consider a quick profit but not consider repeat purchases.

- **Trust** – if a customer trusts an organisation, they have been treated well they are more likely to return. Trust is a two-way process – if the business can trust its customer, they may offer a better deal. If the customer trusts the organisation not to 'rip them off' then they are likely to return.

- **Win – Win** – a better relationship will develop if both organisation and their customers gain by the transaction – both parties will seek its confirmation.

- **Loyalty** – loyal customers will spread the good news about a company and may even champion it. Loyalty is part of the long term, win-win trusting relationship an organisation should seek.

Loyalty is key in the FMCG industry. The key objective behind relationship marketing is to build and maintain loyalty. A loyal customer will identify with your brand on the shelf and choose it over anything else. FMCGs are typically grocery items, and shelf selection of these items needs to be facilitated. Effective relationship marketing (RM) will give your product a clear and distinctive voice thus maintaining loyalty.

A recent survey showed that 90% of in-store retail purchase decisions (a percentage of which are FMCGs) are made in store. A customer who has received regular communications outside that environment will have had their buying motives altered thus making the in-store purchase decision a loyal one.

Problems in Building Relationships with Customers

What can go wrong will go wrong! Unfortunately, some customers will be subject to a terrible experience that sours them permanently. Some of the key problems are as follows:

- Customers do not necessarily want close relationships with one firm as this limits their choice

- Extra time and resources spent trying to build up a relationship can mean other areas and customers are neglected

- The partnership can often be rather one sided. Large multiples (eg Tesco) can use their buying power to influence the relationship, using the threat of withdrawing orders or business. This means that smaller companies are required to bow down to the multiples.

However, combating the problems and building for lifetime partnerships involves:

- Understanding and knowing the customer

- Communications – with good or bad news – stay in close and constant contact with the customer. If customers feel alienated and ill-formed they will go elsewhere

- Feedback – a lack of understanding can often stem from not knowing something in the first instance (Johns, 1994).

- Encourage customer to complain and make it easy for them. A lack of complaints, or feedback does not mean that there is not anything to comment upon.

(b) **ICT and Relationship Marketing**

The use of information technology to build customer relationships and maintain customer loyalty is now in extensive use within the UK and most developed countries. The following are some examples:

- **A database** should be used to build relationships with existing and past customers – eg sending out a customer satisfaction questionnaire to all customers asking them to identify what they like and don't like about the products and the areas they would like to see improved – offering them the opportunity to provide any suggestions.

- **Segmentation of the database** via key variables can allow the company to communicate specifically with key target groups, such as Tesco Baby club members.

- **EPOS (electronic point of sale)** systems can monitor consumer buying behaviour and enable the stores to stock more of what the consumer requires.

- **Electronic loyalty cards** not only offer consumers' added value, but also enable retailers to target promotions at specific customers – therefore increasing customer satisfaction.

- **The Internet** has provided a new platform for many companies. Customers can observe company brochures at their leisure, and order on interactive sites at any time. This has increased the number of channels of communication

- **In Business to Business (B2B) areas** information technology has allowed the integration of shared information in ordering and forecast scenarios. Tesco Geis system on the Internet is accessible only by suppliers and shows sales history, supplier service levels and other EPOS data. This lets suppliers be more proactive and therefore increase customer satisfaction.

An interesting example is Cadburys' who will be launching a campaign where certain confectionery wrappers show what could be winning numbers. The customer logs their wrapper number over a mobile text message service. They then receive a text message in return telling them whether they are a winner. Thus the Cadbury's will have their customers initiating the communication with their own mobile phone details and this can be captured and used for other purposes.

Conclusion

The use of technology to add value, and create efficiencies can be very good for building rewarding relationships with customers. The company is putting E- on the front or creating consumer benefits. A recent KPMG report showed that only one fifth of companies are E-enabled and 'technologically advanced', the report also showed that these sorts of E-advanced companies add value to their offering for the customer.

22 Price policy

MEMORANDUM

TO: **Marketing Manager**

From: **Alexandra Ruth, Marketing Executive**

Date: **14 June 2001**

Subject: **Pricing Strategy**

(a) **Information Required for Setting a Pricing Policy**

Costs

Obviously, for a small organisation, covering costs is a key issues as we have few of the economies of scale that a large organisation may have. We need to consider our fixed and variable costs and determine the quantity of goods we need to sell to breakeven as a basis for pricing.

In the short run, we my cover just the cost of producing garments and the wages, then decide to make a contribution to the fixed cost of rent.

Demand

This is a key determinant for the prices we can charge as consumers will demand less at higher prices. Obviously demand will depend on a number of factors which we will need to consider such as disposable income of our customers, loyalty to our brand, discounts, promotions, seasons and also competitors prices.

Competitors

We need to consider what competitors are pricing goods at to understand the going rate and where we are positioned.

Corporate Objectives

Our corporate objectives and image are key factors in deciding a price. As we are independent retailers, we are concerned with a niche market of high fashions, exclusive goods and our objectives include maintaining image and increased profitability, thus excluding low prices.

Pricing Objectives

This objective is based on the price but should reflect the organisation's objectives. We may wish to try to ensure that we want to penetrate the market with low prices, or always ensure over 50% mark-up, etc.

Communication

Linked to this are the communication aspects of our pricing policy. Our high quality garments would be undermined if sold at a low price.

Other Considerations

Finally, we need to consider supplier costs of materials and current legislation. As a small company we need to consider our position on VAT.

(b) Price Adjustment Policies

I would therefore, recommend a price skimming approach. However, we need to be able to adapt to changing circumstances and therefore, adjustment policies need to be considered. I would therefore suggest the following methods:

Discount and Allowance Pricing

This is where the basic price is adjusted to reward customers for responses such as early payment, large or off-seasons purchases. These can be in the form of cash discounts, quantity discounts for bulk purchases and seasonal discounts for products bought out of season. Trade-in allowances and promotional allowances are price reductions given to encourage purchase.

Segmented Pricing

Companies will often adjust their basic prices to allow for differences in customers, products and locations, the company sells a product at two or more prices, even though the difference in price is not based on differences in costs. Examples may be where different customers pay different prices for the same product such as rail travel First Class and Standard fares. Another example is time pricing where prices vary by the day or the hour such as telephone companies and 'off-peak' calls.

Promotional Pricing

Is where companies will temporarily price their products below list price and sometimes below cost prices. Promotional pricing such as loss leaders attract customers, special-event pricing in certain seasons appeals to certain customers. Cash rebates, longer warranties, free maintenance, low interest pricing policies are all forms of promotional pricing.

Conclusion

It is important to make the correct decisions about the pricing policy as this is the only area where can make profit.

I trust that this is of help. Please let me know if you require any further information.

23 Pet product life cycle

Examiner's comments. This is a tried and tested question which has appeared every session for the past few years but with a different context. The first part of the question required candidates to explain the usefulness of the PLC for cat food products. The answer should have first explained the PLC, identifying each stage, i.e. introduction, growth, maturity and decline stages. The answer should then have gone on to explain how the theory could be used for decision making and possibly identifying the weaknesses of the theory.

The second part of the question required candidates to consider the marketing mix for a current cat food product which was in the maturity stage but appeared to be moving into the decline stage. The answers should have considered the 4 Ps and either some discussion about regenerating the product via repositioning and relaunch using the marketing mix, or by slowing withdrawing the product. Most sensible treatments were considered appropriate for good marks.

(a)

MEMORANDUM

TO: Martin Ford, Marketing Planning Manager

FROM: Mitchell Ness, Marketing Assistant

DATE: 6 December 2001

SUBJECT: The Product Life Cycle and 'Cat Nosh'

1.0 Introduction

We spoke yesterday about the usefulness of the product life cycle concept for decision making for the current 'Cat Nosh' range/. I though that it would be worthwhile documenting this discussion.

2.0 The Product Life Cycle

Sales

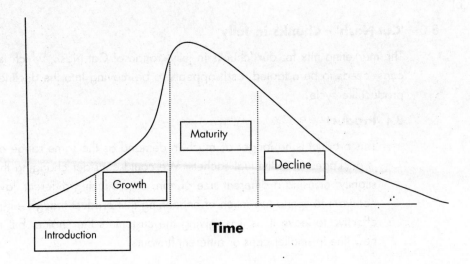

3.0 **Introduction Stage**

The product is introduced to the market, prices are high, demand is low, there are few competitors, promotional costs are high and the product is not widely available. Profits are usually negative at this stage.

4.0 **Growth Stage**

Here, sales begin to pick up, prices fall, more competitors enter the marketing, promotional costs focus on the brand identify, the product is more widely available and profits begin to be make early in this stage and maximise towards the end of this stage.

5.0 **Maturity Stage**

The level of demand peaks and even begins to fall, there are many competitors and prices are generally low. Distribution is wide and promotion is focused on retaining existing customers.

6.0 **Decline Stage**

The rate of decrease in sales begins to increase. Prices will tend to change – either increase or decrease as unit costs increase. Competitors pull out of the marketing as the profits become low (if there are any). Distribution becomes more difficult as retailers stop stocking the product as new products are more popular with customers.

7.0 **Usefulness of the PLC Concept**

The PLC is useful only to a certain extent, with the following problems:

- it is difficult to judge how long each stage will last

- it is difficult to plan for external influences such as the growing demand for cat food to be sold in individual sachets – this has come about as a result of more people having less time and/or inclination to spend time feeding their cat.

- environmental issues have an impact on customer behaviour, such as not wanting to buy cat food in a tin or with excessive packaging.

- Products can not be looked at in isolation, the whole product mix must be evaluated – it would be unrealistic to have a full range of products in any one stage.

(b)

8.0 **'Cat Nosh' – Chunks in Jelly**

The marketing mix for our 'chunks in jelly' range of Cat Nosh, which is sold in steel cans, needs to be adapted, as it appears to be moving into the decline stage of the product life cycle.

8.1 **Product**

This product is no longer as much in demand as the same range of food which is packaged in individual sachets. We could consider changing the ingredients slightly, or using a different size of can, or producing different flavours. We do not want to spend too much of enhancing this product though – it may be more effective to leave it as it is, giving the customers the choice, but introducing a new line in smaller cans or different flavours.

8.2 Price

We may be able to reduce the price if we can reduce the unit costs of producing this range. We should consider removing all must the three most popular flavours to ensure minimum wastage. This would also allow us to reduce production to only three lines in the factory, cutting costs so that we can reduce the price a little (or keep the price the same to increase profitability).

8.3 Place

We need to be more efficient in our distribution, and consider only selling to and supplying larger warehouses in bulk. Again, this will help keep our costs down.

8.4 Promotion

It is too late in the PLC to consider large-scale promotion of this product to the customer, although we could try and shift some of the existing stores of the less popular flavours to retailers who are likely to buy in bulk at a discounted price. This also ties in with cutting distribution costs.

9.0 Conclusions

My recommendation for 'Cat Nosh' – chunks in jelly are therefore to reduce production to only the top three flavours, with a promotion to larger retailers of the existing stock of the other flavours. Prices should be maintained for as long as possible, which in additional to lower production and distribution costs, should maximise any profits that are available from this range which is in decline.

24 Product life cycle

Examiner's comments. The first part of the question required the candidates to explain the PLC firstly and as such answers should have given a good explanation and perhaps an illustration of the PLC. The main part of this section of the question required candidates to discuss the usefulness of the concept and so answers should have considered the positive and negative aspects of using this concept. Disappointingly, many candidates only wrote in general about the PLC rather than discussing the usefulness.

The second part of the question required the candidate to explain how the marketing mix could be adapted for the introduction and growth stages of the PLC for a consumer product of the candidate's choice. Thus the answer should have considered price, product, place and promotional issues for both stages of the PLC and specifically for a product. On the whole, most candidates were able to do this reasonably well.

MEMORANDUM

TO: PRODUCT MANGAGER – SOAPS 'R' US LTD

FROM: MARKETING ASSISTANT, SOAPS 'R' US LTD

DATE: 13 JUNE 2002

SUBJECT: PRODUCT LIFE CYCLE FOR CAMOMILE SOAP PRODUCTS

(a)

1.0   The usefulness of the product life cycle

The product life cycle is a particularly useful concept for our new soap range 'Camomile' and can be used to develop an appropriate marketing mix for the future period.

Stages of the Product Life Cycle

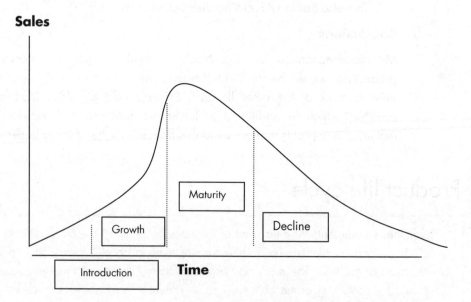

The different stages have the following characteristics:

Introductory Phase

- Lots of investment in the promotional mix
- Secure a few distribution channels
- Use price skimming method to raise revenue
- Basic product features

Growth Phase

- Still promote investment in promotions
- Consider providing extra features to product
- Reduce price to secure market share
- Use same distribution channels

Maturity Phase

- Promote brand image heavily
- Secure new distribution channels
- Price is inelastic in demand at this level
- Use selling as sales promotion – offers, discounts

Decline Phase

- Market share stable and then falling
- Hard selling required – investment into new product features or phase out
- Profits begin to fall
- Price needs to either remain constant or reduced

The usefulness of this concept is that you are able to consider these strategies at each stage when Camomile product level reaches each one. It helps marketing decisions to be made about pricing, distribution etc. It helps to identify an appropriate portfolio of products – i.e. need to consider that the range of our soap products need to have mature products, newly developed products, etc to ensure that there is a healthy balance of products. The entire product range can be plotted against each other and therefore showing where resources can be cut or invested.

There are many limitations in relation to the PLC as follows:

- The PLC concept is most suited to FMCG sectors where products tend to enter all phases
- Strategic or tactical efforts can influence the cycle – i.e. introducing new products which cannibalise our own products
- The length of the cycle varies enormously
- Not all products or services follow the standard pattern as products may have a very short introduction etc
- The pattern does not always follow the normal shaped curve and thus it is difficult to identify when one phase starts and another finishes.

(b)

2.0 Application of the marketing mix in relation to the introduction and growth phases of the plc

The marketing mix could be applied in the following way for the Camomile Soap production within the introduction and growth phases of the PLC.

2.1 **Introduction Phase**

Price – price skimming method could be used – Soaps 'R' Us could use this pricing method as it is a new product. This way the objective of achieving high level of profits could be achieved especially if the product is positioned as an extreme luxury product.

Product – the product itself only has to be at its basic stages. This would mean basic packaging and use, i.e. soap contains camomile for moisture and added cleanliness. Consumers would perceive this as a new, better product.

Place – Soaps 'R' Us should secure a few distribution channels perhaps considering an exclusive distribution strategy i.e. through high class department stores or cosmetics outlets, health stores rather than supermarkets. Once again, this would communicate the exclusivity of the product and reaffirm its pricing strategy.

Promotion - Soaps 'R' Us could use direct marketing to provide samples to a selected number of households and department stores for their exclusive customer database. They could also focus on PR and media to invest in television advertising to promote the brand name.

Consumer advertising would be more appropriate e.g. "Camomile soap ... for healthier looking skin".

Some celebrity ambassadors could be used to promote it by doing specific features for high-class women's' magazines. There could be some cross promotions with another related exclusive cosmetic product.

2.2 Growth Phase

Price - The price could be reduced at this level and may involve perceived value pricing methods, e.g. value for money or promotional pricing methods, e.g. – buy one get one free. Soaps 'R' Us could also focus of pricing offers and bulk buys.

Product - Extra features could be offered at this stage such as a travel soapbox being included in the packaging. More colours or different sizes could be introduced, such as liquid versions and dispensers or shower gel versions.

Place - The same distribution channels could be used, however, this should now be extended to main chains of pharmacies such as Boots the Chemist etc. Internet could be promoted direct from the supplier.

Promotion - This could be target for promotional offers to certain market segments – e.g. older women, younger teenagers etc. The promotion should also consider the seasonal issues such as Christmas. Promotional methods such as leaflets and direct mail could continue.

3.0 Conclusion

The product life cycle is a useful concept to help marketers consider the most appropriate strategies to be embraced.

25 Use of IT

Examiner's comments. The question asks candidates to explain each of the terms Internet, Intranet and Extranet and state how each could be used my marketers working at a tactical level within an organisation of the candidate's choice. The question therefore, was testing not only knowledge but understanding and application of theory. The answers for section a should have considered the Internet as a research tool, direct marketing channel, communication tool and helpful for relationship marketing. The answers for section b should have explained the Intranet as an internal system of communication throughout an organisation explaining such characteristics such as greater management of communication internally, and improved service levels via greater access to real time information, etc. The final part of the answer should have started by explaining the Extranet as an extension of the Intranet used for password protected information for certain trusted suppliers and customers, encouraging trust and relationship building.

(a)

MEMORANDUM

TO: Sandy De Mel, Marketing Manager

FROM: Catherine Cutlet, Marketing Executive

DATE: 6 December 2001

SUBJECT: Report on the Internet, Intranet and Extranet

1.0 Introduction

The following report will detail the terms of:

Internet
Intranet
Extranet

I will also detail how each term can be used by marketers within organisations.

2.0 Internet

The Internet is a global network of databases which are available through Internet Service Providers (ISPs). Available through modems which utilise telecommunications technology, i.e. it is accessed through existing telephone lines, usually through a computer, laptop or a WAP phone.

It can be used for market and marketing research, identifying competitors and researching quickly into their products etc. It can be used for customer research by monitoring those customers who access the organisation's site. It can be used as a market channel i.e. distribution of products and services, it can be used for providing information and communication with customers, suppliers, distributors, etc.

At a tactical level within Thomas C Holidays, the Internet is a very valuable tool. Its main use is to promote the Thomas C Holidays and provide information to its customers of the products and services it provides and how they can be bought. This can be done via a website and customers can log on to the address. The Internet can provide customers with the latest holiday offers, where destinations are features and work as an on-line or interactive brochure.

From a more tactical point of view, websites can be interactive and certain software can tell Thomas C Holidays who is looking at their website, what they are looking at and when. The Internet can also be used to keep an eye of the competition and employees can look up competitors products and latest offers. The main use however, is a means of communication between Thomas C Holidays and its customers.

3.0 Intranet

This is an internal, company site which is usually just available to employees of the company. This will contain times of interest to some or all of them, such as product information, company information, staff handbook and guidelines, procedures and processes, customer databases, news items, press releases, company personnel and structure, corporate objectives, strategies and projects etc. It can be used to communicate internally between departments.

In general it can be used by marketing to influence the culture of the organisation, for training purposes to ensure that all staff are bought into the company policy and strategy, to communication consistently with all staff. It can be used to facilitate feedback and suggestions from across the company and to disseminate information about new product launches or information about new business sales figures as well as news about successes of the company. All staff need to know what their role in this has been in order for them to feel values and worthwhile.

For Thomas C Holidays this can be used to communicate customer feedback from the reservations department to the product and marketing departments. Changes to brochures and prices can be accessed on the Intranet and internal e-mail can take place. The Intranet is a very useful tool as an internal communication and encourages individual and organisational development.

4.0 **Extranet**

The Extranet is a site which is made available to certain individuals and/or organisations, such as the ***IF@zone*** from Standard Life. This site is password-protected and users must register for access to it. It is available to Independent Financial Advisers (IFAS) as well as the sales force and some personnel for other decisions within the organisation. It holds more sensitive information, which cannot be disclosed to unauthorised personnel, but ensures that IFAS can conduct business with Standard Life in an efficient manner.

From a tactical perspective for Thomas C Holidays, they can use the Extranet to communicate with all 8,000 of the travel agents, all airlines and hotel suppliers and any other distributors involved in the supply/trade chain.

This can help ease communication between all levels and provide a quick and convenient method of communication and high level of service within the supply chain.

26 Ansoff matrix and distribution

Examiner's comments. Answers to the first part of the question should have included the Ansoff model an explanation of market penetration, market development, product development and diversification. The candidate's answer should also have related the discussion to a product or service of their own choice, thus contextualising and applying the theory in this area.

The second part of the answer should have included the key issues for new or alternative distribution channels. The answers could have includes a discussion about: customer requirements; product characteristics, after sale service, competitor's channels, distributor characteristics, levels of risk, control and costs involved, experience in alternative countries, logistics management which could include lean and agile considerations, the impact on the other marketing mix elements, etc.

(a)

MEMORANDUM

TO: L Mann, Marketing Assistant

FROM: Ruth Raat, Marketing Manager

SUBJECT: Ansoff Matrix and Growth Strategies

DATE: 6 December 2001

1.0 Introduction

The Ansoff Matrix is an accepted method for helping companies decide on their growth strategies for different products. It relates new and current markets to new and current products. It is best shown in the following diagram:

Ansoff Matrix

	Current products	**New products**
Current markets	**Market penetration strategy** • gain customers from competitors • retain loyal customers • ensure customers buy more frequently	**Product development strategy** * develop new products * adapt existing products
New markets	**Market development strategy** • enter new countries • enter new niche markets • different segments	**Diversification strategy** * usually achieved by mergers and acquisitions * most risky option

2.0 Market Penetration

This is the strategy whereby the company takes current products and increases sales in current markets. This can be done via launching loyalty schemes, increasing promotions, price changes and brand building. This should ensure that customers are gained from the competitors or that customers become more loyal and buy more frequently. This is the least risky strategy which a company could undertake.

3.0 Product Development Strategy

This is where the company develops new products and launches them into current markets. For example a pet food manufacturer who manufacturers tinned food might develop and launch a range of dried biscuits. A new product sold in the current pet food market. The company has experience and understanding of the buyer behaviour and requirements of the current market in which they operate and try to develop more products or adapt products which will increases sales. All organisations should develop new products on a regular basis to ensure sales in the future i.e. 'tomorrow's bread-winners'.

4.0 Market Development Strategy

Here the existing product, for example an air conditioning unit for office space, may be launched into the new market of information technology control rooms where large numbers of computers and servers are kept. They generate large amounts of heat and need temperature control. The air conditioning unit moves from one market to another. Alternatively companies can look to expand into international or different geographic markets. The levels of risk are not as high as new product development but the company will need to learn about the new market's characteristics and buyer behaviour to ensure that the products meet their requirements.

5.0 Diversification

Here the company launches completely new products into new markets. This is a high risk strategy where the company has no experience of the new market and has incurred large research and development costs of the new product. An example would be Marconi who sold their defence products business and launched into a new market of telecommunications. The results have not been as successful as they anticipated. In most cases, this strategy is adopted my companies who acquire other companies via mergers or acquisitions, where the experience of the new product and markets are retained.

(b)

6.0 New Distribution Channels

If we were to consider new distribution channels we would need to take the following into account:

6.1 Customer Requirements

- Firstly, what are the needs and requirements of our customers for distribution?

- Do they require increased outlets?

- Speed of delivery?

- Extended hours?

- These requirements would need to be researched and matched with our corporate objectives to ensure that any changes could be undertaken efficiently and profitably

6.2 Intermediaries

- We would also need to consider the number of intermediaries in our distribution channel.

- Are we looking for intensive distribution – i.e. a large number of intermediaries?

- Are we looking for exclusive distribution – i.e. a very small number of hand picked distribution partners?

- Are we looking for selective distribution – i.e. a larger number that combines elements of exclusivity with slightly more of an intensive approach?

6.3 Length of Channel Chain

- A major consideration would be whether we should distribute directly to our customers.

- This could be via orders and despatch direct from a warehouse or more likely today via a website.

- If we undertake on-line distribution we would need to consider the cost of the development of the website, the cost of order processing, the effectiveness of warehousing, order fulfilment and despatch and the availability of stock

- The longer the channel the less control we have as marketers.

- Our current channel through wholesalers and distributors does put us further away from our customers.

- By going direct we can take back that control.

6.4 Service and Risk

- We would also need to ensure that this is what our customers want

- Our customers who order our tetrapaks of dairy cream for their restaurant and food service outlets would welcome the chance to order on-line with guaranteed delivery as research has already shown us.

- We therefore need to look into the service aspects of delivery, invoicing, tracking orders, complaint handling and after sales issues.

- We also need to consider monitoring of these new channels. How best can their effectiveness be assessed?

- We need to identify the levels of risk and control which we will experience when using these channels.

7.0 Conclusion

We will be able to monitor effectiveness through marketing research, questionnaires on the website, a structured complaints procedure and our after sales contact with our food service clients.

27 Distribution and packaging

Examiner's comments. The first part of the question required candidates to explain and evaluate the changing nature of distribution channels within the marketing mix and consider the role of technology. Many candidates did not evaluate the changing nature of distribution but chose to write in general about channels or technology only. Some candidates wrote about the 4 Ps, which was not required – again, candidates should ensure that they read the question fully and ensure that they are actually answering the question set. The answer should have included issues relating to shorter distribution channels or networks, linkages to the use of relationship marketing concepts and new media such as the Internet, DRTV, telemarketing digital TV, etc. There should have been some mention about the amount of control, loyalty and retention that can be increased by the use of direct distribution channels.

The second part of the question related to the role of packaging and the implications for packaging in relation to direct distribution. The answer should have considered the change in emphasis from emotional to functional as the point of purchase changes. Consideration is required of the users convenience, selling proposition, product protection and communication about the brand on packaging being not as important for direct distribution channels. Again, this was generally, not well answered as candidates tended to write generally about packaging rather than discussing packaging in relation to direct distribution channels.

MEMO

TO: Peter Betts, Marketing Manger, Granary Plc

FROM: Josephine Ashford, Marketing Assistant, Granary Plc

DATE: 13 June 2002

SUBJECT: Technological Advances in Distribution Channels

(a)

1.0 Introduction

Technological advances in today's business are improving and developing the way we distribute our goods. The changing nature of the distribution channels is detailed in the next sections.

2.0 Role of the Internet

This is used as a direct distribution channel and is direct to the customer. Anybody has access to buy goods over the Internet and this is delivered direct to their homes. The increasing Internet usage is becoming more evident every day. Most of the top 5 supermarket chains are now offering this service where customers can do their food shopping 'on-line' and it will be delivered direct to home, thus cutting out the time the customer has to waste in terms of physically going to the store, going round the store and queuing to pay then returning home.

3.0 Using Electronic Data Interchange (EDI)

This is a process of sharing information through databases with suppliers and distributors. They are able to automatically process information regarding stock levels and distribution networks. It improves the speed of delivery and encourages more interactions between distributors and intermediaries.

4.0 EPOS – Stock Distribution (Electronic Point of Sale)

This involves indirect distribution as it is able to determine using EPOS the information on barcodes to identify when stocks need to be updated and a consistent figure on current stocks. This allows distributors to identify timing for each level.

5.0 **The Marketing Mix**

The marketing mix also can be adapted by using the ICT for distribution channels by the following:

Price - this is reduced if distributors can deliver in bulk knowing the required stock needed.

Product - as Granary Plc use perishable FMCGs it is important that stock is delivered to a timescale and also that the distributors can stock it (using amounts of stock needed from database information direct from the intermediate retailer).

Place - the distribution channels can be directed to the correct markets using databases to analyse customer demand on a Database Mining System. Distribution channels such as the Internet for example housebound people such as old aged pensioners. Intensive distribution for people who are ABC1 groups and have a time pressured lifestyle – therefore need easy access to goods on an intensive scale.

Promotion – this needs to be directed to all segments of the market as the speed of distribution using IT such as the Internet and direct distribution is crucial in today's society. As databases are analysing better customer information the distribution channels are becoming faster, more responsive and efficient. Promotion such as useful websites, direct mailing and advertising should be heavily invested.

(b)

6.0 **Packaging and Implications for Direct Distribution**

Packaging is an important factor when adopting direct distribution channels. It involves the following characteristics for effective packaging:

- Size and layout of packaging (use CAD systems)

- Useful knowledge of packaging

- Convenience of packaging for direct end customer

- Easy to access or pick up for handling purposes

- Packaging can be considered as the 'silent salesperson' to help self-selection, however, this is not as important for direct distribution as the item has already been selected.

- Good value for money

- Brightly coloured. Branded to attract attention is not so important with direct distribution

- Easy to dispose or be recyclable

6.1   Direct Distribution and packaging

It is important that packaging is developed as direct distribution often refers to the transfer of goods direct from the supplier to the consumer. It therefore needs to be:

- Easy to stock and pack into bulk parcels for home deliveries

- Use quality material e.g. plastic, paper etc so that the items are not damaged

- Vacuum packed for convenience of distributor

- Easy to identify by both the distributor and the end customer

- Provide information on quantity, stock available, producer information, helpline numbers etc.

7.0   **Conclusion**

The role of packaging is important for both our organisation as the manufacturer, the marketing department who are providing and designing our products and our direct or end customer as they have different needs to an intermediary.

28 Pricing and methods

Examiner's comments. The first part of the answer should have included the role and importance of pricing as the major basis for generating revenue, where prices connect customers and suppliers at the point of exchange. Some explanation of price as a powerful competitive weapon in marketing and a communication tools could have been considered. Some reference to the economist, accountants and marketers perspective of pricing would have been useful here.

The second part of the answer should have related specifically to the explanation of both competitor-based methods and demand or market-based methods, then the answer should have gone on to consider the differences. Hardly any candidates actually complied with this question and mainly just explained the two methods without considering the differences. Competitor-bases methods could have included price matching, going rate pricing, predator pricing, etc. Demand or market-based methods could have included market penetration and skimming strategies, discount and allowance pricing, segmentation pricing and promotional pricing. This was a prime example of an area of the syllabus which still seems very weak with most candidates.

(a)

MEMORANDUM

TO: Janis Hill, Marketing Director

FROM: Emily Clarke, Marketing Executive

DATE: 6 December 2001

SUBJECT: Report on Pricing Methods

1.0 Introduction

As Marketing Executive, I have been asked to produce a report detailing the importance of pricing in marketing terms and also to explain the differences in competitor-based methods and demand-based methods.

2.0 The Importance of Pricing in Marketing Terms

Pricing plays an essential role in the marketing of your product. First of all, you need to cover all of your costs, but the price will help to create an image of your product in the eyes of your customer.

As part of the marketing mix, price will help the perceived quality, value and image. If the price is high, then customers generally take the view that the product is of high standards and is a good quality. This of course, needs to be backed up with the other elements of the marketing mix. If the price is low, there is a danger that the perception is of low quality and is 'cheap and cheerful'. This is only a danger, however, if you want to position your product as a high quality item. In general terms, price will help you to position your product in the market. This can be visualised with as 'perception map':

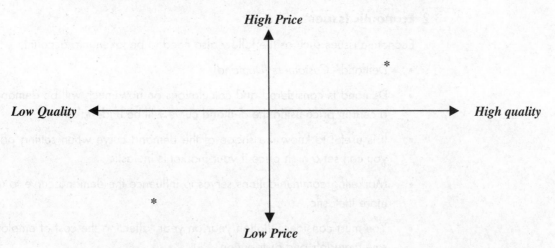

The above map shows two dots, which demonstrate that in positioning your product by price, it will create an image to your customer.

Price can help to gain market share by using methods such as 'price skimming' or 'price penetration'. Penetration will gain a large marketing share as price is set very low, whereas skimming pricing is where the price is set high, usually for new products launched into a market with few competitors and a smaller market share is gained.

3.0 Key Factors that Concern Pricing

There are four key factors that affect pricing decisions, also known as the 4 Cs:

- Cost – related to the actual costs involved

- Consumer/customer – related to the price the consumer will pay

- Competition – related to competitors prices for substitute or complimentary products

- Company – related to the company's financial objectives

3.1 Financial Issues - Cost

- This is the lower level of a price – often accountant use cost when deciding on the pricing structure. There are at least 4 different types of costs in regard to a product or service:

- Fixed cost – a cost that does not change according to the increase in the number of units produced i.e. rent and rates for the premises

- Variable Costs – a cost that changes according to the number of units produced such as raw materials

- Total Costs – a sum of fixed and variable cost times the quantity produced

- Average Cost – this is the total cost divided by the number of units produced

- Contribution - allows the Accountant to analyse whether the product can be sold at less than cost for a period of time, but making a contribution to the costs.

- Breakeven analysis - indicates the amount of units that must be sold at a given price to cover costs.

- Company's Financial Objectives – the company's objectives in terms of profitability also need to be taken into account when consider the price.

3.2 Economic Issues

Economic issues such as the follow also need to be taken into account:

- Demand - *Customers (Demand)*

- Demand is considered and calculations on how much will be demanded at a certain price using the demand curve will be undertaken

- It is useful to know the shape of the demand curve when setting prices as you can set a high price if your market is inelastic.

- Marketing communications serves to influence the demand curve to make it more inelastic.

- You must consider inflation year on year, affecting the cost of employment, raw materials and distribution.

- This is also a consideration for customer's disposable income

- The possibility of the Euro currency in the UK must be anticipated.

3.3 Competitors

- Competitors must be taken into account

- The marketer looks at competitors, macro environment, internal environment, stage in the product life cycle and sets a price at what the market will bear.

All of the above factors and perspectives play a key role in finalising a final price.

(b)

4.0 Competitor Based Pricing

This method is where the pricing policy is based upon competing prices in the market of industrial packaging tape. This is different to cost-plus pricing in that it takes into consideration how the other competitors are pricing their products and how their products are perceived by their customers. Cost-plus pricing does not do this, and merely covers costs and leaves room for a little profit. The price does not necessarily have to be cheaper than competitors, as discussed before, it depends upon how you want your products to be perceived by your customers, and compared to your competitors.

Some of the methods used for competitor based pricing include price matching, going rate pricing and predator pricing.

4.1 **Price Matching** – this is where the company guarantees that the product cannot be bought for less anywhere. If it can be bought for less, they usually refund the difference. Therefore, the price is very much based on the competitors in the market place.

4.2 **Going Rate Pricing** – here the pricing policy is determined by the competitors pricing strategy and a similar price is set (but not guaranteed as above).

4.3 **Predator pricing** – this is where the pricing policy is set low so that the competition has problems in competing for market share.

5.0 Market/Demand - Based Pricing

The final method is more suitable to take into account market needs and wants and relates to what is in demand. Compared to competitor bases pricing, it takes demand into consideration. As customers are becoming more demanding, this is a more suitable method of pricing. Economic issues and the elasticity of demand are considered here.

There are a number of methods such as penetration and skimming strategies, discount and allowance pricing, segmentation pricing and promotional pricing. I will explain a number of these methods below.

5.1 **Skimming** – this is where a high price policy is undertaken to 'skim the cream' of the market. This is more advisable if you have a product which is new into the market and there are few competitors. It is important that you are able to lower the price once you have established a customer base and need to gain more market share.

5.2 **Penetration** – this is where the price starts off with a low price and the market share is gained quickly. It is difficult however, to increase the price one this has been undertaken.

5.3 **Segmented Pricing** – companies will often adjust their basic prices to allow for differences in customers, products and locations, the company sells a product at two or more prices, even though the difference in price is not based on differences in costs. Examples may be where different customers pay different prices for the same product such as rail travel First Class and Standard fares. Another example is time pricing where prices vary by the day or the hour such as telephone companies and 'off-peak' calls.

6.0 Conclusion

I hope that this has helped in your consideration of the pricing policy to adopt for the industrial packaging tape. Please contact me should you require any further information.

29 Life cycle hindrance

> Examiner's comments: summary/extracts. Problems centred on an absence of comment on the issues raised by the question.

Notes for this debate to assist your presentation

I propose to **agree with the motion that the product life cycle is a hindrance** to marketing planners.

The concept of the product life cycle refers to the stages a product passes through from its initial introduction and launch onto the market through to its decline. Conceptually we can understand and accept the relevance of this model in explaining that different products will have different shapes and different lengths of life spans. In fact historically such life spans can be mapped out. However the product life cycle model has limited predictive value and therefore is of limited value in assisting marketing planners.

What are the critical limitations of the product life cycle concept as a planning tool?

(a) It is virtually impossible for marketing planners to establish the exact stage at which a product is at in its life cycle. Whilst a broad estimate can be made the degree of accuracy that can be established is of little value in a planning context.

(b) A product's life cycle can be influenced by a complex array of variables ranging from changing consumer needs and wants, Government legislation, technological breakthroughs and competitor activity, many of which are unpredictable. The only assumption that a planner can make is that at some stage a product will become obsolete. Therefore an organisation should constantly be looking for 'creative obsolescence' of its products irrespective of their current position in the market place. The simple adage that 'if you don't someone else will ' should focus planners minds far more than the 'simplistic life stage assumptions' that underlie the product life cycle concept.

(c) The product life cycle is a concept not a predictive model. It has no scientific foundation to establish its validity as a planning tool. There is no agreed formula for predicting the shape of the life cycle and it is likely that different planners using the same data could predict widely different life cycles simply on the basis of their methodology.

(d) The two axes, level of sales/profits and time can only be predicted with any accuracy in the short term and both can be influenced as much by the activities of the organisation as by external events. As with any forecasting tool the best assumption is that the forecast will be wrong and the longer the time span the greater the degree of error is likely to be.

(e) The product life cycle concept does not provide the planner with any underlying conceptual framework to support its predictive capabilities. Empirical evidence is sparse to support its value as a planning tool.

I will conclude my comments with an extract from a quote outlining the findings of research conducted by Dhalla and Yuspeh who examined over 100 product categories to assess the value of the product life cycle as a planning tool.

'Our results suggest strongly that the life cycle concept when used without careful formulation and testing as an explicit model, is more likely to be misleading than useful'.

I ask you to support the motion.

30 Development of new products

(a) **The importance of the development of new products**

In the face of increasing competition, changing customer needs and rapid rates of technological innovation, the new product development has become an essential part of an organisations marketing strategy.

(i) Organisations must find new products to replace older, declining products.

(ii) Organisations must innovate to maintain their leadership position in the marketplace.

(iii) Profit performance can only come from ongoing product development.

(iv) Product improvement is an important part of the new product development process and customers will demand ongoing product improvement.

(v) Increasingly market segments are fragmenting therefore product development has to keep in touch with a wider diversity of customer needs.

(b) The stages of the new product development process

(i) **Idea generation**

Market trends and Ford's market research indicated that the existing product range and Ford's brand images were becoming tired and boring. Competitors were becoming more innovative in car design and branding, and this was affecting Ford's market situation and profitability. Teams within Ford were established to identify more closely with the attitudes, values and needs of the market place. From this research, key findings were identified that pointed to new ideas in terms of driving dynamics, branding and styling etc.

(ii) **Idea screening**

A range of possibilities was identified for Ford to investigate. These ranged from redesign of existing ranges, introduction of American ranges into the UK market and total redesigns. Past experience, market research, competitor analysis and longer term strategic marketing positioning factors were considered in this screening process.

(iii) **Concept development and testing**

The **redesign product strategy** was selected and a range of concept designs was developed and tested. In particular, the concepts were tested against market research data, which had identified distinct market segments with specific needs and requirements. The Ford Focus design grew from this process including an indication of what the brand's personality would be. The design had to conform to Ford's stringent brand specifications.

(iv) **Marketing strategy**

The **Ford Focus brand** was targeted at a specific market segment that had distinct attitudes, values and driving dynamics needs. The positioning of the brand was paramount as the brand had to reflect the personality and attitudes of this target market. Age was not an issue for the Ford Focus. The key motivator behind all Ford's product development activities was to establish a range of innovative cars with a distinct positioning but with a broad market appeal. The brand image of Ford was being repositioned from it's tired, dull, outdated image to an image that was modern, exiting and innovative and the Ford Focus strategy reflected this repositioning.

(v) **Business analysis**

The business analysis was ongoing throughout the NPD process. The need for an innovative strategy was determined from the market research and competitive trend analysis. Full cost analysis of the strategy was made, and timings of product divestments and introductions were planned. Dealer analysis was conducted to ensure that dealers' needs would be met as a result of the new strategy. The price position of the Ford Focus was determined first, and then manufacturing costs calculated, to ensure this price point could be reached. The level of investment needed to implement the new strategy was budgeted for. No new manufacturing platforms would be needed as the new design could be built on old platforms.

(vi) **Product development**

The manufacturing and design processes were fully integrated into the brand planning process to ensure that the Ford Focus specification met the needs of its target market. The Ford Focus had to meet stringent design and driving dynamics requirements.

(vii) **Test marketing**

Stringent tests and research were carried out on the Ford Focus before its launch. Customer attitudes were taken into account and fed back into the manufacturing and seeing process. Overall the test markets met with strong approval for the brand both from consumers and dealers.

(viii) **Launch**

The Ford Focus was launched in the UK in 1998 with a major advertising campaign and dealer support programme. The brand has been well received and is meeting its launch targets.

31 New product development and buyer behaviour

Examiner's comments. Most of the steps of the new product development process are discussed, although there are a few issues which could have been developed further such as the commercialisation section. This question was often answered last on the candidate's script and as such these answers seemed to have suffered from the lack of time in many cases.

(a) REPORT ON NEW PRODUCT DEVELOPMENT

To: Trainee
From: Marketing Manager
Date: 7th December 2000

1.0 **Introduction**

This report covers the stages of New Product Development process that need to be considered.

1.1 Idea Generation

Idea generation is where all ideas for the development of the new product are created from inside and outside of the organisation. Sources of ideas can be the Sales and Marketing Team, Customers, Suppliers, Market Research process or suggestions from other employees. This first step can use techniques such as Brainstorming to create a wide range of ideas for consideration.

1.2 Screening

The purpose of this activity is to reduce the number of potential ideas to those that have merit to develop further within the overall direction of the business. Usually a series of criteria are used to assess the worth of the idea against business potential.

1.3 Concept Development and Testing

This is the process by which the screened ideas can begin to be developed and refined into a product concept for testing with potential consumers. At this stage the product or service will still be only an idea and it can be difficult to assess potential customer reaction. Concept testing has developed into a sophisticated activity where product descriptions and possible technical and customer benefits can be determined. Again where possible concepts fail to meet business objectives they are eliminated from the NPD process.

1.4 Business Analysis

The financial viability of the proposed new products are assessed with regard to financial payback of resources, such as people and equipment. Both indirect and direct costs associated with each new product are evaluated eg for marketing and production capability to supply the product or service.

1.5 Product Development

It is at this stage that small scale volumes of the product are produced for development and testing These prototypes are developed to confirm the potential with the targeted customer segment and evaluate feedback from the marketplace. The process of fine tuning the offering to meet more closely the customer needs is undertaken in this phase. If the reaction from the market place is poor then an option to withdraw the product could be considered to minimise incurring unnecessary costs.

If the Product development has been successful then preparation of the product or service for launch can proceed. This decision is crucial and should be based on exhaustive analysis and appraisal of various scenarios that the product or service will encounter.

1.6 Test Marketing

This is the final check to ensure that the product or service can be successfully marketed into the marketplace. The object of test marketing is to investigate the appropriateness of the proposed marketing strategy, to refine the tactics that will be employed and to predict the likelihood of achieving the planned performance of the product or service from the limited test marketing. It is therefore important that the chosen testing activity is as representative as possible to the eventual market conditions.

1.7 **Commercialisation and Launch**

This is the final stage where a viable proposition has been selected for launch. Production, financial, quality as well as other commercial considerations have been extensively examined, with the potential risk of failure minimised and suitability to the chosen market maximised. The marketing mix is set and the product or service is ready for launch

(b) 2.0 **Potential problems of Identifying Buyer Behaviour for the New Product**

An organisation's buying behaviour is a complex process involving a decision making unit (DMU) to decide where the new product or service is sourced.

Some of the main considerations are:

- Changing the source of supply requires the Buyer to take a risk to move to a new supplier which will require initial trials with no guarantee of success. They will need convincing that the benefits to be gained by changing to the new shrink packaging system will far outweigh the risk involved in making the change. The Buyer will need reassuring that support will be available to ensure a smooth, trouble free and timely installation and commissioning of a new machine.

- It can take a considerable amount of time for organisations to make a decision to buy a product. This is often because authorisation to make a purchase requires a number of people to collectively commit to a decision.

- The user of the machine may not be the buyer of the equipment which creates a problem for the marketeer. They may have to market the new product to the buyer who does not understand the technical attributes of the machine and is only interested in cost considerations.

- The buying procedures and systems within organisations may be very varied as some companies will need to undertake a number of tenders or quotations if they are to purchase capital equipment. It is very difficult to find out the internal systems of an organisation and to be timely in submitting information to the organisation's timescales

It is crucial for the Marketeer to understand the organisations structured decision procedure for purchasing new machinery. It starts with identification of requirements and concludes with ensuring performance against technical specifications after commissioning of the machine.

32 Decline stage marketing

Examiner's comments. This was a very popular question and in the main, was completed reasonably well. However, a number of students wasted valuable time by going into depth on the stages leading up to the decline stage and then only offered one or two characteristics – indicating that the question had not been read fully. Many offered a diagram which was appropriately labelled and referenced, which gained some marks.

(a) **Report**

Date: 9 December 1999
Re: Decline stage marketing

Characteristics of magazine in decline phase

The likely characteristics of the special interest photography magazine during the decline phase of its product life cycle are as follows:

- Falling levels of profitability
- Dated format
- High number of competitors
- Use of dated technology

It is likely that the product has witnessed falling levels of demand and therefore these falling sales volumes will reduce income from the magazine. This is likely to be accompanied by increased promotional and pricing activity to boost flagging sales which will result in **falling profitability**.

It is also probable that the **format** of the magazine has become dated and less relevant to its target audience either through changing market trends and developments in photography or customer needs which will over time have changed.

If the magazine publishers have not monitored these changing trends or needs and adapted the magazine format, this will open up opportunities for **competitive magazines** to enter the market thus further increasing the pressures on the volume of magazine sales.

New technologies can also increase the likelihood of the magazine entering the decline phase particularly through access to digital technology and the Internet, but also through improved printing techniques and scope for customisation.

(b) **Marketing mix strategy to be adopted**

The marketing mix strategy that the publisher could adopt for the magazine will range from withdrawal of the publication from the market to refreshing the magazine or repositioning it. Different variables of the marketing mix will be relevant for each strategy.

Withdrawal should only occur if the market for this particular magazine has declined to a level where **no economic justification for continuing** with it exists. It may also be applicable to withdraw the title if **new titles are being launched** which offer scope for growth and require funding. Withdrawal can be immediate or gradual. If gradual, sales promotional activity and pricing tactics can be used to encourage the consumer to purchase.

Refreshing the magazine would involve making changes to the product. This could be new editorial, new colour, design and format or special features. Through this process existing custom can be maintained and possible new readers attracted to the new format. Such activity can result in extending the life of the product.

Repositioning the magazine would require an extensive communication campaign outlining the new position. A revised editorial and magazine format would probably be targeted at a new set of customers. While the traditional values of the magazine would probably be maintained, the proposition is likely to be different. Repositioning the magazine can potentially revitalise the title, creating fresh demand and new growth. It is likely that celebrity endorsements would be used to support the communication campaign.

The strategy adopted by the publisher will therefore determine the marketing activity that should be implemented. For gradual withdrawal, the focus will be on **pricing and sales promotions activity**. Refreshing the magazine will primarily involve **product adaptation and some communications**. Repositioning will involve heavy emphasis on communication and possibly extensive product adaptation.

33 New product pricing policy

> **Examiner's comments.** This question was answered quite well. Most candidates were able to identify the key factors when setting a price although they were not able to offer examples often within their answers. Weak candidates only gave a range of pricing policies without relating to the question and did not consider the main factors.
>
> Part (b) was not answered as well as part (a). Many identified a pricing policy but did not go into explain it. Many offered inappropriate policy without further justification. Some candidates forgot to produce their answer in a business format and therefore lost easy marks.

(a) **Main factors to consider when setting price of new range of flavoured milk targeted at children.**

There are a number of factors that need to be considered when setting price. The nature of the target audience is a critical issue alongside how the product is to be positioned and its relative perceived value. The user of this product is the child but the buyer and probable decision maker is the parent. The price therefore has to be targeted with the parent in mind. The price should reflect the brand's positioning and will be determined by whether it is to be a premium, middle or mass market product. If the product has unique attributes, special appeal or a strong brand proposition it can potentially attract a price premium over competitors and still capture volume. A good example of a product that achieves volume sales at premium price points is the Nike trainer. It has a unique proposition supported by good quality products which are endorsed by top sports personalities.

A second consideration is the cost structure and desired profit margin not just for the manufacturer but also distributors. A key goal must be to recover costs of up front investment as quickly as possible and provide a future healthy revenue and profit stream for the channel. Low profit margins will make this task harder. Trade-offs might be necessary within the product and packaging. If the desired price points for this product are to be achieved. A good example of improved price positions at lower manufacturing cost can be found in the automobile industry, where several car manufacturers are improving efficiency of manufacture whilst at the same time enhancing product offers at higher price points than previously.

Where the new product fits within the existing product range is an important consideration. Product range pricing requires the price points to be selected with care to avoid unintentional cannibalisation of existing product lines. A good example of this is Persil tablets which are priced at a premium to Persil washing powder. The benefits to the user are accrued through more efficient use of powder therefore lower cost. The price premium reflects this value whilst at the same time controlling the degree of cannabalisation of sales of the traditional washing powder.

(b) **Identification and justification of one pricing policy**

My recommended pricing policy for this new range of flavoured milk is to price it at a premium to traditional milk and milk shake products and emphasise its freshness which is a clear product attribute. The new range is unlikely to be a complete substitute for traditional milk and may be drunk more as a snack. The premium price will enable us to establish a higher profit margin particularly in view of the fact that the additional costs incurred in producing the flavoured milk will be marginal. The product should therefore be positioned at a premium emphasising its unique attributes and health benefits. It will be possible to achieve good volume of sales fairly quickly after launch if the premium price is supported with strong marketing activity, particularly with brand, and at the point of distribution.

34 Pricing

> **Examiner's comments.** Due to its financial theme, this was not a popular question. Candidates who did attempt this seemed not to fully understand the differences between the financial or economic issues considered.

(a) **Financial and economic issues which may affect the marketer's pricing decision for a consumer product**

Product – new car launch

Financial issues

(i) **Cost and profit margin**

The marketer must consider the relationship between cost and price. Trade offs may well be made in terms of features, design and build quality to ensure the desired price position can be attained at an acceptable profit margin.

(ii) **Breakeven quantities**

The volume of anticipated sales and contribution attained from each unit of sale must be considered. Ideally breakeven should be attained as early as possible from launch to avoid resources being diverted to support the new product.

(iii) **Return on capital employed**

This is a useful measure of profitability which relates investment to returns and can be compared with other investments possibly to determine levels of and direction of financial support. This is a key issue particularly where high levels of investment in capital and plant are required to support production.

(iv) **Financial risk**

The level of risk that the investment exposes the organisation should be a key consideration. A radical product development strategy to achieve a turnaround in fortunes has to be weighed against the potential for cash flow difficulties and not achieving targeted sales and profit targets.

Economic issues

(i) **Economic growth and prosperity**

The level of economic growth and prosperity will influence consumers purchase decisions. Confidence, level of disposable income and a general feel good factor will increase the likelihood of a consumer renewing their car and upgrading to a higher specification.

(ii) **Exchange rate fluctuations**

Exchange rate fluctuations will impact upon imports of materials, components and export prices. Profits can be distorted as a result of fairly insignificant changes in exchange rates. The current strength of Sterling over the Euro is creating problems to UK car manufacturers.

(iii) **Demand and price elasticity**

Marketers need to understand the relationship between price and demand. Price elasticity will vary dependant upon the degree of differentiation and quality offered, the extent of brand loyalty, the extent to which the car has close substitutes and whether the car is perceived as a necessity or luxury.

(iv) **Inflation, taxation and interest rates**

These economic factors all impact upon the rate of economic growth and level of consumers disposal income. In periods of low inflation, taxation and interest rates, disposable income and willingness to take on loans is likely to be high. Levels of indirect taxation on petrol can also influence purchase decisions.

(v) **Investment in transport infrastructure**

Government investments in road and alternative transport infrastructure need to be considered as the drive to encourage consumers to not use cars increases.

(b) The extent to which the product is differentiated and its intended brand position in the market alongside the quality and range of features that are included in support will influence the pricing decision. Service offers made to augment the product such as free help lines, delivery or warranties also need to be considered.

The needs and expectations of members of the distribution channel need to be taken into account. Each will have a desirable profit margin to cover the costs of holding and handling stock. Required level of sales and service support will also incur additional costs to the manufacturer. Direct distribution to the consumer may enable lower price points to be achieved.

The level of investment available for marketing communications to support and build the brand and offer incentives to encourage sales and distribution will influence the likely price premiums that can be achieved. Price is often a crucial positioning factor that requires the other elements of the marketing mix to be used in support.

35 Customer care

Tutorial note. This answer has managed to identify some good practical tactics that could be adopted by the airline and has been able to illustrate knowledge about effective customer care well. The answer is also well presented and thus received marks for this.

Examiner's comment. There was a general tendency to deliver answers in a general context and not in the context of air travel.

(a) **Report on Improving Customer Care**

To: C Broomfield, Marketing Manager
From: D Brindly, Trainee Marketing Executive
Date: 7th December 2000

Introduction

This report will highlight the key practical approaches which our company could undertake to improve the standard of customer care for passengers who have experienced problems within our organisation.

Customer care aims to close the gap between customer expectations and their experience. It is a policy and a set of activities used by a business to bridge this gap.

(i) **Practical Approaches to Customer Care**

To improve customer care it is important to describe the shortfall between expectation and experience. In this case a one hour delay to the journey time occurred in both directions. Our organisation must understand the extent of the problem fully and implement a strategic response within the operating procedures of the business.

We need to ensure that the problem is then corrected. In this case, we need to make sure that effective communication is introduced to inform the customers of any difficulties and also to offer some compensation commensurate with the failure of the service in order to retain customer loyalty. In understanding that some customers will be continuing their journey on connecting flights it would be sensible to provide personal assistance by our staff for these passengers.

This may include complementary meals and drinks, use of the executive lounge as well as accurate, alternative flight details. We also need to provide information and explanation of the cause of delay including likely waiting times and ensure regular updates are provided to the customers. For longer term delays, suitable accommodation would also have to be provided. Particular customer needs would have to be understood as part of the decision making process.

The personal service offered to the delayed passengers should include the collection of personal details to enable correspondence to be understaken after the event to retail the customer loyalty and make the customer feel appreciated.

The use of IT could be embraced in this process, as the Internet and teletext can be used to provide minute to minute accurate information for customers facing such problems, to make alternative arrangements prior to departing for the airport.

It is important to demonstrate a proactive approach to the solutions being offered to customers to ensure the reputation of the organisation is maintained.

(b) **Steps in Establishing Effective Customer Care**

The practical steps in establishing an effective customer care programme should be as follows:

(i) **Customer Orientation**

Fundamentally, the company must establish a customer-wide orientation. A well-defined mission statement is needed, unifying all members of the company.

(ii) **Customer Requirements**

Customers' needs and requirements must be researched and clearly defined.

(iii) **Management Commitment**

There must be commitment from all staff and most importantly from top management levels.

(iv) **Up-to-date Information**

This must be collected regularly from marketing research, and disseminated throughout the organisation. Customer feedback, for example from surveys, is vitally important to identify changes in the market, the macro-environment and competitors' actions. This information must be used to inform decision making and to design the products and services which we offer.

(v) **Regular progress report**

These should be distributed to keep the staff informed.

(vi) **Customer Care Specifications**

Specifications or plans will aid understanding of the process and improve staff motivation.

(vii) **Measurement and Control**

The measurement and control of the whole cycle of planning, implementation and control is very important. Monitoring our customer service levels and customer satisfaction will enable the company to improve its service – a key to customer care.

(viii) **Conclusion**

Customer care is a crucial company wide method of securing customer loyalty and is key to ensuring long term profitability for the organisation.

36 New distribution channels

Examiner's comments. The first part of this question was rarely completed. Candidates failed to apply the Ansoff matrix to the context of the question. In some cases, candidates confused the Ansoff matrix with the BCG matrix. Many candidates only had a vague idea of the concept.

The second part of the question was not completed well in many cases. Often the candidate tended to take a narrow view of the criteria which could have been employed. An attempt did attract some marks.

(a) **Ansoff Matrix**

The Ansoff matrix identifies four options that an organisation can consider when developing its growth strategy. They are shown in the diagram below.

Products

	Existing	New
Existing	Market penetration	Product development
New	Market development	Diversification

Markets

The small manufacturer for electrical components to the computer industry can achieve growth through any of the four options in the diagram.

It should initially consider market penetration as this is the lowest risk option. This involves selling more components to the existing market. Market penetration is attractive if the market is growing or if customers are dissatisfied with current market offers. Market research should be undertaken to see if these conditions exist in the market.

If research shows that limited scope for growth exists then market development and product development options can be considered. Market development involves finding an new market, either through a different market segment, that is another industry which would use electrical components, or by considering regional, national or even international expansion. Product development requires the organisation to implement new product development procedures and encourage innovative ideas. Customers in this industry are constantly looking for new ideas therefore this may prove an attractive option to consider.

Diversification is the highest risk option open to the electrical component manufacturer. This involves developing new products to be sold in different markets. It is unlikely to be appropriate for a small business due to the high risk and cost involved.

These options need to be researched and evaluated before the growth strategy is developed.

(b) **Key issues to consider in distribution decision**

The key issues which the marketing department will have to take into account when considering alternative or new distribution channels are as follows.

Target segments

The marketers need to consider whether the new channel would offer good coverage of the target segment. It is also important to consider what quality of relationship distributors within the channel have established with customers. Selecting the wrong channel or channel members may result in the failure of the entire marketing strategy.

Organisation objectives

The organisation's marketing objectives must fit with the goals of the new channel. It is also important to ensure that the channel has the capability to deliver the required orders to secure the organisation's objectives. The required length of relationship with the channel partners must also be considered.

Cost of distribution

Cost of distribution is a significant proportion of an organisation's marketing costs. It is vital to ensure that the new channel will provide both efficiency and effectiveness gains. Identifying new and lower cost distribution can significantly improve profitability but needs to be balanced with ensuring that customer service levels are maintained or improved.

Size and power of channel member

A new channel may appear attractive initially as a result of its newness. This needs to be evaluated against the negotiating power of channel members. A small manufacturer is in danger of being squeezed on price and therefore profitability even though it may secure large order quantities.

Competitors' channel choice

The strength of the competitor in the channel needs to be considered. Presence in the channel may still be critical for the small manufacturer, but alternative routes to market may offer more attractive long term prospects if direct competition is avoided.

Expertise of channel member

It is vital to the organisation that the new channel member has the necessary technical expertise to satisfactorily distribute the electrical components. This is a key consideration if the distributor is to effectively sell and service the product line.

Ability to handle tasks

It is necessary for the distributor to be able to provide adequate sales force coverage and activity, required service levels, stock handling and administration of accounts. Ineffectiveness in these areas will result in dissatisfied customers and poor sales performance levels.

Conclusion

These considerations are all essential before decisions to enter the new channel are made. Careful planning at this stage will minimise the possibility of potential channel management problems in the longer term.

37 Distribution

> Examiner's comment. Many candidates [did] not consider the role of IT within their answer.

(a) (i) **Key issues to take into account when considering alternative distribution channels**

Cost

The Marketing Manager needs to consider the costs of alternative distribution channels. Costs can be occurred through giving profit margins, cost of holding stock, and service support. By going direct to the end user some of these costs may be reduced but potential new costs will be incurred in terms of order processing and administration. These costs need to be assessed against any competitive advantage.

Market coverage

The degree of market coverage that the distribution channel can provide is a key consideration. This includes closeness of relationships with customers. The market strategy being considered will influence this decision. Where market share and volume is a primary goal mass distributors will be utilised. More specialist services may required selected distributors who cover targeted segments. Traditionally market coverage required an extensive distributor network but organisations are increasingly exploring the developments in direct distribution particularly through the Internet.

Control

It is important to consider the degree of power and control distributors have over the channel. Multiple retailers dominate the grocery market and manufacturers have to decide whether they wish to do business with these majors or go for the second tier multiples whose negotiating power is not as strong. Lower volumes may result but at higher profit margins.

Logistics and service support

The questions of who holds stock, owns stock, closeness of links between buyers and suppliers, and position in the supply chain will all be important considerations. Increasingly markets are operating as networks and partnerships, therefore selecting the right channel partner is crucial.

Competitor activity

Competitor strategy and position in the channel will need to be considered, for example whether the competitor have exclusivity deals, how entrenched are they in the market, what basis of their competitive advantage is whether existing channels are viable. Daewoo Cars could not find any car distributors available to stock its cars. It therefore developed a new channel selling its products in out of town retail parks and locating next door to Halfords. Halfords provided all service and repair facility. Attempting to compete directly with established competitors may prove too high a cost.

(ii) **Reasons for the recent growth in direct marketing channels**

New technologies

New technology has enabled organisations to more effectively and efficiently communicate directly with the consumer. This technology has enhanced data, acquisition techniques, data analysis, market segmentation, customer monitoring and communications and response and handling. With the telephone for instance it is now possible for an automated systems to handle many hundreds of calls simultaneously reducing the risk of losing potential respondents. The developments now occurring on the internet and through digitalisation will fuel this growth allowing for increased opportunities for interaction to occur.

Media and market segment fragmentation

Market segments are fragmenting in that the needs of customers are more complex and the consumer is more demanding. Increasingly behavioural motivational and lifestyle factors are determining purchase behaviour and traditional forms of segmentation such as age and socio economic grade become less meaningful. Customers also have a need for more individualism as their expectations rise. This has meant that the mass markets of the past are less evident today and marketers need to utilise more targeted communications at more clearly defined target audiences.

The increasing number of advertising media reflects this fragmentation and has enabled marketers to consider more targeted communication campaigns and move away from mass communication. The growth of satellite TV, specialist and lifestyle magazines, alongside opportunities to utilise the internet makes it easier to locate a defined segment and build in direct response mechanisms because a higher proportion of the audience will be interested in the communication.

Increasing customer confidence

Consumers have developed a greater trust and confidence in dealing direct initially via post, telephone and through catalogues. Now many consumers are searching and purchasing online which enables direct marketers to establish immediate opportunities for dialogue.

Customer relationship management

Direct marketing has enabled marketers to establish, build and maintain closer relationships with customers. In business to business and consumer marketing, direct marketing is a key communication tool to ensure that customers remain loyal. This can include account management, loyalty cards and 'membership clubs' such as the AA.

Improvements in management of logistics

The improvement in logistics management has meant that orders can be despatched and delivered with increased reliability and reduced cost within 24 hours of the order being taken. This, coupled with the increased range of merchandise that can be stocked and displayed, and convenience factor, cutting out the time and hassle of shopping, has led to distribution becoming increasingly acceptable.

(b) (i) ### Cash and carry warehouses

Cash and carry stores are large stores carrying an assortment of goods ranging from groceries to computers to office equipment and furniture. Makro and Nurdin and Peacock are examples of this type of retailer. Cash and carry stores act as middlemen between the manufacturer and small businesses. Makro have a dual customer base of consumers and small businesses and retailers. Nurdin and Peacock do not sell to consumers. Customers can take advantage of bulk discounts when they shop.

Superstores

Superstores are increasingly located on out of town shopping centres with large car parks. They cater for the household weekly shop. They primarily stock groceries, household products and clothing. A range of new services such as banking and petrol forecourts now supports this range of products. In recent years new superstores have been opened by non grocery organisations such as IKEA and Toys R Us.

Catalogue showrooms

A catalogue showroom sells a wide selection of fast moving brand name goods at discount prices. This includes jewellery, cameras, toys, sporting goods and garden equipment and furniture. These showrooms make their money by cutting costs and margins to provide low prices that will attract a higher volume of sales. The customer can select a product from the catalogue. It is checked to see if it is in stock. The item is paid for and then collected from a distribution counter. Only one of each item is commonly shown on display. Argos and Index are examples of successful catalogue showrooms. In recent years 24 hour telephone ordering service and free delivery have been offered to augment the showroom.

(ii) **Intensive distribution**

Intensive distribution involves the product or service being made available in as many outlets as possible. Market coverage and availability are the key goals. Organisations such as Coca Cola, Mars and Macdonalds adopt such as strategy and utilise extensive distribution channels to ensure their success.

Selective distribution

Selective distribution involves the selection of a few carefully scrutinised distributors or outlets to sell products or services within a given defined territories or region. Complex products such as computers or cars are likely to be sold through selected distributors. Similarly many industrial products are sold through specialist distributors who can provide sales, service and specialist support.

Exclusive distribution

Exclusive distribution involves the selection of one distributor to look after a total region or market. The exclusivity may fit with the products exclusivity or it may be a decision that reflects the power and size of the distributor. Close partnerships and support will frequently be evident in such a strategy between supplier and distributor. Contractual arrangements will probably exclude that distributor from selling competitor products. Some car manufacturers such as Ford and Jaguar operate exclusive dealerships.

38 Service industry

> Examiner's comments. Many candidates were able to refer to the elements of intangibility, inseparability, perishability, heterogeneity and ownership and went into explain the problems which these characteristics pose. Some seemed to be guessing and waffled, some candidates did not discuss the problems associated with marketing services.
>
> Part (b) required a consideration of the 7Ps, applied to the service organisation chosen. Many candidates were able to consider their own organisations and gave valid answers.

(a) **Identification and explanation of the characteristics of services**

Services are characterised by five factors that differentiates them from product. These are:

Intangibility	-	Services cannot be touched tasted, smelt or seen. They can only be experienced.
Perishability	-	Services cannot be stored. Services are not like products which can be held in stock. They have to be consumed at a moment in time. If an airline has empty (unsold) seats it cannot store these for another day. It has to fly.
Variability	-	Services are delivered primarily by people via processes. It is extremely hard to manage both to ensure the same consistent level of service time and time again.
Inseparability	-	Services are frequently delivered at the time and place of consumption. If something is going to go wrong it will occur at that moment in time.

BPP PUBLISHING

Lack of ownership - When a service is purchased the owner often only has ownership for a limited period of time. A holiday is experienced but at the end the holiday has no residual value its only benefit is in use (and any memories).

Problems presented for marketers

These five factors present unique problems to service marketers.

(i)   Service marketing is primarily about managing service experiences and ensuring that customer expectations are met by the delivery of that service. Clear understanding of customer needs and management of customer expectations become critical in service marketing as does the importance of marketing communications.

(ii)   Demand management is essential in service marketing. In particular maximising customer throughput in line with resources and avoiding periods of under-demand and over-demand. Poor management of demand can result in lost revenue and dissatisfied customers.

(iii)   Managing people and processes to minimise variability of service delivery is an extremely difficult function. Training of staff and close monitoring of service are important tasks. Management of systems and process to ensure consistent and reliable service can present major problems for service organisations.

(iv)   If a mistake is going to occur it is going to occur at the moment in time that the service is often being consumed. Minimising this potential is a crucial task of service marketers. Service recovery becomes an important management task.

(v)   Due to lack of ownership service marketers must offer more to customers than the service experience. Membership of clubs, frequent flyer or hotel loyalty cards and the offering of tangible service products such as badges, balloons etc all provide opportunities for some form of ownership of the service.

(b) **Tactical issues relating to a small business.**

The local independent travel agent can be selected to demonstrate the tactical issues which should be considered relating to the extended marketing mix. (People, Process and Physical Evidence). These types of travel agents are faced with competition from large national chains whose buying power and resource far exceeds that available to the independents. Service is therefore an important weapon by which these independent agents can compete. The personal (and local) service factor can be exploited. Employees knowing customers on first name terms and keeping in contact throughout the year can establish stronger relationships. Setting up internal processes within small organisations is simpler than for many national organisations. The purchase of a good database and establishment of a appointments process can be highly effective. Visits to customers own homes and acting as a broker would all be of potential value to customers. Small travel agents should also be able to offer a more flexible and customised service because their internal systems have less bureaucracy. Consideration of the physical ambience and layout of the agency in which customers experience the service delivery could also be improved in order to create a user friendly and relaxing service environment.

By these tactics small independent agents can compete successfully against larger national chains and prosper through their service orientation.

39 Grey market promotion

(a) **Key considerations for packaging**

The range of biscuits is to be repositioned to target the grey market. The key considerations in determining the packaging for the product range are as follows.

(i) **Distribution**

It is important to consider how the product is going to get to the customer, in other words, the channel of distribution. In the case of these biscuits, thought needs to be given to the weight of the product, its transportability, the need for protection of the product and the likelihood that the product will be stacked on shelves.

The costs of distribution are high. Therefore any design considerations within the packaging that can reduce cost and improve distribution effectiveness should be incorporated within the design. An interesting concern in the grey market is the sizes offered in packaging. Purchase quantities are likely to be smaller than for a middle-aged household with family. Consideration should be given to this at the design stage. While cost is important, the target market will also be interested in quality and value, so these factors must be balanced.

(ii) **Branding and package design**

Innovative packaging can create instant product recognition and give a company a competitive advantage over the competition. Branding and package design should work together to help consumers to have instant recall of the product and awareness of it on the shelf.

Consideration should be given to the needs of the target market in terms of the main function of the packaging when determining size, shape, colour and text and brand name. Packaging has a powerful communication role and therefore must be consistent with the needs of this market. It is probable that quality, brand image and design are important considerations to this target group.

(iii) **Convenience**

Various package designs should be tested to determine which offers the most convenience in use. This could be factors such as ease of opening, dispensing or carrying. Such issues are likely to be important to this target group and therefore are important in product differential.

(iv) **Regulations**

As the product is food, there are likely to be requirements that ingredients and other such details are clearly displayed on the packaging. Also, issues such as safe handling and usage and warning relating to health are frequently determined by law. Clarity and visibility of such instructions is particularly important to the older consumer who may have hearing or sight impairment.

(v) **Merchandising**

It is important to consider the needs of the retailer when designing packaging. Convenience in terms of handling, space efficiency, and innovation at point of sale are important to them. Merchandising is an integral part of ensuring that the product is seen on the shelf or in store. It should be given careful consideration alongside the other points above.

(b) **Push and pull promotional techniques**

The strengths and weaknesses of push and pull promotional techniques which could be used for this repositioned product range are illustrated in the following diagram.

Push promotions

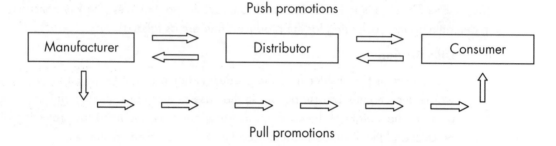

Pull promotions

Push techniques

Push promotions are promotional activities targeted at the channel of distribution. They aim to encourage retailers to purchase, stock and sell the brand. Push promotions 'push' the product through to the consumer. Associated marketing activity consists primarily of personal selling and trade promotions.

Pull techniques

Pull promotions are promotional activities targeted at the consumer. They encourage purchase of the product from retail outlets. Pull promotions 'pull' the product through the distribution channel by creating demand from the consumer. Associated marketing activity consists primarily of advertising and brand communication, merchandising and sales promotions.

Advantages and disadvantages of push promotions

(i) **Advantages**

Push promotions provide an important communication and incentive function to the channel of distribution. Without effective push promotions, many brands would not be stocking in the required quantities to ensure effective coverage of the market.

Distributors need encouragement to stock products and the sales force play a vital function in this process. Incentives play an important role in maintaining distributor loyalty and enhancing relationships. A discount or free product for volume provides a reason to buy. Similarly a prize for reaching specific sales targets acts as an incentive to purchase more stock. Push promotions can also provide useful trade information if they are tied into a process of data acquisition. This data can be used in future campaigns to target specific channel members with special offers.

(ii) **Disadvantages**

Push promotions can be misused. Overuse of price promotions can lead to price competition in the channel. This reduces profit margins and subsequent future investment in the brand.

Overuse can also lead to distributors expecting the incentive and therefore eroding its effectiveness. Investment in push promotions may be at the expense of pull promotions in particular brand building.

Push promotions might also lead to overstocking. This would result in heavy discounting being required to clear shelves of the product.

Advantages and disadvantages of pull promotions

(i) **Advantages**

Pull communications offer and opportunity to communicate directly with the end consumer. They can be used to build brand awareness, provide incentives for purchase decisions and provide reassurance to distributors that the manufacturer is prepared to invest to support the brand.

Pull promotions particularly suit mass distribution brands where national exposure is an important requirement of the promotion. They are equally effective for more selective coverage if used through carefully targeted and appropriate media.

(ii) **Disadvantages**

The major disadvantage of pull promotions is the cost of promotions. This is has been particularly true recently, with a rapid increase in media inflation and potential for weak targeting. Competitor campaigns are plentiful and it can be difficult to ensure 'share of voice'. These factors can result in less effective advertising and promotion at higher costs. The increasing fragmentation of market segments and media has created increasing difficulties for marketers to justify the levels of expenditure required to ensure effective pull campaigns.

Conclusion

In reality, a combination of push and pull techniques are usually used. The two strategies support each other and the advantages of both can be enjoyed and the disadvantages minimised. This minimisation of the disadvantages is achieved through planning and implementing integrated push and pull strategies.

40 Services marketing

Tutorial note. This is quite a comprehensive which has included all of the characteristics of services (ie 5 rather than the 4 required) although 4 would have been sufficient for the marks. The answer has been contextualise and references to financial services have been included throughout. The answer goes on to identify the key issues or problems for the marketer and in some cases solutions for these. This part of the answer received top marks. It was also presented well and thus received marks for this also. This is a very good example of a top-level answer for this part of the question. The answer highlights the key extended mix elements and highlights not only some of ways in which organisations should address these areas but it also highlights the problems if they do not.

Examiner's comments. Some candidates did not include the problems facing marketers, thus losing marks. The second part of the question was completed well, although a minor weakness was that candidates did not customise their examples of the extended marketing mix to the context of the examples they had cited.

(a)   MEMORANDUM

To: C Rewelorr, Marketing Assistant
From: L N E Srewot, Marketing Manager
Date: 7th December 2000

Characteristics and Problems of Service Provision

Following our discussions earlier I have put together an explanation of the different characteristics between services and products and problems that relate to service provision. This will, I hope allow you to understand the attributes of the financial services that we offer.

There are five characteristics of a service which are described below:

- *Perishability* A service cannot be stored or saved. It has an immediacy that cannot be held over until sometime in the future. For example with a loan the repayments start immediately after it has been set up. If there is a delay with the loan the lost revenue cannot be recovered. Marketeers have to give incentives for customers to purchase at off-peak times to counter this potential problem.

- *Intangibility* You cannot touch or feel the service offering as it has an abstract delivery. Unlike a product which you can touch (and smell and see) a service has no physical presence. It is only the paperwork that accompanies the service which has a tangible element. This can give problems since customers cannot see what they are getting for their money and they can only make a judgement based on experience of the service.

- *Inseparability* A key distinguishing feature of a service is that the provider and receiver of the service are inseparable from consumption and the consumer. The customer has to be present for the service to take place which presents a problem for the marketeer as they cannot always ensure that the process is enjoyable for the customer.

- *Heterogeneity* The delivery of the service will vary each time to the customer. This is because a service is dependant on the unique interaction of the provider and the customer which will vary depending on the interaction between the two individuals. The variability is created by the influence of human behaviour in the transaction and consistency can become a difficult problem to manage.

- *Non-Ownership* Ownership of a service remains with the provider. For instance with banking services they serve only to allow the customer to make use of the services such as credit cards but they are not owned by the customer.

These are the differences between a service and a product and their associated problems for the Marketeer. If I can be of any further assistance please do not hesitate to contact me.

(b) **The Extended Marketing Mix**

The extended marketing mix is comprised of People, Process and Physical Evidence and is to applied to a small independent firm of management consultants in order to derive the following benefits:

- *People* There should be a strong emphasis on staff training to ensure a consistently high quality of provision. Poor customer service is the most commonly quoted reason for a change in sourcing services and is the most difficult problem to overcome to recover lost custom. The high level of people involvement in management consultancy demands that their customers are treated in a very professional manner throughout the delivery process. As their customers will judge the quality of the service by the conduct of the staff the close proximity of the staff working in a small business magnifies the need to adequately train all employees. This can include such areas as personal presentation, dealing with enquiries, providing quotations and maintaining technical competencies in line with current developments.

- *Physical Evidence* The image of the branches of the consultancy and any correspondence that is sent out in response to enquiries, including from the web site need to be consistent and include company brand identity such as logo or accreditation awards. This is crucial as it is one of the means that current or prospective clients will evaluate the consultancy.

  The staff uniforms, interior decoration of the branches, tidiness and signage should reflect a common and consistent quality image for the management consultancy. It should believe that the colour scheme and logo reflect its professionalism and trustworthy image which should be maintained to retain its fresh feel. All its literature and web site content should be regularly updated to provide an impression of current thinking for its clients that enhances quality perceptions for the offering.

- *Process* As part of customer service efficient administrative processes underpin a high quality of provision. For instance if a client has spent an unnecessary amount of time trying to contact a Management Consultant they would become very frustrated and annoyed at the waste of their valuable time. It sends all the wrong messages concerning the offering and will become a source of friction between the two parties that will have to recovered. The small business will need to consider putting procedures and resources into place to ensure these problems are carefully managed and that the clients expectations are at least achieved, if not surpassed.

Conclusion

Many companies, large and small often treat these areas of the marketing mix with limited attention which results in a poor perceived level of customer service. By paying due attention to the quality of all the people, the physical evidence and the process involved in the Management Consultancy operation will enhance the service marketing provision.

41 Packaging

MEMO

To   Product Manager - Segge
From   A N Other
Date   10th June 1999

(a) **Role of packaging for CD ROM games**

Packaging performs two primary roles. One is to offer a product protection from damage. The second is to act as a communication medium that promotes the product off the shelf and provides a channel for product information.

For CD ROM games the protection primarily comes from the clear plastic boxes. Inserted in the box is a special CD holder which keeps the CD secure. Small booklets and colour covers can also be inserted in much the same way as a music CD is packaged. For new CD ROM games a further layer of packaging is added in the form of a cardboard box/carton that in scale dwarfs the CD inside. These boxes are highly visible, stack well on retailers shelves and provide a perception of added value through the packaging design, colour and size. Inside the box is contained the CD along with other product information and leaflets.

The role of the outer box is purely communication as it provides no protection to the CD inside. Product details can be added to the box along with clear visuals of the application.

(b) **Key issues for new packaging to be considered in relation to the marketing mix.**

The following packaging issues should be considered in relation to the marketing mix.

The packaging is an integral part of the product offer to the customer and should therefore reflect the brand image and position. Specific details of product specification and application can be reinforced through visuals or copy on the packaging, but must be truthful and not misleading.

The packaging should be consistent with other forms of marketing communication. Integration of promotional message within packaging can be a powerful reinforcer of that message and encourages product recognition and trial. Special promotional offers can also be included on packaging. It should also be remembered that good packaging design can sell a product, therefore careful thought should be given to this issue.

For distributors packaging plays an important role. A key issue is maximising shelf space therefore packaging designed to stack well in secure / strong materials is a benefit. Damage to goods is of no value to distributors and should be avoided within the design. For postal distribution strong but lightweight packaging should be considered to minimise mailing costs.

Good packaging design can enhance a brand's image and encourage customers to pay higher price points. The same product in a premium style package will be perceived as better quality than that product in a more basic package.

Customer care information and product usage information can be provided on packaging thus enhancing the service element of the marketing mix.

As you can see from the above comments, packaging plays an integral role in the marketing mix of a product and should be given careful attention when developing the marketing strategy.

42 Services marketing mix

Examiner's comments: summary/extracts. A very popular question which most candidates seemed to handle well. Weaker answers identified the service characteristics but did not discuss the implications from a marketing perspective although this was clearly required.

(a) **Identification of marketing characteristics for services**

There are five key characteristics of the marketing of services. These characteristics need to be understood and considered when developing and implementing service marketing strategy.

Intangibility

A product is tangible. It can be seen, touched, heard, tasted or smelt. These factors will help a consumer examine and evaluate what is on offer and make choices between competing brands.

It is more difficult to use the senses in the same way to make a purchase decision about a service. The service experience can only take place once the decision to purchase has been made. The service marketer is marketing an experience. He has to ensure that it meets the expectations of the consumer.

To overcome the problem of intangibility, service marketers can provide tangible suggestions about the service. This is done through choice of location, colour schemes, décor, customer care, uniforms or additional services. These can all have the effect of upgrading the consumer's experience and making it easier to evaluate different service offers.

Inseparability

Products can be purchased before they are consumed and the production staff rarely come into contact with the consumer. Service providers are not distant in both space and time in this way. Production, purchase and consumption often happen at the same time with services.

Inseparability means that a purchaser comes into direct contact with the service provider. The service provider has to ensure that the service encounter is well managed to avoid service delivery failure through poor service delivery systems or poorly trained employees.

To overcome the problem of inseparability, the service delivery system has to be efficient and effective. A long wait, poor communication and disruption are three key causes of a poor quality of service provision. Three important factors in ensuring high quality service delivery are highly trained staff, close monitoring of systems and a clear service recovery strategy.

Perishability

Services are often manufactured at the same time as they are consumed. An airline delivers its service at a specified moment in time. The service cannot be stored for the future. If the service is not fully taken up, the service provider loses revenue. A manufacturer of products can usually hold stock to be sold in the future.

In periods of over demand, it is frequently difficult for service providers to increase capacity. Restaurants and hotels also face these difficulties of demand management.

To overcome this problem, service marketers require a range of marketing strategies to try and even out demand to fit the capacity. These might include pricing, special offers, improved scheduling or forecasting. If possible, the service capacity can be adapted to cope with peaks and troughs through strategies such as using part time workers or setting up partnership programmes.

Heterogeneity

It is relatively straightforward to ensure the consistency of most products from one period of consumption to the next. It is more difficult to ensure this consistency when delivery service due to the number of variables that can impact on the service experience because the service is consumed at a particular moment in time. Each service experience is likely to be different. The problem of standardising the service experience is a significant challenge to the service marketer, particularly when that service is delivered in many different locations.

Service providers have to develop ways to minimise the variability that can occur in a service experience. They have to focus their attention on systems and procedures, employees and the physical environment. Many organisations utilise standard colour schemes throughout branches. Employees are also required to follow strict guidelines about complying with standardised procedures, behaviour and appearance.

Ownership

On purchase, a consumer takes ownership of a product for a period of time. With services, there is no transfer of ownership. The consumer is essentially buying the right to utilise the service for a period of time. Service marketers face the challenge that their consumers do not own the service they are providing and therefore may not value it highly.

Service marketers must ensure that the service experience creates a willingness and desire in the consumer to continue or repeat the experience. This repeat consumption can be encouraged through incentive schemes such as loyalty cards or membership clubs such as the AA or RAC.

(b) **The extended service marketing mix**

The traditional marketing mix of product, price, place and promotion provide only partial relevance to the issues and challenges faced by service marketers. Three further marketing mix elements are required to explain how service marketing strategy is developed and implemented. These three factors are people, process and physical evidence.

People

Services depend on people and interaction. This includes both front and back office staff. As the customer is often a participant in the creation of the service and delivery experience, the management and understanding of people is crucial to the delivery of high quality service.

The ability of staff to deliver service reliably, to the required standard and to present an image consistent with the organisation is a vital concern to the service provider. First Direct bank is an example of an organisation which has set up sophisticated recruitment, training and development policies. First Direct initially employ people on the basis of attitudes and then provide training in the required skills. Telephone operators at First Direct undergo several weeks of intensive training before being allowed to serve customers directly.

Process

The production and delivery process must be organised both an efficient and effective manner to serve the needs of the customer. Consistent and reliable levels of service are important to good service delivery. The systems and processes that are engaged when a customer comes into contact with the service organisation such as data processing, service delivery systems and communications networks must be managed to ensure that systems failures or delays are minimised.

Front and back office staff procedures need to be understood by everyone involved in the serving process. Many processes that work behind the scenes impact directly on the customer service experience. Organisations such as Northern Rock Building Society have reduced the time it takes to get mortgage applications approved from several weeks to less than one hour, through the introduction of new technological processes.

Physical evidence

This comprises the management of the physical environment within which the service is delivered. This can include the design and ambience of a building, the cleanliness of a kitchen or consistency of use of the corporate colours.

Physical evidence communicates and can leave strong impressions in the minds of customers as to the quality and positioning of the organisation. British Airways, The Body Shop and McDonald's are examples of organisations that manage physical evidence as a key part of their corporate identity.

43 Customer care

Examiner's comments. The candidate was asked to identify the relevance of customer care to the hotel section. The answer should have commenced with the explanation of the importance of customer care in this service sector especially when considering the maintenance of standards, perceptions, expectations and the monitoring process.

The second part of the question required candidates to propose a new customer care programme for the company. Thus answers should have considered: the identification of customer needs and perceptions; the establishment of a mission statement; the setting of service level standards and specifications, (TQM systems, customer systems, good communications, staff and customer, responsive to customer complaints, minimise waiting times, bottle necks, etc), the establishing of management processes and communication of this to all staff; the definition of tasks according to time factors; the setting of a basic minimum level; the insurance of systems for effective response to complaints; the management commitment; the implement effective and continuous measurement and control systems.

Many candidates were not very good at answering specifically and many tended to waffle about customer care in general for both parts of the question.

(a)

REPORT

PREPARED FOR;   P Rhodes, Sales Manager

PREPARED BY: E F Sodje, Customer Relations Manager

DATE: 13 June 2002

SUBJECT: Customer Care

1.0 Introduction

After my recent appointment as Customer Relations Manager I will be looking into implementing a new customer care programme for Horizon Hotels. I would hope that this would increase the levels of repeat business throughout the chain.

2.0 The Importance of Customer Care

In our service sector customer care is an extremely important factor. With the increase of customer expectations and the effects of consumerism it is important that there is a high quality of service and that we aim to get it right first time. We should be aiming to close the gap between our guest's expectations and their experience.

3.0 Gap Analysis

The following model is an adaptation of the famous 'SERVQUAL' model, which was devised by Parasuraman, Zeithaml and Berry in 1985, (commonly known as PZB).

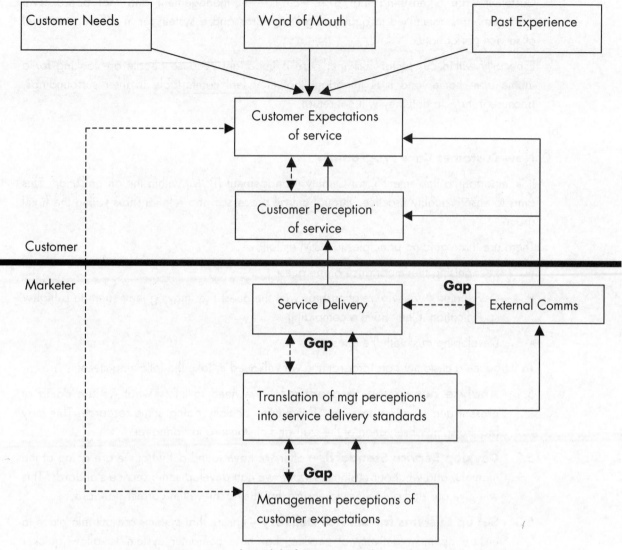

Customer Needs

Word of Mouth

Past Experience

Customer Expectations
of service

Customer Perception
of service

Customer

Marketer

Service Delivery

Gap

External Comms

Gap

Translation of mgt perceptions
into service delivery standards

Gap

Management perceptions of
customer expectations

A Conceptual Model of Service Quality and its Implications

This model shows the problems that can occur in the delivery of a service as there are a number of gaps in terms of customer perceptions, expectations and management expectations and perceptions.

4.0 The Identification of Gaps

It is important that the gaps are identified.

- The gap between management perception and customer exceptions will illustrate that the management may not appreciate the customers' needs

- The gap between service quality specifications and management perception – which means that the management does not set standards of performance

- The gap between service quality specification and the delivery of service – which means that operational personnel may be inadequately trained to meet the standards required

- The gap between service delivery and external communications – where the expectations from the promotional activity are not matched in practice

- The gap between perceived and expected service – where customers envisage a better service than the one that has been provided.

Customer care is ensuring that a service is well management and that board level management is committed to quality, high standards and a system for monitoring the level of service performance.

Especially within our sector customer care is important because people are looking for a 'home from home' and it is important that they feel comfortable in their surroundings, because if they do not, they will not return.

(b)

5.0 New Customer Care Programme

It is important to implement Total Quality Management (TQM) within the organisation. This aims to ensure quality practices throughout all processes and relationships within the hotel group.

There are three guiding principles to TQM as follows:

- Recognising the importance of the guest

- Developing ' win-win' relationships with the guest (i.e. moving their room to a higher specification if they have a complaint)

- Developing trust with the guest

To introduce a customer care programme we will need to take the following steps:

5.1 **Analyse our current procedures** – we need to know what we are doing at present and what guests want. This means actually doing some research. This may require some observation of the staff and customer questionnaires.

5.2 **Develop Service Standards -** after we have found out what we are doing at the moment, and what our customers want, we can develop some service standards. This will give our staff guidelines to ensure that they achieve the correct standard.

5.3 **Set up Systems for Service Delivery** – ensure that systems are put into place to ensure optimum delivery of service. I.e. new computer system to allow quicker checkins

5.4 **Analysis of Staff Training Needs** – Find out what our staff need to be trained on i.e. should our room service staff be trained in food hygiene or the reception staff go on a customer care course?

5.5 **Introduce Staff Training** – ensure that all training requirements are met. We cannot expect our staff to deliver good service if they are not trained to do so.

5.6 **Set up Monitoring and Measurement Systems** – this will allow us to check that service delivery meets our standards. This will keep staff on their toes and may identify areas for further training. This could be done using a 'mystery guest' programme on a regular basis.

5.7 **Introduce Performance Related Pay and Reward Schemes** – this recognises the staff who do well and rewards them, it may also incentives poorer performing staff to try harder.

6.0 Conclusion

I do hope that you can now see the importance of customer care and will agree with my proposal for the commitment of the Senior Management Team to the implementation of our customer care programme.

44 Customer care process

Examiner's comments: summary/extracts. The question asked for the service marketing mix. Candidates confused 'people' with customers. There was no real need to launch into the 4Ps, unless they could be directly related to customer care.

Customer care can be defined as the management and control of all elements of an organisation's relationships, processes and transactions that impact upon its customers, the aim to deliver customer satisfaction and delight.

Customer care is an important part of an organisations marketing activity. It is essential for any organisation that strives to achieve a greater degree of marketing orientation. Customers' service expectations have been steadily rising and to remain competitive organisation's have been required to respond.

Customer care focuses upon a customer's 'consumption' of a service. It attempts to see the organisation's service through the customer's eyes. It focuses upon the nature of the relationship established between the customer and the organisation and the nature of the experience the customers receive when coming into contact with the organisation or when consuming the service.

The primary objective of customer care activity is to manage all aspects of an organisation's activities that create gaps between customers' expectations and customers' perceptions of the service they received. Customer care activity includes, management of customer / employee contact points, external and internal communication, management of systems / processes and design and maintenance of the physical service environment. The three key elements of the marketing mix that can have a strong impact on the achievement of high quality customer care are people, systems and processes, and physical evidence.

People

Employees and staff associated with an organisation require an understanding of their role in the service delivery chain. This applies equally to those employees who have direct contact with the customer and those providing support services. Employees have to be committed to providing excellent service and this requires significant investment in customer care training. The organisation has to assess the extent to which staff feel motivated and empowered to deliver the required service standards. Good employee relationships and morale are essential.

Systems and Processes

In an ideal world all systems and processes would be able to provide flexible, efficient and effective responses to customer demands. Systems and processes refer to ordering and inquiry systems, queuing systems, internal communication systems manufacturing and logistics processes, and can relate to manual or information technology systems. All systems and processes should be under scrutiny to ensure consistent delivery of customer service.

Physical evidence

Physical evidence refers to the design, ambience and atmosphere that surrounds an organisations physical environment. It can be created through layout, choice of fixtures and fittings, colour schemes etc. It also includes factors such as good signage, informative communications and appearance of staff. All these factors impact upon a customers perception of their experience of the service.

BPP
PUBLISHING

Customer care is not a quick fix solution and requires continuous investment and attention to detail over a period of time. It can involve significant change within organisation's to ensure customer care standards are achieved. Programmes such as Investors in People and Total Quality Management can play an important role in the development of customer care programmes, with their focus upon quality of service and products through systems and people.

45 Target markets

> Examiner's comments. This question required an introduction to the meaning of segmentation, giving reasons for segmentation strategies. Candidates seemed to show some difficulty in identifying the variables for industrial markets. Some candidates ignored this part of the question. They did, however, seem able to attempt to illustrate the variable for consumer segments and go on to use examples.

Definition of market segmentation, targeting and positioning

Market segmentation is the subdividing of a market into distinct subsets of customers, where any subset may conceivably be selected as a target market to be reached with a distinct marketing mix. (Kotler)

Targeting is the evaluation and selection of market segments that offer the best potential and ideally best fit the capabilities of the organisation. Marketing activity can be tailored to the target segments selected.

Positioning is the perceived attributes, feelings and emotions that a customer attaches to a product or service in their mind. Positioning of products and services can be managed by marketers through their marketing activity.

Reasons for segmentation

The primary reason for market segmentation is to identify within markets distinct groups of people with similar needs, characteristics or behaviours that can be targeted with an appropriate marketing mix. Customers benefit because they are supplied with products and services that more closely relate to their requirements. Organisations benefit in terms of improved competitiveness, more efficient use of marketing resource and the potential to identify new market opportunities.

The product selected is car and truck tyres. Outlined below are the major categories of variables by which the market for tyres for both the consumer and truck tyre markets can be segmented.

Consumer segment variables	Industrial segment variables
Demographic	Organisational characteristics
Socio- economic	Regional
Lifestyle	Product / service application
Attitudes / motives	Benefits sought
Geodemographic	Complexity of DMU / purchasing policy
Benefits sought	Nature of business relationship

The basis for segmenting the consumer market may initially be based upon broad demographic and socio economic criteria but these descriptors may not be precise or appropriate classifications by which to target the different groups of consumer who purchase tyres. More precise segmentation may be available through identifying individual lifestyles eg 'boy racers', 'collectors clubbers' 'suburban drivers' etc or exploring attitudes and motives for purchase.

Similarly segmenting markets by benefits sought may provide more accurate segmentation data than the broader demographic and socio economic criteria.

For the industrial market similar broad based segmentation criteria may be used. In particular breaking markets down by regions or by type and size of company provide general segmentation data but these are not precise. Greater detail can be obtained by considering the various potential applications that a product could be used for. At the end of a truck tyres life it has to be disposed of. Truck tyres are now used as garden ornaments for flower beds, or are crushed, revulcanised and the rubber used to make the flooring seen in playareas or on roads.

Similarly by considering benefits that truck tyre users are seeking can highlight new market segments. Heavier duty side walls, thicker treads, specific performance characteristics such as fuel economy are all potential benefits that may be required by customers. The market can also be segmented by considering the different purchase processes that may be used in the industry or by the complexity of this process. Different strategies can then be adopted to target these segments.

Finally the nature of the relationship sought is a very powerful behavioural technique that can be utilised in this sector. Some buyers will seek full service support and close relationships regarding fleet management whereas others will seek simply the best price and only be interested in the transaction.

Market segmentation is crucial to marketers in both consumer and industrial markets . By considering the tyre markets for cars and trucks illustrates how market segmentation techniques can be successfully and usefully adopted in both sectors.

46 Marketing concept

> Examiner's comments: summary/extracts. Many candidates chose not to answer this question as it was quite demanding .... those who did answer it seemed to be rather vague in their approach. It is important that candidates are able to answer this type of question in the future as there is now a 15% weighting on the syllabus for advances in IT .... it is likely that further IT questions will be appearing regularly on the examination paper.

(a) **Successful adoption of the marketing concept**

(i) **A business to business organisation**

Trend Heating and Lighting, a division of Trend plc, faced a period of increasing competition and declining demand in several of its traditional core markets. It held a position as market leader selling heating and lighting systems to construction companies, architects, electrical installers and through specialised distributors.

Profitability was in decline and the company had reached a crisis point in terms of its future viability. Cost cutting had taken place in an attempt to maintain margins but frequently this was in areas such as marketing research and development and training. Limited research and development activity was taking place and reliance placed on an established sales force who were increasingly being forced to sell systems at lower price.

The company took actions to re-orientate itself. Extensive research of the market highlighted two significant trends. The first involved the increasing use of information technology in both the design and installation of systems. The second trend identified changing customer needs. A segment of the market was identified that required

BPP
PUBLISHING

complex heating and lighting systems integration and solutions rather than just systems application and installation.

Trend proposed to its top design and installation engineers that it would support them in setting up their own independent distribution companies to service this segment. The company worked in partnership to identify markets and provide full service back up to these new distributors in return for exclusivity. As a result of this innovative market led strategy, Trend established itself once again as market leader in a growing and profitable market segment.

(ii) **A non-profit organisation**

The Inland Revenue has undergone a significant internal and external reorientation in an attempt to reposition itself from an 'enemy to be feared' to a 'friend to be trusted'. Traditionally the Inland Revenue provided limited services other than to send out tax demands, administrate tax collection and prosecute late payers and tax evaders. None of these processes were customer orientated, the Inland Revenue primarily being seen as answerable to the government. Evidence of this lack of customer orientation fed down to the contact that was available between the consumer and the revenue with no contact name being provided just a district and reference number.

As a result of the introduction of self assessment the Revenue acquired a new identity and position to support its tax collecting and administration duties. A new openness was introduced that enabled direct contact to named revenue employees providing support and advice particularly on the completion of self assessment tax returns.

A more flexible and friendly face of the Revenue was introduced that was more supportive to the consumer. Employees were trained in the new work practices and the change was supported by an internal communications plan. Consumers were informed through an extensive advertising campaign to communicate this repositioning.

As a result of this reorientation the Revenue has succeeded in changing peoples perceptions of its role and services. It is a good example of a non profit making organisation successfully adopting the marketing concept.

(b) **How the use of information technology could assist in the management of a customer oriented culture in Trend Heating and Lighting**

Information technology can assist in the management of a customer oriented culture through the following ways.

(i) **Marketing Information Systems**

Gathering market and customer information and analysing and disseminating it, enable management to make speedier decisions and adopt a proactive rather than reactive approach to their market place and customers. These improvements feed into understanding the behaviour of customers and identification of potential market segments. The MKIS can also provide improved monitoring and control of marketing activities.

(ii) **Communication systems**

Internal and external communications systems can be developed enabling better communication between internal and external customers. The use of email and the Internet are offering significant improvements in both speed of communication, targeting and response. Customer Relationship Management activity is enhanced through using such systems. These developments should result in improved service performance, improved efficiency and responsiveness to customer demands.

(iii) Logistics management

Management and planning of logistics systems including transport, materials handling and stockholding can all be improved through the adoption of information technology. Networks can be established along the total supply chain offering management information and order and payment capabilities. Information technology is now being used by the organisations to control their European logistics systems.

(iv) Marketing strategy and planning

The marketing and strategy development process can be improved through investment in applications software, decision support systems and the application of knowledge management. Strategic Planning software is available to support company adoption of planning techniques and processes.

(v) New product development

Information technology can support the NPD development process through enabling marketers and researchers to work closely together on market led technological innovations. Developments such as Quality Function Deployment, which bring the voice of the customer to the engineers and designers are being enhanced through investment in information technology systems.

47 International distribution channels

Memo

To: Managing Director
From: A N Student
Date: 10th December 1998

I have outlined below the advantages and disadvantages of the following three different distribution channels in terms of achieving your objectives of expanding into new international markets.

(a) Franchise operations

Franchising is an arrangement whereby our organisation would grant a dealer the right to sell our products under our brand name in return for a capital sum and an annual royalty normally based on value of sales. It is likely that we might also finance the furnishing of the shop and provide ongoing marketing support as part of this arrangement.

Advantages

(i)   The franchisee will benefit from investing his/her capital in an established brand and gains marketing support to help establish the brand in their region. This substantially reduces the risk and capital commitment.

(ii)   The franchisee will benefit from our advice and guidance in terms of managing the business to maximise sales and profitability.

(iii) We (the franchiser) will benefit from the lower risk in terms of capital investment, as we can use Franchisees' money to support launching the franchise.

(iv)   We will benefit from the local knowledge of franchisees in their area.

(v)   We can establish our own retail outlets as opposed to selling through already established retail outlets therefore gaining access to distribution outlets and maximising our control.

Disadvantages

(i)   Franchisees will have to give up a degree of autonomy and control in running their businesses which may result in conflict of interest.

(ii)   The Franchisees potentially will not earn their desired income because of the requirement to pay royalties on sales etc. They may resent this arrangement over time.

(iii)   We may be tied to a franchisee that is not performing. Depending upon the contract we have agreed, this may be an unprofitable arrangement.

(iv)   We will limit our flexibility in terms of developing more intensive distribution through established distributors.

Overall, franchising does offer our company a means of gaining access to international markets but it will require us to manage the franchise with care and invest heavily in support of franchisees' operations to ensure success. Selecting the right locations and franchisees will be key to our operations. We have to accept that our brand will only be sold through our own distribution outlets.

(b) **Mail order direct to potential customer**

Mail order is a marketing technique that primarily sells product through a catalogue or from 'off the page' advertisements. It is one aspect of the field of direct marketing and would require us to develop a database of potential customers in the countries we are targeting. The mail order operations will require call handling, service desks, stock handling control and a mail handling distribution network in support of the system. It is possible that mail order could utilise the new interactive technology of digital television and the internet.

Advantages

(i)   Mail order negates the need for distribution outlets at retail level as we can deal directly with our customers.

(ii)   It offers us the opportunity to build relationships with our customer base that would not be as accessible through retailers.

(iii)   It is possible to enter all our international markets with limited investment in terms of distribution set up costs. Our major investment will be in catalogues, advertisements and operations / logistics.

(iv)   New technology opens up the opportunity for this medium to be exploited more fully particularly in terms of targeting, reach and cost.

Disadvantages

(i)   Potential response rates may be low particularly because we are only selling our products into a specialist area of mountaineering and sports.

(ii)   We will have no 'shop front' to support brand awareness in the markets we select.

(iii)   Mail order systems will vary in quality from country to country and there may be cultural barriers in some countries that limit the use of mail as a means of selling products.

(iv)   There is a high cost attached to preparation of catalogues and supporting the mail order operations.

Overall, mail order direct to our customer base does offer us opportunities to get closer to our customers and may provide better opportunities for repeat custom. We would require particular skills in managing mail order operations as well as direct marketing to ensure we maximise response rates and customer acquisition. We would be reliant upon advertising to build our brand as we would have no retail exposure. Whilst a mail order operation with a specialist product range does offer potential it is a high risk strategy.

(c)   **Agents in selected countries**

The value of using agents in selected countries works best at **market entry** stage in international markets. The agents do not purchase stock but simply sell on commission. The organisation will use the agents existing network of customers and relies upon the agent to represent it effectively. The company can consider a sole agency where only our product is sold or an agency that sells products from a variety of manufacturers.

Advantages

(i)   Low risk, in terms of forward investment in setting up distribution channels.

(ii)   Low risk, in terms of bad debts as ownership of the product remains in our hands.

(iii)   Utilisation of existing distribution channels exploiting local agents knowledge of markets and contacts.

(iv)   Low cost, in early stages of market entry as payment of commission is only paid on sales.

Disadvantages

(i)   The firm relies on the agents to sell product and maintain good relationships with customers with limited control from supplier. Similarly loss of agent would result in loss of customer base.

(ii)   As sales rise, commission costs increase until it may be cheaper for a firm to manage its own sales network.

(iii)   The agent may not be able to cope with large or small customer's dependant upon their size and resource. Market potential may not be exploited to the full utilising an agent's service.

Overall, using agents in selected countries offers a relatively low cost and straightforward method of gaining entry to international markets. Access is gained to distribution networks and, in the early stages, this can be extremely beneficial to our organisation. In the longer term, there is a danger that agents will not exploit fully the market opportunities that arise. The costs of agents relative to our own salesforce has to be considered against the value we attach to the agents' contacts.

48 Relevant marketing mix

Examiner's comments: summary/extracts. Candidates had difficulties developing the business-to-business marketing issues in the components manufacturer and the haulage company, although examples from banking and the car industry were better handled. However, 'for those choosing the service company, the opportunity to bring out the extra three Ps was generally missed'.

(a) **A large banking group**

A large banking group, such as Barclays has to focus on four key sectors.

(i) The consumer market
(ii) The corporate market
(iii) The small/medium business market
(iv) The financial markets

In all these sectors both international and domestic considerations are necessary.

The bank, whilst essentially a service, offers its customers a range of products. Although some of these products are intangible, they are nevertheless perceived by customers as offering specific benefits and meeting specific needs. It is important for a large banking group to engage all the elements of the marketing mix for these sectors.

In the consumer market distribution has become a major issue, particularly with the advent of direct banking. Service is an important element of the bank's response to an increasingly competitive marketplace. New products are being launched as the bank's marketing environment poses new opportunities and threats. Communication is critical both in terms of customer acquisition and retention. The heavy use of advertising and direct marketing are evidence of the importance attached to these components of promotion.

Within the corporate market a different range of tools will be utilised. In particular, relationship marketing and sponsorship become important elements of the mix. A range of financial services is offered to corporate clients particularly with investments. The product mix, communication and distribution structure will vary from the consumer market, with the sales function becoming more dominant.

For the small/medium business the role of the business adviser is important, along with the various services the bank provides to assist the business in managing its financial affairs more effectively. It is not uncommon to see TV advertising targeted at entrepreneurs. Each element has an important part to play in the bank's competitive position.

(b) **Electric component manufacturer**

A company that manufacturers electronic components for computer manufacturers will focus its marketing activities on a relatively few number of customers in the business sector. The need for consumer marketing activity will therefore generally be unnecessary although organisations such as Intel have gained a strong market position in the supply of computer chips by building a strong brand reputation with consumers. The assumption in this case is that this manufacturer is focused upon its business customers.

The predominant marketing mix activities will focus upon product quality and delivery with strong sales force and technical support. It is likely that corporate entertainment and the building up of relationships throughout the customer's organisation will be important aspects of the company's marketing programme. The role of distribution is important particularly in terms of product availability and speed of delivery. There is a danger that this market can become price driven as technological change means new products are copied or become obsolete very quickly. A strong commitment must therefore be made to research and new product development.

Packaging and branding are less critical components as tools of communication, although they can play a role in supporting the manufacturer's overall positioning. Publicity, particularly in the trade press, can be an important tool of communication. The supply of support literature and price structure alongside easy to access order processes will enhance the competitive position of this company. With a focus on fewer customers, direct marketing techniques should predominate. The relationship that the manufacturer has with distributors in the supply chain will also be important to ensure wide availability of component parts.

As can be seen from the above, whilst all the elements of the marketing mix are evident in both examples, the nature of the mix varies considerably depending upon the nature of the market and sector in which the organisation operates. The marketing mix seen simply as the 7Ps does not divulge the diversity and choice that marketers have in managing and implementing their marketing activities. The above examples also demonstrate that some organisations gain competitive advantage by 'breaking the rules' through innovative use of the marketing mix.

49 Theme park customer care

> **Examiner's comments:** summary/extracts. A less popular question, rarely completed well. In part a candidates tended to concentrate only on the customer care aspects rather than the wider strategic implications of customer orientation.
>
> Part (b) was again, not handled well. Candidates generally ignored the need to discuss the importance of customer care at the expense of practical issues. There was a tendency to discuss operational aspects of practical issues such as the provision of facilities that would indicate high levels of customer care.

INTERVIEW PRESENTATION TO SENIOR MANAGEMENT OF THEME PARK

(a) Customer orientation

Customer orientation is when an organisation wants to understand the complex needs and behaviours of its customers and wants to deliver the required levels of products and services to ensure high degrees of satisfaction and loyal purchase behaviour.

Customer orientation should be shared throughout the organisation. A divisional director of a major competitor of the theme park has highlighted the importance of customer orientation, saying:

'We believe that real customer focus has to start from the top down and the bottom up and it has to be totally accepted by the workforce. Otherwise the lines of communication will fail.'

The goal of a customer orientated organisation is to build customer satisfaction into everything that they do. Successful organisations will establish better and longer term relationships with their customers than those which are not driven by the same goal.

It usually costs more to attract new customers to a theme park than it does to retain existing customers. Loyal customers are up to six times more profitable than new customers attracted. Recommendations from highly satisfied customers will also lead to new customers which will generate further profits.

Achieving customer orientation will involve considerable change and investment. The longer term benefit will considerably outweigh any short term increase in costs and difficulties. The future success of this theme park is dependent on achieving greater customer orientation.

I would like to finish my presentation with a video of the Disney Corporation which demonstrates an organisation whose activities are driven by their desire to meet customers' needs. After the video I am happy to take any questions.

(b) **The importance of customer care and practical approaches for improving customer care in a theme park**

Customer care can be defined as the interaction of all the factors that affect the process of making products and services available to a customer. Customer care covers every aspect of a customer/supplier relationship including consistency and reliability of deliveries, availability of staff, good communications, ease of administrative process and complaint handling.

Clutterbuck describes customer care as:

'...a fundamental approach to the standards of service quality. It covers every aspect of a company's operations, from the design of a product or service to how it is packaged, delivered and serviced.'

Customer care emphasises the importance of attitude to customer. Through instilling this attitude of care throughout the organisation, and managing the customer's visit to the theme park, the experience of customers can be transformed by the manner of service they receive.

The aim of management should be to monitor customer experience constantly and through good customer care, strive to close the gap between their experience and their expectations. Visitors to this theme park should remember how well they were treated.

A customer care policy should be developed, which should incorporate guidelines for the implementation of a customer care programme. This should ensure that customers to the theme park are welcomed and find staff accessible and helpful. The quality of service should meet their needs.

I will be happy to take questions regarding how such a policy could be implemented and developed.

50 North Wales food

Examiner's comments. There was a problem with the wording of (c) and the marking scheme was adapted. In (a) some candidates were not familiar with the concept of objectives. Part (b) was not a pure marketing research question, nor was it just about surveys at the exhibition.

To: (i)   North Wales Food Producers
     (ii) Welsh Development Agency

From: A N Student

Date: 11th June 1998

Subject

(a) Setting appropriate objectives for attending the London Food and Drink exhibition

(b) Methods to evaluate / measure performance

(c) Bases for segmenting the consumer confectionery market

This report is prepared in two parts which will cover issues (a), (b) and (c) above relevant to:

(i)   North Wales Food Producers
(ii) The Welsh Development Agency

(a) **Setting appropriate objectives**

As indicated in the case study, a major advantage of exhibitions is the potential to bring buyer, seller and competition together for a number of days so that products and services can be demonstrated and personal contact can be made with a large number of relevant decision makers in a short period of time.

The exhibition is therefore primarily an opportunity to communicate directly with potential or actual customers.

North Wales Food Producers

Objectives for the four North Wales food producers should encompass a range of opportunities that the exhibition provides.

(i) The raising of buyer/media awareness of the range of products/brands supplied.

(ii) The raising of buyer/media interest with regard to the range of products/brands supplied.

(iii) Increasing the knowledge of buyers/media about the company through the provision of brochures and product literature.

(iv) The encouragement of trial of new products and product samples to encourage desire and interest.

(v) The gathering of data on prospective customers for follow up after the exhibition.

(vi) To gather information about competitors and related industry activity.

(vii) To promote the benefits of North Wales as a region.

Objectives for Welsh Development Agency

(i) The identification and gathering of information on prospective clients .

(ii) Raising awareness of international and UK food processing companies with regard to the relocation opportunities and benefits offered within the two identified Welsh regions.

(iii) Generation of interest with existing organisations to expand their current levels of operations within the region.

(iv) Generating publicity via press conferences etc to promote the region outside of the exhibition.

(b) **Methods to evaluate performance**

The evaluation and measurement of performance can be assessed in terms of criteria related to performance during the period of the exhibition and performance over a designated period after the exhibition has ended.

North Wales Food Producers

During exhibition

(i) Number of confirmed appointments acquired
(ii) Number of inquiries generated on the stand
(iii) Number of orders taken in relation to inquiries
(iv) Value of orders taken
(v) Visitor level on stand relative to competition

After exhibition

(i) Ratio of confirmed leads followed up to actual order
(ii) Cost of exhibition per value of orders achieved

(iii)   Quality of leads generated

(iv)   Number of appointments made per general inquiry generated

(v)   Quality / quantity of publicity generated through media coverage

Welsh Development Agency

During exhibition

(i)   Level of confirmed interest generated on stand

(ii)   Analysis of type and size of companies

(iii)   Number of general inquiries received on stand

(iv)   Evaluation of awareness / recall of exhibition stand

(v)   Quantity of leaflets / brochures handed out

(vi)   Regional analysis of inquiries

After exhibition

(i)   Number of confirmed appointments leading to further action/consideration of relocation/further development

(ii)   Cost of exhibition relative to inquiries generated

(iii)   Generation of publicity via media

(iv)   Quantity/cost of leaflets/brochures per generation of post exhibition inquiry

(c)   **Bases for segmenting the consumer confectionery market**

The Welsh manufacturer of sweets and candy can segment the consumer confectionery market against a range of potential segmentation classifications

(i)	Geographic	By country or by region. It is likely that regional differences will exist with regard to taste, economic development and cultural / legal factors.
(ii)	Demographic	Age / sex / ethnicity population profiles will provide useful statistical data for profiling segments and ascertaining potential size of market segments.
(iii)	Socio - Economic	Social grading and income groups may be found to relate closely to purchase behaviour, attitudes or media usage/shopping habits.
(iv)	Psychographic	Understanding of motivation/attitudes or lifestyle analysis will provide more sophisticated segmentation variables which can be closely monitored in relation to potential target groups behaviour.
(v)	Behavioural	Nature of purchase, purchase occasions, benefits sought and frequency of purchase can be utilised to provide information directly related to the consumer behaviour.

51 Battle of the brands

(1)   **Report**

To: Research and development department
From: Marketing department
Re: New Product Development Process.
Date: 9 September 1999

(a)   The country of my choice in the United Kingdom.

New product development process

1.1   The stages of the new product development process that should be adopted for casual footwear new product design are shown in the following diagram.

Idea Generation
Idea Screening
Concept Development and Testing
Marketing Strategy and Development
Business Analysis
Product Development
Test Marketing
Commercialisation

1.2   It is recommended that this process is implemented to ensure the successful launch and commercialisation of the new product. This is because effective product development should be guided by a definite product and marketing strategy. If there is no clear strategy and objectives for the new product, the new product development process will lack direction, investment, support and cohesion.

Stages of the process

2.1 **Idea generation**

This should be a continuous process within the organisation. There should be a system in place to encourage new ideas. Senior staff should formally respond to new ideas and be seen to consider them and act upon them. There are many sources from which new ideas can be generated. These are both internal (employees) and external (customers, suppliers, competitors).

2.2 **Idea screening**

Many ideas will be generated, but only a few can be acted upon. A screening process is required to adopt the best ideas. Criteria must be developed by the product management team against which new ideas can be evaluated.

The criteria should require information about the target audience for the product, an assessment of competitors, the size of the market, the potential price of the product and the attractiveness of the market. For example, in the United Kingdom, there is extensive information available on the youth market, from industry publications, market research publications and various other sources. Making use of this information will aid the screening process.

It is also important at this stage, to consider the new product idea in the context of the current product strategy, to see if the idea fits the current marketing skills and experience of the organisation.

2.3 **Concept development and testing**

Attractive ideas can be developed further. The casual footwear the Nike are considering needs to be defined in greater detail. Design prototypes should be drawn up and shown to representatives of the target audience. The concepts could be shown symbolically or physically and Nike could invite customers to be involved in the design phase.

Technology enables this concept development phase to be carried out more effectively and efficiently through computer generated designs. Nike can use the feedback from this phase can be used to look for ways to refine the concept and make it more appealing to the target audience.

2.4 **Market strategy development**

This can now be considered for the product concept. The product's positioning in the segment can be defined along with sales, market share and profit goals. The pricing, distribution and promotion strategy can also be outlined with detailed costings and budgets.

The casual footwear market is a new market for Nike. Therefore considerable planning will be needed to ensure that market entry will be successful. It is important to consider the current purchase behaviour and attitudes to brand and prices of the target market. The youth market is a notoriously difficult market to reach. The strategy must therefore be considered with care.

2.5 **Business analysis**

Once a product concept and marketing strategy has been decided on, a business analysis of the proposition can be carried out. This will involve a review of the sales, costs and profit projections for the new product to assess whether these meet the overall business objectives of Nike. To estimate sales of the footwear, Nike will have to consider the market segment trend, likely investments in trade support and competitive activity.

2.6 Product development

If the product passes the business analysis phase then product development can commence. This will require investment in manufacturing, raw materials stock and new tooling needs to take place. The first prototypes can be manufactured and tested to make sure that the product does what it is intended to do. For casual shoes intended to be a fashion accessory, both emotional and functional aspects need to be considered.

2.7 Test marketing

Once the product has passed functional and consumer tests it is ready to be test marketed. A suitable region in the UK should be selected. The region should be fairly representative of the full target market. Over a period of months, the marketing programme can be tested to learn how the consumers and retailers respond to product and marketing activity. Nike should extensively test market the casual shoe as it is a new area for them. This should maximise its chance of success at launch.

2.8 Commercialisation

When the test marketing has been completed, the product will be ready for launch into the whole market. The optimum date for the launch should be decided, bearing in mind events that Nike could associate the launch with, for example the European football championship. It is also important to decide whether to saturate the market or be more selective in terms of region or distribution. The information from the test market phase will be critical in making these decisions.

The marketing plan will be developed from launch to market development with a full programme of marketing activities and communications. The launch phase of the product is frequently the most critical phase within the NPD process. It is vital to ensure that distribution channels are in place, necessary stock is produced and that sales support is available to enable the customer to be introduced to the new product.

(b)

3 Information required for the formulation of a pricing strategy

3.1 The pricing strategy for the casual shoe must be in line with other Nike products. Nike has a positioning strategy in all of its product ranges and the casual shoe should be consistent with them.

3.2 It is recommended that the following information be obtained to support the pricing strategy decision.

- Nike's corporate guidelines on pricing and brand positioning
- Marketing objectives for the new brand
- Market research which gives information about probable consumer demand
- Consumer perceptions of price and value
- The ratio of expected demand to price (obtained from test marketing)
- Estimates of costs, profit margins and breakeven quantities
- Agreed distributor or retailer margins (whether standard or negotiable)
- Promotional support budgets
- Competitor price positions in target market
- Competitor marketing activity and likely response at launch

3.3 With this information it will be possible to make more informed decisions on pricing strategy. As Nike tend to follow a premium brand strategy, it is likely that the casual shoe will be similarly positioned.

3.4 Nike will aim to have their product endorsed by someone who will sway public opinion, such as a well-liked England player. This will support the quality, positioning and image of the product. It will also support the niche nature of the brand and will acknowledge the discerning nature of the target group.

3.5 Nike must ensure that the new product does not damage the Nike brand position in its sportswear markets. It should also recognise the differences in the competitive nature of the casual footwear market where it has not yet established itself as a recognised brand. Low initial volumes at high profit margins should therefore be expected, with gradual increases in volume being obtained as the new product is established.

52 Interflora Worldwide flower deliveries

Examiner's comment. (a). Candidates did not address the question fully, though this method could be agreed as appropriate to a certain extent. Some candidates chose to write about the people element of the marketing mix although this was required for the second part, and only attracted very few marks in this instance. (b) was answered more appropriately. (c) was answered reasonably well. There was clear evidence of candidates putting down 'all that they know' about the promotions mix rather than being specific and relating it to their own country.

(a) **Report**

To: Directors of Interflora
From: A Student
Date: 15 June 2000

Practical approaches that Interflora should consider to improve the standard of customer care and satisfaction across the participating florists include:

Customer research

Interflora should invest time and money into researching current levels of customer satisfaction. This can be done on a national basis providing a useful information resource and identifying best practice. Mystery shoppers can be utilised to contact and visit Interflora outlets and assess the quality of service and customer care.

Staff training and development

Interflora should identify training needs of Interflora staff and organise training and personal development programmes. It is essential that staff be given the appropriate levels of skills and knowledge to deliver high levels of customer care. This should include customer handling skills, management skills, and technical skills.

Internal communications

Interflora should ensure that clear channels of communication exist to all its outlets. Staff within outlets should be kept informed of plans and developments. Internal recognition and awards for performance should be recognised and communicated. A series of meetings can be arranged to ensure regular and open dialogue.

External communications

A national campaign to support the Interflora brand and local outlets should communicate the levels of service that a customer can expect from Interflora. This external communication will form an important part of the staff's identification with the Interflora brand name. Staff must feel they are an important asset to Interflora and critical to the service offered. This importance should be communicated as a fundamental part of the brands value.

Standardised systems and processes

Interflora should support its outlets with the introduction of standardised systems and processes to ensure that customers receive the same level of service quality whichever Interflora outlet they contact. These systems and processes should be designed for the customers benefit above all else.

Establishing performance standards and monitoring systems

Evaluation performance is an essential activity through which good and poor performance can be identified. Prompt actions can then be taken where problems occur. We should adopt a policy of prevention rather than cure to ensure high levels of customer satisfaction. Benchmarking performance can form part of this process to explore best practice.

(b) **How people, process and physical evidence could be developed for this service**

People

Employees and staff associated with Interflora are a key asset that must be invested in to ensure that customer service goals are achieved. The ability of staff to cope with customers, to deliver service reliably to the required standard and to present an image consistent with that which the organisation would want is a vital concern. A staff development and training programme should be introduced to ensure that each employee has the required levels of skill and knowledge. Many service failure stem from staffing problems.

Remuneration schemes should be introduced that reward development and performance. Particular attention should be paid to how staff interact with customers and their responsiveness to customer demands. Through the introduction of improved recruitment and selection processes management should try to influence the type of individual that outlets employ. This will also serve to improve the longer term profile of Interflora staff.

Process

Interflora needs smooth, efficient, customer friendly procedures. This includes both front office and back office procedures. The design of the service process and introduction of more advanced technology can both help to improve service level performance. The introduction of automated call handling, where orders can be made without interacting with staff is a good example of both improved process and introduction of advanced technology. Data software and data processing systems are now offering applications that enable organisations to provide better forecasting, measurement and control and keeping track of customers via the database. Well designed processes also ensure that the customer can place an order without any unnecessary delay. Interflora should also develop and expand its online ordering service via the Internet.

Physical evidence

Interflora should establish clear guidelines as to the design, ambience and atmosphere of its outlets. This can be achieved through coordinated colour schemes, shop layout, use of logos, staff uniforms and signage. Investment support should be given to outlets to enable this to happen. At all points where the customer contacts Interflora, physical evidence should reinforce these images as it can have a strong influence on brand image and perception of their experience of the service. Physical evidence can also provide a point of differentiation between Interflora and competitors. If this can be shared across all outlets then Interflora will reinforce its identity in the marketplace.

(c) **Major promotional methods for inclusion in a campaign to raise awareness of Interflora's products and service**

A range of professional methods can be considered to raise customer awareness of Interflora's products and service. These include advertising, direct marketing, public relations, sales promotion, selling and production of literature. The utilisation of new technology in particular the Internet and digital interactive media should also be considered as a high proportion of the target audience are now 'on line'.

Advertising is defined as any paid form of non personal presentation and promotion of ideas, goods or services through mass media by an identified sponsor. Advertising is delivered through media channels such as television, newspapers and radio but also includes posters and banner advertising on the Internet.

Direct marketing is defined as an interactive system of marketing which uses one or more advertising media to effect a measurable response at any location, forming a basis for creating and further developing an ongoing direct relationship between an organisation and its customers. Direct marketing enables personal communication through channels such as the telephone, catalogues and direct mail but also utilises direct response advertising (such as freephone numbers) and sales promotions (such as coupons and competitions) to generate awareness, interest and action. Data is captured on a database which enables targeted communications to named individuals.

Sales promotion is defined as short term incentives to encourage purchase or sale of a product or service. This includes gifts, coupons, special offers, loyalty cards, promotional price discounts and competitions. Sales promotions can be utilised to stimulate trial, encourage more frequent repeat purchase or simply as a reward for loyalty.

Public relations is defined as the deliberate, planned and sustained effort to institute and maintain mutual understanding between an organisation and its publics. Public relations activity includes media relations, publicity, community programmes, internal communications, corporate identity programmes and sponsorship.

It is recommended that Interflora invests in a communications campaign utilising the above promotional methods and technologies. The following plan of action should be followed.

Conduct a national advertising campaign within selected mainstream media supported with a direct marketing campaign. Advertising should contain strong brand imagery in visual media alongside detailed product and service information within press adverts. This advertising campaign can be supported with direct mail campaigns to targeted households. All adverts and mail shots should have a response mechanism enabling the customer to contact Interflora to place an order or ask for further information. Literature should be prepared and sent to all enquiries.

The Internet should be utilised with banner adverts supporting the Interflora web page. Adverts should be placed on sites where flowers might be a primary purchase such as weddings, funerals and birthdays. Information gleaned from visitors to the site can be held on database and passed onto outlets.

Public relations activity should be running in conjunction with the above campaigns to maximise publicity and gain high media coverage.

53 Energy Power Systems launches a new battery system

Tutorial note. This answer was started quite well, with the candidate presenting their answer in a report format, which makes the work easier to read and follow. The answer has related to the case and has identified the areas which are to be recovered in the report. The corporate objectives have been taken from the case and the marketing audit includes the PEST analysis. The answer includes applying PEST to the case well, although this was not specifically requested and may have cost time. Candidates should remember that this part of the question was only worth 15 marks and as such there was quite a lot to cover for the marks.

Examiner's comments. This question generally produced answers that indicated a varied performance. The variation in quality largely depended on the treatment of question 1a.

(a)

REPORT

MARKETING PLANNING PROCESS FOR THE LAUNCH OF 'SMART' BATTERIES

To: Marketing Director - EBC

From: Marketing Executive – Towers Communications

Date: 7 December 2000

REPORT CONTENTS

1.0	Introduction
2.0	Marketing Planning Process
3.0	Marketing Mix Decisions for the launch of the 'Smart' Battery
3.1	Product
3.2	Price
3.3	Place
4.0	Promotional Mix for the Launch of the 'Smart' Battery
5.0	Conclusion

1.0 Introduction

The marking planning process should be considered in the launch of the new batteries, which is due to take place next year.

2.0 Marketing Planning Process

The stages in the Marketing Planning Process are described as follows:

2.1 Corporate Objectives

This is the overall objective of the organisation. The corporate objectives of the organisation should also be considered and discussed before any action is taken concerning the launch of the new product. The objectives could be as follows:

- To increase profitability by 8% within the next two years
- To be the first entrant with 'smart' technology in the sector

2.2 **Marketing Audit**

Marketing auditing is the systematic gathering of information about the marketing environment , including the activities of competitors. This analysis is known as the PEST analysis. This includes:

- Political concerns such as the European directive in 2008 which will have an impact on the market for the company's products

- Economic concerns such as the level of consumer confidence in mobile technology etc

- Social issues such as changing lifestyles and the use of electrical consumer accessories

- Technical issues such as increase of product performance incorporating new technology and competitors reaction to this.

2.3 **SWOT Analysis**

This takes into account the company's strengths, weaknesses, opportunities and threats from the environment. It also analyses the company's position within the market. In short, the SWOT is a summary of the marketing audit and each element should be prioritised.

- Strengths for example should have considered that the brand is know world-wide and the company is the world's largest producer of battery and flashlight products.

- Weaknesses for example could have identified that the 'smart' batteries are a totally new product and the first of its kind, therefore, more risks are involved. The batteries which they currently produce will be banned by the year 2008

- Opportunities could have included the fact that Energy Power Systems is already a very successful company and so they have a large market share currently. The growth in consumer mobile technology offers the company a growing market.

- Threats could include competitor activity, which will be very high.

2.4 **Marketing Objective**

These are the objectives set by the marketing department within the organisation.

An example of these could be to increase market share or to become market leader of this sector within 3 years. It should be remembered that objectives should be SMART i.e. specific, measurable, achievable, realistic and time based.

2.5 **Marketing Strategy**

This stage requires that strategy is set, which includes consideration of the Ansoff Matrix (see below):

	Current product	New product
Current market	**Market Penetration strategy**	**Product Development strategy**
New market	**Market Development strategy**	**Diversification**

As already stated market penetration and product development strategies have been considered.

This strategic stage also involves looking at:

- Segmentation of the sector, ie industrial and consumer
- Targets, ie splitting down the segments even further
- Positioning the product

2.6 Marketing Tactics

This stage involves looking closely at the marketing mix and adjusting each element (price, product, place, promotion – people, processes and physical evidence for services).

- **Product** – the consideration of the five levels of product management which includes: the core product, the actual or basic product, the expected product, the augmented product and the potential product.

- **Price** – the consideration of the pricing policy such as cost based methods, competitive based and demand market based

- **Place** – consider of the which channels of distribution and the logistical issues

- **Promotion** – consideration of the advertising, personal selling, sales promotion, direct mail and public relations for the industrial and consumer purchasers in each segment

2.7 Monitor and Control

The monitoring of the effectiveness of the marketing plan, in order to evaluate whether the correct marketing mix is being used, or needs modification. This also indicates whether the corporate objectives are being met.

This can be completed by:

- Regular feedback from customers
- Analysis of sales figures against the objectives

(b) 3.0 Marketing Mix Decisions for the launch of the 'Smart' Battery

The marketing mix element to be considered are product, price and distribution applied to the case for both the industrial and consumer markets.

3.1 Industrial Market

3.1.1 Product

The battery should be designed with long lasting characteristics and appearances so as to be accepted by the business to business segments. It should be perceived to be of high quality otherwise it would not generate enough sales for the company because these days, everyone wants quality and long lasting batteries for use. The product will have to be adapted to fit our various business customers needs. The capacity, size, weight etc will vary for mobile communications, power tools and computer based companies.

3.1.2 Distribution

We will have to secure adequate transportation and supply to get our product to the customers directly. It any of the business customers are following 'Just in Time' production, we may have to synchronize our production/distribution to meet their needs – perhaps through an electronic data interchange or extranet.

3.1.3 **Price**

Our relationship with our customers will have to be considered. The long term gain for EBC will benefit the organisation more than a short term skimming strategy.

3.2 **Consumer Market**

3.2.1 **Product**

A variety of different sized batteries will need to be available to suit various consumer needs. Small batteries for cameras and Walkmans and larger batteries for toys.

3.2.2 **Distribution**

It is very important that our products are stocked in retail outlets that can be supported by the distribution system. Different retailers will have different product demands which will be reflected by their differing customer profiles.

3.2.3 **Price**

The development costs and the position of the product in the PLC determines a skimming pricing strategy to maximise revenue.

3.3 **Conclusion**

All these factors should be considered for B2B and B2C. Further research is required for each stage of the marketing mix. I should be happy to discuss this further at our next meeting.

(c) 4.0 **Recommendations for the Promotional Mix for 'Smart' batteries.**

> Tutorial note. The answer considers each segment and their understanding about products. Appropriate references to the augmented product and core product indicates the candidate's understanding of this theory. Also consideration of packaging also indicates understanding of the positioning required for this product and how the packaging for consumer products can help to communicate such positioning.

4.1 **Product Launch for Industrial markets**

- Personal Selling or Key Account Management – using the existing personnel selling or Key Account managers to promote the product benefits/negotiate terms, etc. The message can be tailored to the industrial buyers and the 'added value' of using the 'smart' battery can be used as the key message.

- Trade Advertising – the use of advertising in certain trade press may be appropriate here.

- Public Relations – again the use of perhaps a special event for industrial buyers to attend, which communicates the 'smart' benefits of the product which can be moved on to their customers.

- Promotions – one of the key methods may be to offer trials of the product at no extra cost from the existing products and asking the businesses customers to comment on the product – testimonials.

4.2 **Product launch to Consumer market**

4.2.1 **Introduction phase**

- Need to create awareness of new product through media campaign.

- To create brand awareness and to inform and persuade customers to buy.

- Try to target the innovators by stressing the benefits of the new technology

- Use of PR stunts to communicate the 'smartness' of the battery – i.e. invite journalists to a 'technically smart' and cool event, which encourages them to look at the product and write about it. Run competitions in target magazines – 'Name your top 5 Smart accessories' with joint companies offering products such as electric toothbrushes or cameras and batteries as prizes.

4.2.2 Post launch phase

- Reduce price slightly – using price promotions as demand increases and company takes advantage of economies of scale.

- Continue to promote the advantages of purchase

- Target the early majority

- Try to get some PR promotion by submitting an environmental article to the newspapers, to stress the benefits to the environment compared to the old rechargeable batteries, in order to target the 'green' consumer

- Send mail-shots, with coupons for 20% off to encourage further sales

- Point of sale advertising – with cameras/ mobile phones etc.

4.2.3 Second phase

- Slightly modify the product – eg handy size packs/bulk packs to gain more sales

- Advertise to re-enforce the benefits of the product to gain brand loyalty

- Comparison advertising – how much better the product 'smart' batteries compared to the 'Energizer' batteries.

- Improve the product further and promote further benefits

- Increase brand equity by promoting bow much better 'smart' batteries are

- Give the consumer a good image of the product, if they perceive the product as good value for money, they will remain brand loyal and make repeat purchases.

5.0 To summarise, the promotional mix elements should include:

- Sales Promotions – discount vouchers used for the purchase of batteries i.e. 'buy one get one free'.

- Advertising – used to raise awareness of the new product and promoting the benefits, as it is a completely new innovative idea.

- Direct mail – depending on the cost involved, this form of communication could be used to target certain segments.

- Public Relations – use of events and stunts for media journalists to encourage them to write about the product as a new innovation. Latterly to send press releases to target consumer press to communicate the benefits of being environmentally friendly with the use of such batteries.

54 W Moorcroft plc – Art Pottery

REPORT FOR W. MOORCROFT POTTERY

MARKETING RESEARCH PROPOSAL

TO: Hugh Edwards, Chairman, Moorcroft plc

FROM: Alison Jones, Solutions Research Agency

DATE: 14 June 2001

REPORT CONTENTS

1.0 Terms of Reference
2.0 Introduction
3.0 The Marketing Research Proposal
    3.1 Recognise the problem & set objectives
    3.2 Determine the research plan
    3.3 Secondary research sources
    3.4 Primary research methods
    3.5 Research instruments
    3.6 Sampling issues
    3.7 Data Collection
    3.8 Analysis of data
4.0 Report findings and conclusions

1.0 Terms of Reference

The following report has been requested as a proposal for the marketing research required by Moorcroft Plc for the new Okra glass range. This research agency has considered the information provided and this report suggests the most appropriate strategy for this type of research.

2.0 Introduction

The process of marketing research can be defined as the 'systematic process of designing, collecting, analysing and reporting the data and findings relevant to a marketing situation currently facing your company.' The situation currently being faced by your company concerns the need to discover more about the levels of awareness and the perceptions of the newly acquired Okra glass range in the current marketplace, and I propose to do this using the marketing research plan outlined below.

3.0 The Marketing Research Proposal

The proposal should follow the following format:

- Identify the problem and define the objectives
- Design of the Research
  ○ Secondary research from internal and external sources
  ○ Primary research decisions

- Sampling Issues
  - Random or non-random
  - Size of sample
- Data Collection and Pilot Phase
  - Qualitative methods (eg in-depth interviews or focus groups)
  - Quantitative methods (eg survey by postal questionnaire)
- Data Analysis
- Findings Related to the Interpretation and Completion of Report

The proposal will follow this format, specifically related to Moorcroft.

3.1 Recognise the problem and set objectives

We first need to consider why Moorcroft needs to undertake marketing research. Moorcroft has recently purchased the company which produces the 'Okra' range of glassware and therefore needs to evaluate the target audience for this new range and consider how this fits in with the company's other products.

The objectives for the research must be SMART, that is, specific, measurable, achievable, realistic and timed. In this particular case we need to find out current awareness levels, attitudes and perceptions relating to the Okra glass range and other Moorcroft products for the end customer and trade target segments.

3.2 Determine the research plan

Before we begin the research process, we need to exhaust the possibilities of any secondary research data you may have, that is data that has been collected from internal or external sources, already for other purposes. Then the next stage will be to identify the primary data that is required and consider the methods of collection for this.

3.3 Secondary research sources

We must first consider secondary or desk research. This is often cheaper than primary research and can give us an overview of the current situation. We can look at Moorcroft's existing customer database and other internal records for example from the accounts department. We could also look at published data, which relates to our target audience, for example from appropriate trade journals and published statistics on websites such as www.statistics.gov.uk and www.ons.co.uk, (Office of National Statistics).

3.4 Primary research methods

We must then undertake primary research, which can take the form of questionnaires, interviews, focus groups etc. Staff need to be carefully recruited to undertake this research. They should be pleasant and approachable.

3.4.1 Quantitative Data

Firstly we need to collect quantitative data. This can be done by sending out surveys to our current client database and putting and on-line survey on our website. This will give us data that is easy to analyse and quick to collect.

3.4.2 Qualitative Data

The second and more involved and time-consuming stage is qualitative data collection. This should be collected by interviewing customers and potential customers – both end and trade. We also need to set up focus groups where deeper discussions should take place, which is how we can find out perceptions, which are usually deep rooted.

3.5 Research instruments

As discussed earlier, the most common instrument is the questionnaire, although there are many different types of questions that are used. Dichotomous (yes/no), multiple choice and closed questions would be suitable for our quantitative research and a ratings scale using Likert scales, with some open questions would be suitable for this.

We would devise semi-structured schedules for the interviews and focus groups, to allow the respondents the freedom to embellish their answers and offer deeper thoughts.

3.6 Sampling issues

We have already identified two trade segments and five end customer segments that should be used for the data collection methods. There are two types of sampling methods that can apply to each group. Probability, whereby you take the target population and randomly sample until you reach your chosen size that is, 200. You could also apply stratified random method, if you wanted to focus particularly on one sample and just a handful from the rest. Another method is non-probability quota, where you would choose a certain number from each segment.

3.7 Data Collection

This is the area where the most costs are involved, as our staff will undertake the data collection, via postal questionnaires and running focus groups and interviews. This requires specialist trained interviewers, who collect the data and input that into the computer programme set up for this. The survey of the trade customers will also be fed into the computer.

3.8 Analysis of data

Once the information has been collected and input into the computer programmes, we can analyse it using a variety of different methods using our specialist analysis software such as SPSS or on our Excel programme. The qualitative data will be analysed using content analysis.

4.0 Report Findings and Conclusions

As soon as the analysis process is completed, we will report back to you with the findings, separated into trade and end users and by each segment. From the response from the qualitative research we will find out the customers' perceptions about the Okra range and from the quantitative analysis we will find out how many of the customers are aware of the Okra range. From here 5 copies of the report will be presented to you and a verbal presentation if required. You will then be able to consult the analysis and make decisions about your marketing mix for the Okra range.

(b)

```
┌─────────────────────────────────────────────────────────────────┐
│                         MEMORANDUM                                │
│                                                                   │
│   TO:       Marketing and Sales Staff, Moorcroft plc              │
│                                                                   │
│   FROM:     Percy Towers, Marketing Executive                     │
│                                                                   │
│   DATE:     14 June 2001                                          │
│                                                                   │
│   SUBJECT:  Importance of Understanding the Behaviour and         │
│             Perceptions of Customers                              │
└─────────────────────────────────────────────────────────────────┘
```

Importance of Understanding Customer and Trade Perceptions and Behaviour

I wish to briefly outline the importance of the above to the marketers and staff at Moorcroft plc. In order for any marketing plan to work it is imperative that all parts of the organisation are involved and there is total support and commitment at management level.

We need to remember the consumer buying process, which includes:

- **Need recognition,** what makes customers buy Okra products and how this can be influenced?

- **Information search** – where do Okra customers get their information and how do we influence them? What media do they consume?

- **Evaluation of alternatives** - what will make Okra product stand out – ie use of branding, promotion pricing and product placement which we have meaning for our customers.

Purchase

Post purchase evaluation : how can we ensure that our customers return to buy the Okra range?

Similarly, we need to understand the trade buying process also which includes responding to specifications and a more rational buying process.

Therefore, it is vital that our staff understand the target markets for the following reasons:

- So that any perceived problems by the customers can be addressed

- So that the market can be targeted according to spending patterns

- To increase the effect of positive perceptions.

- The sales pitch can be altered to correspond with the buyer's needs and wants.

- In the large retail outlets, we must reach the key people in the decision making unit (DMU) to be effective.

- Trends in spending and behaviour should be identified to maximise potential sales and profit.

- The marketing mix needs to be adapted to ensure that the products appeal to the target markets and develop new products.

Understanding customer behaviour will provide us with a solid customer base, which gives us a competitive edge and important aspect for this new range. I hope that this helps, please contact me should you require further information before I leave for my holidays in the USA.

(c)

REPORT FOR W. MOORCROFT POTTERY

Communications Mix for Okra and Moorcroft Ranges

TO: Hugh Edwards, Chairman, Moorcroft plc

FROM: Percy Towers, Marketing Executive

DATE: 14 June 2001

REPORT CONTENTS

1.0   Terms of Reference
2.0   Introduction
3.0   Elements of the Promotions mix including:
          Promotions mix for Trade
          Promotions mix for End Customer
4.0   Conclusions

1.0 Terms of Reference

Market research has been carried out regarding the Okra range of products since the purchase of the company in April. This report uses that information and outlines the most appropriate promotional/communications proposal for the relaunch of the range.

2.0 Introduction

When planning a promotional campaign, we need to consider the communications strategy, which would probably include push, pull or a combination of both elements.

- **Push** strategy – this is where the communication messages are targeted at the channel intermediaries (trade channels) such as Liberty's and international dealers and other retailers. This should allow the trade channel members to facilitate the distribution of the products to consumers or end users – thus 'pushing' the products to the consumers.

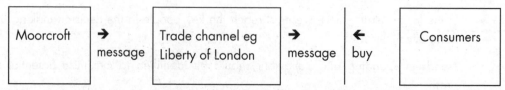

- **Pull** strategy – is where the communication is directed at the end consumer or buyer. The objective is usually to generate increased awareness, build attitudes and provoke motivation within this group of buyers. This is known as a pull strategy as the buyers should then demand the products from the intermediaries or trade channels

message

| Moorcroft | ← buy | Trade channel eg Distributor | ← buy | Dept Store | ← buy | Consumer or buyer |

Or customers buy direct from Moorcroft

In reality we will use a mixture of both of these strategies, however, and we will apportion different weightings of their communications budget to the push and pull strategy.

3.0 Elements of the Promotions Mix

The elements or tools of the promotion mix are as follows:

- **Advertising** – this will include a range of different types of advertising: to include the trade, consumer and corporate issues. Advertising is an effective tool for raising awareness about a consumer product or service, however, it is not as effective for actually achieving sales. Other elements need to be used with advertising to ensure sales increases. We need to consider the media which our customers consume before making decisions about this element.

- **Sales promotions** – includes incentives designed to encourage purchase such as free offers, limited editions etc. These can be aimed as the trade channels the sales force and the consumers. This element is most effective in actually motivating trials and re-buys.

- **Personal selling –** this type of communication can be very effective. This is where one to one contact between the out Key Account Managers and the trade customer is made, or our retail sales assistants in the factory shop. This is one of the most effective methods as the message can be tailored to each individual buyer and often it is a highly complex and technical product or service. Again, this method is very effective at ensuring actual purchase.

- **Public relations** – these are activities designed to create understanding and goodwill between an organisation and its publics. A wide range of activities can be classed as public relations such as press conferences, press released, open days, etc. This method is difficult to evaluate and control. However, press releases are often seen as being more credible than an advert by the consumer and therefore can be used effectively with advertising to raise awareness, especially when launching our new Okra range.

- **Direct mail** – Kotler adds this fifth element to the traditional promotions mix, and can be considered as one of the most effective method of communication when linked to our customer database and loyalty scheme via the collector's club. We will want to develop a new and exciting catalogue to be mailed out. This method can building consumer relationships and is very easy to control and evaluate.

- **Website** - we may wish to introduce the new product range on the website. We could offer information on the products, provide a virtual tour of the factory and give the customer an excellent insight into the workings of the organisation. The use of the website will ensure that we are able to capture markets globally. The monitoring of the hits to the website will enable use to establish were and when and how popular the site is globally.

4.0 Conclusions

By adopting a spread of distribution channels, we can ensure that our product is reaching all of the target markets identified in the market research analysis. We also need to ensure that we monitor our promotional plan to achieve the objectives which we will set.

55 Botswana Telecommunications Corporation (BTC)

Examiner's comments. The first part of the question required candidates to identify with reasons the steps for introducing a marketing orientation within BTC and also to explain how the effective use of IT could have contributed to this aim. Therefore, candidates should have commenced by explaining what is meant by the marketing orientation concept. Then the answer should have considered BTC and related to the actual steps involved i.e. to define BTC's customers' needs, gain top management commitment for change, BTC should have invested resources and set up information systems and adapted the services where necessary to meet the needs of their customers. There should have been some consideration of the communication and training of the philosophy to internal staff to ensure customer-driven shared values and set up customer care systems, ensuring measurement and control was undertaken on a regular basis.

The second part of the question required the candidate to explain the key differences between services and products and, importantly, the problems that these differences offer for BTC marketers. The answer should have considered intangibility, inseparability, perishability and heterogeneity. Problems should have been discussed such as image problems, service quality, customer's perceptions and expectations, positioning issues relating to value etc.

The final part of the question required the candidate to discuss the elements of the marketing mix. The answers should have included pricing, product, place, promotion and the extra elements: processes; physical evidence and people. Each of these elements should have been related to BTC as much as possible.

(a)

REPORT FOR BOTSWANA TELECOMMUNICATIONS CORPORATION
MARKETING ORIENTATION

To: M Bosco-Wallace, Marketing Manager, BTC
From: JP Hyde, CIM Candidate
Date: 6 December 2001

Contents

1.0   Terms of Reference

2.0   Introduction – Defining Marketing Orientation

3.0   The Steps involved in becoming Marketing Orientated

4.0   The Use of Information Technology

5.0   The Difference between Marketing Services and Products and the Associated Problems

6.0   The Extended Marketing Mix which BTC could adopt

7.0   Report Conclusions

1.0 Terms of Reference

Due to the changing technological environment in which the telecommunications industry now operates, Botswana Telecommunications Corporation need to reappraise its position within the market. Therefore, this report will identify the steps required for introducing a marketing orientation within BTC and how the effective use of information technology may contribute. It will then go on to explain the key differences between services and products and the problems that these differences may present to BTC. The final section of the report will then discuss the elements of the marketing mix which BTC will need to consider when marketing its services.

2.0 Introduction – Defining Marketing Orientation

At present, as outlined in our company's Annual Report, we as a company are product orientated. Therefore, being able to produce certain products and services, we sell these to our customers whether or not they fit the needs of our customers.

As this is the case, a marketing orientation is necessary. Theodore Levitt suggests that a marketing orientation is superior to a production orientation. Therefore, no longer can an organisation expect to concentrate on efficient production. The concept suggests that the organisation needs to be customer focused and market driven in order to succeed in today's competitive environment. Marketing orientation is a co-ordinated marketing effort that involves many things such as market research, market led product/service development, etc.

3.0 The Steps involved in becoming Marketing Orientated

Marketing orientated organisations put the customer first, therefore, this means that the customer will need to become central to all business and marketing decisions and planning. The customer has to be taken into consideration before any other aspect.

The main steps are as follows:

3.1 Assessing the customer requirements

Before any decisions are made, BTC needs to assess their customers and decide what their needs and wants are and how they will meet those needs. This can be done by looking through past records and any networks and customer access lines. The corporation already knows that access lines to customers have increased by 19% to over 102,000 in the last two years. This is essential in a marketing orientation as the customer comes first and their needs need to be met and exceeded in order to be successful.

Levels of customer satisfaction should be tested and analysed to identify the areas where the organisation is failing the customer. Areas such as complaints systems, down-time technical reports, new customers gained and old customers lost should be identified and analysed.

3.2 Making sure management is committed to customer requirements

There must be support from senior management that marketing orientation is important and it is essential to ensure that the orientation is widespread throughout the whole of the corporation. If management levels are customer focused, then it is inevitable that the orientation will filter throughout the rest of the corporation. Indeed, this should lead to the planning of a change in the organisation's internal culture.

3.3 Focus the whole of the Corporation

This can be done by introducing Total Quality Management systems. Here, systems need to be set in place to make sure the whole staff knows what your objectives are and how you intend to meet these objectives. BTC are already aware that customer care and responsiveness at all levels within the organisation is one of their main challenges. To ensure this, every member of staff needs to be aware of what you are aiming for, how you intend to do it and why. Feedback needs to be passed back to management from the TQM system and evaluation needs to take place on a regular basis.

Departments must work together, breaking down any barriers that exist currently between them. Effective and efficient communication is vital for marketing orientation.

3.4 Setting Service Standards

Using customer feedback from the analysis undertaken (see 3.2), should allow service standards to be agreed which the internal systems will fulfil. For instance once service standard might be concerned with the length of time customers are expected to wait to access services. If the waiting period is caused because BTC cannot install lines quickly enough, measures must be put in place which will rectify this situation and keep the customer fully informed at all time.

3.5 Identify Staff Training Requirements

BTC's new philosophy and culture needs to be communicated to all staff. Where staff are unable to deliver the required levels of service because of the lack of training needs to be identified. A training plan must be put in place to resolve the situation. This could include such things as delegation and empowerment training, technical product training and customer handling skills. Reward schemes and staff motivation should also been considered as this will help with the success of the new culture. Staff are in prime positions to give feedback about customers as they are dealing with them at front of house or moment of truth situations.

3.6 **BTC's Model for marketing orientation**

The following model will help in the implementation of such a programme:

Determine Customer Needs

Top Management Commitment

Invest in Resources
continuous
assessment
Develop service standards

Staff training and customer care
programme launched

Marketing the services

Monitor and control through
customer feedback

3.7 **Potential Problems**

Adopting a marketing orientated approach is a timely process and training and costs need to be invested therefore it may be difficult to convince top management about the benefits as they will be long term rather than quick fixes in relation to the investment made. Therefore, there may be a resistance to change within BTC. Barriers may exist between departments that are tough to break down.

4.0 **Use of Technology**

The effective use of IT would come into two areas mainly, which are:

- To help facilitate market research
- To offer customer friendly services

4.1 **IT and Marketing Research**

This could include monitoring user frequencies, sales data, conducting surveys via the Internet, researching competitors by viewing their websites, conducting telephone surveys to establish both business customer and private customer satisfaction levels. In addition a database could be set up to make best use of the customer information that is already available to BTC. This would help to achieve their objective and retaining customers by employing relationship-marketing techniques. Data could be collected for instance via Internet registration forms and used to establish preferences which would subsequently be used for specific targeting and planning new products. An effective MKIS could be set up within BTC.

4.2 **IT and Customer Services**

BTC could improve Internet services for customers by offering them good levels of information about new products, potential problems. Text messaging in relation to customer information could be used for those customers who have access to mobile technology.

The key element to becoming marketing orientated is the recognition that identifying, anticipating and satisfying customer requirements is vital. Information technology should be utilised effectively to support this, such as implementing call handling systems in call centres, ensuring that calls are placed in the appropriate queues, that levels can be monitored to ensure adequate resources are in place to meet customer demand.

(b)

5.0 The Difference between Marketing Services and Products

There are five major areas where services differ from products and they present challenges to the company, which can be overcome by the use of effective marketing.

5.1 Heterogeneity

This means that services can differ from time to time and from person to person who is delivering the service. The same telephone operator can provide an excellent service to one customer then provide a poor level of service to the next service, dependant on how the member of staff is feeling at the time or whether they have had to work in their lunch-hour and resent this. Service involves human contact, which introduces the problems of human effort and human behaviour which is difficult to control precisely. Therefore, ensuring continuity of service standards is difficult.

To counter this BTC should ensure that there are delivery standards which are monitored closely, taking customer feedback to support the research.

5.2 Inseparability

The service cannot be separated from the provider – the producer of the service is also the retailer of it, unlike products which can be made in a factory and then sold to the end-customer in a different country. BTC needs to consider this to ensure that the service provided is consistent with the brand values that they want to project. This could have implications for standards of delivery where the reputation of the organisation is at stake each time the customer takes up the service – known as 'moments of truth'.

Vigorous control of the standards to ensure excellent delivery is required here. Careful recruitment, staff training and a rewards philosophy is required to ensure that quality staff are delivering the service.

5.3 Perishability

This means that the service cannot be kept to use later, it must be consumed at the time that it is offered. There is no second chance – each customer interaction must meet customer requirements. This can produce difficulties for the organisation in ensuring that both the service and the staff to deliver it are available, when the service is most in demand. Overstaffing leads to wasted resources, but understaffing leads to customer frustration.

BTC should use promotional techniques effectively to increase off peak demand, such as reduced rates. This should go some way to evening out demand fluctuations.

5.4 Intangibility

Services are intangible i.e. there is nothing physical to hand over to the customer, unlike a product. This means that customers will judge BTC more on the personal experience they get from each interaction with BTC, so it is imperative that a consistently high level of service is provided from each member of staff within BTC.

Therefore promotion methods should be used to illustrate the value and benefits of the service or brand. Testimonials from satisfied customers are useful here to add value to the service.

5.5 Ownership

Ownership of services is sometimes complicated. For example, a business may pay BTC to provide telephone and Internet services to their office premises. BTC retains ownership of this service and can change the timing or layout of the service as they like. The business does not receive anything until BTC chooses to deliver the service.

(c)

6.0 The Extended Marketing Mix which BTC could adopt

In marketing its services, BTC will need to consider the extended marketing mix which relates to product, place, price, promotion, people, process and physical evidence. BTC will need to consider the following points when making their decisions about the marketing mix:

6.1 Product

- What is the core customer need?
- What basic service is required to meet this?
- The augmented service should exceed customer expectations
- Continual monitoring of services in relation to changing customer needs

6.2 Price

- How much should the service cost the customer?
- What pricing strategy should be used?
- What are the competitors doing?
- How will the price affect market share and the volumes of customers?
- What features can be added to justify different prices for different segments of the market
- Should BTC differentiate in pricing strategy between business and household customers?

6.3 Promotion

- What is the most effective means of promoting BTC's services?
- Nationwide above-the-line advertising or localised, more personalise promotions?
- Should BTC use advertising only?

6.4 Place

BTC need to consider their distribution channels and networks

- The infrastructure is on of the most modern in Africa and international access is provided.
- BTC needs to look at mobile technology however

6.5 **People (Staff)**

- Staff must be polite, friendly and helpful

- They must be able to handle complaints and deal efficiently with customer complaints

- Staff must be trained to work the systems

- Staff must embrace the marketing orientated philosophy

- Staff are the front line people and it is vital they satisfy the customer in every way.

- It is the level of service from the staff that the customer will remember.

6.6 **Processes**

- All systems supporting the front line staff must be efficient to avoid errors and time delays

- Security measures should be taken for customer confidentiality

6.7 **Physical Evidence**

- BTC infrastructure should continue to remain modern and should professional to convey the image of a quality service to the customer

- The brand needs to be supported and communicate the brand values

- Front line staff should have uniforms with the corporate logo to communicate a quality service.

- Business cards, customer bills, invoices should include the brand name and portray the values of the organisation – contributing to the brand values.

- Corporate colours and logos should be present on all forms of communication.

7.0 **Report Conclusions**

All of these considerations will go a long way towards achieving marketing orientation within BTC. However, in addition BTC must ensure that the values of the whole organisation reflect this orientation and the customer is central to every through the organisations from the most senior managers through to the cleaners.

This should offer the company ample reward by way of competitive advantage, profitability and better targeting.

56 Pix Cinemas

Examiner's comments. The first part of the answer required candidates to identify and explain the key characteristics of services and as such should have discussed the intangibility, inseparability, perishability, variability and ownership issues as related to the cinema experience. The question also required candidates to discuss the problems for marketers when considering the repositioning of the offer and issues such as the level of education of the consumer, image problems, service quality, changing economic environment, customer's perceptions and expectations, positioning issues, customer care etc. This was worth 15 marks and it should have been quite easy for candidates to pick up such marks.

The second part of the question required the candidate to discuss the ways in which PIX could adapt its promotions/ communications mix, which again is a very common area of the syllabus, which often appears on the examination paper. This time, the mix should have been considered in relation to the market penetration strategy. Therefore, the answers should have identified the elements of a market penetration strategy and the implications for the communications mix. This said, the answer should have considered the communications mix in relation to gaining customers from competitors, developing loyalty schemes to try to get existing customers to visit the cinema more frequently. The Examiner's looked for a good mix of advertising, sales promotion, public relations, and personal selling and direct marketing elements, which were justified and related to a market penetration strategy.

The third part of the question related to buyer behaviour. This was an easy question, as it did not require a model to be identified, but a discussion, which illustrated the understanding of buyer behaviour especially in relation to the social environment. The answer should have considered not only a buyer behaviour model but also the issues relating to the social environment for PIX such as lifestyles, work patterns and leisure time etc.

As usual there was a number of marks available for the presentation of the candidate's answer and the tone of the reports written. These were easy marks, which all candidates should have been able to acquire.

(a)

REPORT FOR PIX CINEMAS

SERVICES, COMMUNICATIONS AND BUYER BEHAVIOUR ISSUES FOR PIX CINEMAS

To: Nigela Towers, Managing Director, PIX
From: Bob Ritchie, Marketing Executive, PIX
Date: 13 June 2002

Contents

1.0   Terms of Reference/Introduction

2.0   Findings

3.0   Conclusion and Recommendations

(a)

1.0 Terms of Reference/Introduction

PIX cinemas have decided to reposition their brand which will involve a number of developments within the services areas. It has come to my attention that the majority of PIX market share is within the service sector. There will be a strategy to develop in this area defined using the Ansoff Matrix (see section 2.2). This report has been requested by PIX marketing research and will be submitted on 13/6/02. The sources of information used include Primary and Secondary research data.

2.0 Findings of the Report

2.1 Key Characteristics of Services

Services are, by nature:

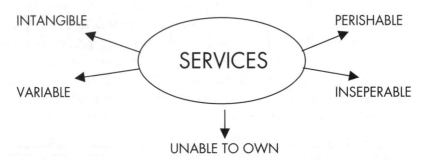

Perishable – once the cinema experience is over, it cannot be relived without an added cost, and e.g. you must come to the cinema again. It cannot be stored so if a 6.30 pm showing of a film only attracts 30 customers and the capacity of the cinema is 200, then the ticket fee for the remaining 170 is lost and cannot be regained for that 6.30 pm slot although it would cost PIX the same amount of money to show the film to 30 or 200 customers.

Inseparable – the service provider i.e. PIX and customer must both be at the same place, e.g. you cannot experience the cinema in your car or house. Therefore, the experience of watching a film is consumers at the time of purchase.

Ownership – the customer only pays for the service for a certain duration, and has no claims on it thereafter, e.g. to see one film in the PIX cinema once or a hotel room once checked out. Services cannot be taken home.

Variability – since humans are involved in the service provision, in one way or another, their performance will vary from day to day, e.g. the mood of the ticket person collecting the tickets at a 12.30 am showing of a film late at night might be much different than their mood at 8.30 pm and thus the person may not be as polite or helpful as he/she is tired etc. This could have an impact on the customer's perception of the service encounter.

Intangibility – services cannot really be touched, smelt or tasted generally, and there for the quality will be evaluated by the experience only. Thus, a customer visit to PIX cinema to see a new film such as 'Spider Man' will be evaluated by their experience of not only the film but the cleanliness of the cinema, the queuing time, the noise levels in the cinema during the film, the service provided by the ticket people, etc.

2.2 Problems relating to the Repositioning of the Service

We must take all these issues into consideration when putting together a marketing plan. The marketing of services is different from that of products due to these characteristics. To combat this along with *product, price, place and promotion,* the extended marketing mix for services also includes people, process and physical evidence.

People – those who work in ticket sales, as ushers etc are part of this. The problems faced are intangibility, inseparability and perishability. The experience had to have something which customers could relate to before purchasing it i.e. friendly, smiling faces. Inseparability meant that the quality of the service provider had to be high and convenient. Perishability meant services would last only the duration of the film, thereby high quality staff, friendly, helpful and knowledgeable is essential.

Process – the delivery of the service must be on time and high quality. Films need to be brought to the UK in time, ticket sales must be opened well before the movie is to be screened, booking in advance should be permitted. There must also be a good way of seating late customers.

Physical Evidence - this is perhaps the greatest tool that should be used to combat the problems of satellite TV and rentals of movies. The cinema should be marketed as state of the art, with fantastic sound and visual quality, comfortable seating, great snacks etc.

Some of the key problems are that the PIX cinema currently has no real image. Therefore, the service quality and communications messages do not effectively differentiate the cinema from its competitors. The marketing mix is not fully considered and applied to communicate a specific positioning in the consumers' mind.

A perceptual map must be created to map the perceptions of the consumer in relation to PIX's competitors and the current offering. A new positioning will need to be considered such as the seriousness with which PIX considers its films.

(b)

2.3 Promotions Mix within Marketing Penetration Strategy

PIX cinemas must adapt its promotional/communications mix in order to achieve its objective and develop a useful and effective marketing strategy. Kotler describes five main factors in the promotional mix as below:

- **Advertising** – posters, TV, radio, etc

- **Sales Promotion** – film review discounts, reduced rates for children, OAP, students

- **Personal Selling** – door salespeople, promoting offers and new services – such as the 'Unlimited Pass'

- **Public Relations** – shows, entertainment venues, TV

- **Direct Mailing** – leaflets, flyers, Intranet

- Effective communications mix may involve all of the above in an external mix: press advertising, billboards, TV and internal communications i.e. reports, effective teamwork, telephone sales.

A marketing strategy must be adopted and according to the Ansoff Matrix – a Marketing Penetration strategy must be applied:

ANSOFF MATRIX

	Current Product	**New Product**
Existing Market	**Market penetration** * Gain competitors' customers * Add value, bonus for existing products * More sales from existing customers – loyalty schemes * Buying in bulk (family tickets) * Buying off peak times	**Product development** * New product features * Brand new products eg cafes
New Market	**Market development** * Target new segments	**Diversification** * Different new series ie clothing

This strategy will mean PIX must use the promotions mix such as:

- Promotional Offers – reduce tickets for certain market segments such as OAPs, free tickets after 5 visits, joint promotions with a newspaper or magazine.

- Discount Prices – use direct mail to promote 2 for 1 offers to everyone in the local area

- Advertising – advertise in competitor's areas eg shops that sell satellite dishes and other substitute goods, eg TVs, video shops to raise awareness of brand name.

- Public Relations – interview internal staff to promote image of good service, good value for money, i.e. perceived value offers and promote the company itself. Make the staff dress up in costumes from the main movie and get publicity about this.

- Internet – set up a webpage where competitions can be run, questions could be answered online and tickets maybe won.

The 'Unlimited Pass' is a good way to build a loyalty scheme and capture data. It could be marketed better to reach more of the market by offering more sales promotions such as:

- Discount if 10 friends join

- A 3 and 6 month subscription at higher prices than the year subscription

- Invitations to movie premiers for Pass holders

- Priority in booking tickets for Pass holders

(c)

2.4 Buyer Behaviour and Social Environmental Issues

The buyer behaviour is important when creating a marketing plan. Maslow considered a hierarchy of needs as detailed below:

Maslow's Hierarchy of Needs

This can help organisations to consider the behaviour of their customers by understanding what motivates them.

Apart from recognising the psychological buyer needs the process of buying should also be considered.

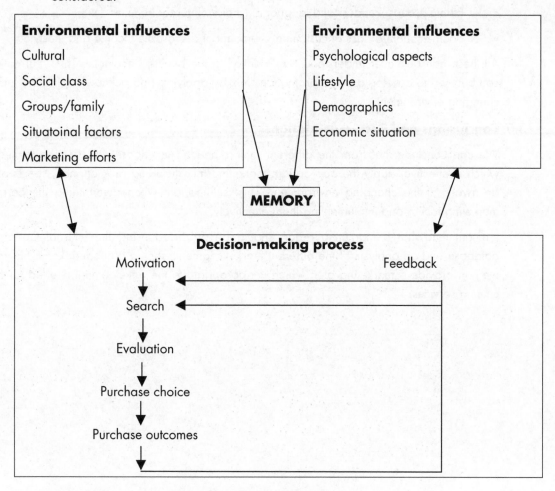

A Framework of Consumer Buyer Behaviour

(adapted from Lancaster, Massingham and Ashford, 2002)

- Motivation – what should I do tonight? Where should we go?

- Search – memory of previous visits to cinema, advert in paper

- Evaluation – remember last visit to PIX as OK, think about other cinemas or renting a film

- Purchase choice – watch major film a big screen at PIX cinema

- Purchase outcome – was it a good night out? Will we go again?

People will often decided to do something considering the above decision making model. PIX should be aware of the different stages of the buying behaviour process and be able to adapt the marketing mix to ensure that the potential customer chooses PIX cinemas.

The environment is consistently changing in both social and technological areas.

Such changes may include:

- Use of the Internet, computer on a larger scale

- Population distribution and age range

- Tastes and preferences within the market environment

- Change in demand for cinema services

- Changes in age groups that are highest users of cinemas

- Geographical spread – ease of getting to the cinema

- Ethnic groups – understand language, foreign film requirement

- Socio-economic class of customers – amount of disposable income and lifestyles.

All these can be better understood buy identifying the buying behaviour. This information can be used to develop a useful promotions mix by applying and acknowledging the future changing environment.

3.0 Conclusions and Recommendations

We can conclude that from the different factors needed to choose a marketing strategy, which is effective, apply the appropriate marketing mix including promotional aspects and be aware of the changing environment. This is important when determining the correct marketing tactics and implementing them effectively.

I recommend that a marketing report should be produced using the Internal Customer database and an analysis of the different market segments should be undertaken. This way we can provide a marketing plan which is appropriate to the development needed for PIX cinema services.

Specimen paper and suggested answers

The Chartered
Institute of Marketing

Certificate
in Marketing

Marketing Fundamentals

5.24:   Marketing Fundamentals

Time:

Date:

3 Hours Duration

This examination is in two sections.

PART A – Is compulsory and worth 40% of total marks.

PART B – Has **SIX** questions; select **THREE**. Each answer will be worth 20% of the total marks.

DO NOT repeat the question in your answer, but show clearly the number of the question attempted on the appropriate pages of the answer book.

Rough workings should be included in the answer book and ruled through after use.

© The Chartered Institute of Marketing

BPP
PUBLISHING

Certificate in Marketing

5.24: Marketing Fundamentals – Specimen Paper

PART A

Energy Power Systems Launches a New Battery Range

Energy Power Systems is a division of the Ecco Battery Company (EBC) and manufactures **rechargeable** batteries. Ecco is the world's largest producer of battery and flashlight products, with twenty production facilities supplying over 500 products into 165 countries worldwide. The key corporate objectives are to increase profitability by 5% within the next two years, and for the battery division to be positioned as the number one supplier of state-of-the-art technology in batteries.

Energy Power Systems (EPS) manufactures rechargeable nickel cadmium, nickel metal hydride and lithium ion cells and battery packs for equipment manufacturers, and for the consumer market. The cells are produced at the company's headquarters in Florida, and then either sold directly to the equipment manufacturers or assembled into battery packs by one of three assembly facilities in Mexico, Newcastle (UK), or Hong Kong.

Energy Power Systems' Rechargeable Battery Product Range

EPS produces a particular range of rechargeable batteries, most of which are used in either cordless power tools, emergency lighting or mobile communications. However, the relatively inexpensive technology employed in current manufacture is being replaced by a new technology. A European directive has been issued to ban all of this type of battery by the year 2008, due to the negative impact that the cadmium electrode within the cell has on the environment when consumers dispose of these cells.

Core Markets

Energy Power Systems employs a differentiated segmentation strategy, modifying the marketing mix for each of its targeted segments. This allows the company to concentrate on markets that offer high returns and opportunities for growth, which is consistent with the corporate objectives of its parent company EBC.

EPS segments the market into an industrial segment and a consumer segment, and further segments these as follows:

Industrial Segment

- Mobile communications manufacturers such as Ericsson, Motorola, etc.
- Cordless power tool manufacturers.
- Computer manufacturers.

Consumer Segments

- Audio visual equipment – e.g. Sony Walkman.
- Personal care – such as the cordless toothbrush.
- Photographic – e.g. camera batteries.
- Toys and novelties.
- Hand-held equipment – such as cordless car vacuum cleaners.

New Product Range – 'Smart' Batteries

The company is about to launch a new range of 'smart' batteries, using a relatively new type of technology. These batteries have the ability to control their own charging when fitted into a compatible charger. They also have the ability to report back information to the user of the battery – information such as the time left till empty, manufacturer's name, age, etc.

EPS is one of the only battery manufacturers that offer in-house design and manufacture of these smart batteries. For the core industrial markets, a completely 'customer-smart' battery can go from concept to production in as little as five months.

The brand name 'Energy' is the name used for all batteries produced by the company. Recently commissioned marketing research has shown that within the consumer segments, the brand is known worldwide. However, this is less important to industrial users, who usually prefer to display their own logo on the batteries. This research has also highlighted the fact that consumers are mainly interested in the length of the battery life and reliability. The company is aiming to secure the market by being the first entrant with this 'smart' technology.

PART A

Question 1.

The launch of these new batteries is due to take place within the next year. You are to prepare a report to be used as the basis for discussion within the organisation's Marketing Department which considers:

a.   The principle of market segmentation and the advantages that it offers the company.

(10 marks)

b.   The various stages involved in the new product development process for the new batteries.

(15 marks)

c.   The composition of the different marketing mix programmes that are adopted for the launch of the batteries into the consumer and business-to-business segments to be targeted.

(15 marks)
(40 marks in total)

PART B – Answer THREE Questions Only

Question 2.

You work for a children's clothing manufacturer that intends to grow its business through new channels of distribution.

a.   Identify the range of alternative distribution channels that may be available to your company.

(7 marks)

b.   Identify the factors that should be taken into account when deciding which distribution channels to select.

(7 marks)

c.   Identify how the effectiveness of your distribution channels may be measured.

(6 marks)
(20 marks in total)

Question 3.

a.   For a service organisation of your choice, illustrate how the extended marketing mix for services is used to effectively meet customer requirements.

(12 marks)

b.   Examine the part played by new information and communications technology in providing additional value for the customers of your chosen organisation.

(8 marks)
(20 marks in total)

Question 4.

You are employed by a global car manufacturer that is regarded as being a leading exponent of contemporary marketing practice. Using illustrative examples from your industry:

a.   Explain what you understand to be the advantages of marketing to both consumers and business organisations.

(12 marks)

b.   Identify some of the ethical and social responsibility issues that face modern marketers.

(8 marks)
(20 marks in total)

Question 5.

Your organisation, which manufactures TV and hi-fi equipment, is in the process of developing a marketing plan.

a. Describe and illustrate the structure of its outline marketing plan.

(10 marks)

b. Examine the factors that it should consider when setting its marketing budgets.

(10 marks)
(20 marks in total)

Question 6.

You have recently taken up a position as a Marketing Manager in a small computing software house that has little understanding of some of the fundamental principles of marketing. You have been asked to explain and illustrate the following in the context of this organisation:

a. Variations in the marketing mix at the different stages of the product life cycle.

(10 marks)

b. The range of internal and external factors that influence pricing decisions.

(10 marks)
(20 marks in total)

Question 7.

For a large financial services company of your choice (such as a bank):

a. Explain the concept and importance of branding.

(10 marks)

b. Explain the significance of relationship marketing and customer retention.

(10 marks)
(20 marks in total)

PART A

Question 1

REPORT

**Market Segmentation approach;
EPS Rechargeable Battery Product Range**

To: Ms Alexander Raat, Marketing Director
From: Mr Arthur Tring, Marketing Assistant
Date: 6 June 2002

1.0	Report Contents
2.0	Introduction
3.0	Market Segmentation process
4.0	New Product Development stages
5.0	Marketing Mix for the launch programme
6.0	Conclusion

1.0   Introduction

The market segmentation approach should be considered by the Marketing Department for the launch of the new EPS Rechargeable Battery Product Range with regard to the industrial and consumer marketplaces.

2.0   Market Segmentation process

The growth of specialised segments in a market has resulted in firms producing goods and services that are more closely related to the requirements of particular kinds of customers. Instead of treating customers as a unified entity, firms have identified sub-groups of customers whose precise needs can be more effectively met with a targeted approach. There are three stages of target marketing, which are

Market Segmentation
Identify basis for segmentation
Determine important characteristics of each market segment

↓

Market Targeting
Select one or more segments

↓

Product Positioning
Develop detailed product positioning for selected segments
Develop a marketing mix for each selected segment

As businesses began to pay greater attention to the needs and wants of the marketplace, they began to realise that constituent people and organisations that collectively make up the marketplace are unlikely to have identical preferences. The result of this approach was to conclude that it was unlikely that one product would satisfy all the requirements of the marketplace.

For our business this means dividing the marketplace into an industrial segment and a consumer segment which each consider different variable that need to be accommodated in the launch program.

2.1 Industrial market segmentation

A number of variables are considered for this segment of the marketplace

Size of firm; this could be based on sales turnover, number of employees, number of products produced or market share of their particular sector

Type of industry; different sectors will have different requirements with regard to product specification, price, after sales service and warranty demands.

Geographical region; adapting the marketing mix to different national or regional considerations such as with distribution requirements for multinational mobile communication manufacturers

Type of buying organisation; how an organisation purchases its products affects the way we negotiate and communicate with it. Larger customers of ours tend to have formal procedures that we must adopt, whereas smaller firms operate in a much more informal manner.

2.2 Consumer market segmentation

The main discriminating variables to be considered are listed below.

Demographic; Age, gender, family size, social class and disposable income, and education

Perceived benefit; different people buy the same or similar products for quite different reasons. As our new battery range will deliver improved performance we need to determine the major benefit consumers are seeking from the particular grouping of product, to identify the profiles of the consumer seeking those benefits and to recognise existing competitors products that are similar to delivering each of those benefits.

Loyalty; Analysis of brand loyalty can tell us much about our customers attitude to their end consumers

Lifestyle and cultural considerations; Understanding how consumer groups spend their time and money, reflecting their cultural attitudes and beliefs will be seen in the take up and targeting of products incorporating our new range of batteries.

2.3 Targeting

Once we have identified and evaluated the different segments we will then need to decide on the level of market involvement. This will identify if there are any segments that we would not want to service and would determine the targeting approach. The result would be to adopt an undifferentiated, a differentiated or a selective marketing strategy.

2.4 Product Positioning

Having designed the new range of batteries we will need to adopt a marketing mix to fit a given place in our customer or consumer's mind. Using marketing research we should establish the position of our competitor's products in any given market segment and then determine how to position our products in the most favourable way.

3.0 New Product Development stages

The benefit of utilising a NPD approach is to gain advantage in a competitive marketplace in the quickest time possible and to co-ordinate the contributing activities in the most effective and least costly way. It also allows for the process to be managed and all risks to by identified and controlled throughout the NPD stages. There are eight steps in the NPD process.

Idea generation
Systematic and structured to capture all sources
|
Idea screening
Devise a method to rationalise, based on market potential
|
Concept development and testing
Convert ideas into meaningful consumer terms
and test with targeted audience
|
Business analysis
Determine forecasted sales, costs and profit levels
Relate to corporate objectives
|
Product development
Develop the concept into prototypes
and pre-production samples for product evaluation
|
Test marketing
Following successful functional and consumer testing,
the product is introduced into more realistic market analysis
|
Launch
Full scale commitment to commercialise product
Timing, targeted roll-out markets and planning considerations

4.0 Marketing mix for the launch programme

The marketing mix element to be considered are product, price and distribution applied to the case for both the industrial and consumer markets.

4.1 Industrial market

4.1.1 Product

The battery should be designed with long lasting characteristics and appearances so as to be accepted by the business to business segments. It should be perceived to be of high quality otherwise it would not generate enough sales for the company because these days, everyone wants quality and long lasting batteries for use. The product will have to be adapted to fit our various business customers needs. The capacity, size, weight etc will vary for mobile communications, power tools and computer based companies.

4.1.2 Distribution

We will have to secure adequate transportation and supply to get our product to the customers directly. It any of the business customers are following "Just in Time" production, we may have to synchronize our production/distribution to meet their needs – perhaps through an electronic data interchange or extranet.

4.1.3 Price

Our relationship with our customers will have to be considered. The long term gain for EBC will benefit the organisation more than a short term skimming strategy.

4.2 Consumer market

4.2.1 Product

A variety of different sized batteries will need to be available to suit various consumer needs. Small batteries for cameras and Walkmans, and larger batteries for toys.

4.2.2 Distribution

It is very important that our products are stocked in retail outlets that can be supported by the distribution system. Different retailers will have different product demands which will be reflected by their differing customer profiles.

4.2.3 Price

The development costs and the position of the product in the PLC determines a skimming pricing strategy to maximise revenue.

5.0 Conclusion

To summarise, I have described the use of market segmentation, the new product development process and different marketing mix programmes for the launch of the EPS range of rechargeable batteries. We should now collectively consider the implications within the Marketing department.

PART B

Question 2

REPORT

**Children's clothing manufacturer
New Channels of Distribution**

To: Mr Percy Basil, Managing Director

From: Miss Josephine-Anne Foley, Marketing Assistant

Report Contents

1.0   Introduction

2.0   Alternative distribution channels

3.0   Selecting Distribution channels

4.0   Measurement of distribution channel performance

5.0   Conclusion

1.0 Introduction

This report has been prepared to review potential opportunities for new channels of distribution.

2.0 Alternative distribution channels

It is a growing trend that many producers do not sell directly to the final consumer. Instead the majority of goods and services move from producer to user through a series of intermediaries, who perform a variety of functions. Collectively these intermediaries are known as the distribution channel and provide a link between production and consumption. They can undertake a range of key functions

2.1 Completing the transaction

Information. Gathering and distributing marketing research and intelligence information

Promotion. Developing and distributing marketing communications materials

Contact. Sourcing and communicating with prospective buyers

Matching. Shaping and fitting the offer to the buyer's need

Negotiation. Reaching agreement on the terms of supply including price, delivery and quality requirements

2.2 Fulfilling the transaction

Physical distribution. Transporting and storage of goods

Financing. Acquiring funds to cover cost of the channel work

Risk taking. Assumes the risk of carrying out the channel work

The choice we have to consider is do we want to undertake these activities or incorporate them into the activities of the distribution channel.

Distribution channels are characterised by the number of levels involved in the intermediary activity. These range from a direct marketing channel that has no intermediaries, where we would sell direct to the consumer to an indirect approach using multiple intermediate levels.

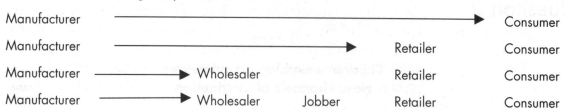

Normally we would expect to sell via the retailer but we may consider the other channels, such as using a jobber who buys from wholesalers and deals directly with smaller outlets. The direct route to the consumer may include using various communication routes such as catalogue, mail order, telephone or the Internet. Also we may consider setting up branded retail outlets for our products as an alternative route to market.

3.0 Selecting distribution channels

The key issues that the Marketing department will have to consider in selecting the most appropriate distribution channel are as follows:

Target segments. The marketers need to consider whether the new channel would offer good coverage of the target segment. It is also important to consider what qualities of relationship distributors within the channel have established with their customers. Selecting an inappropriate channel or channel member can result in the failure of the entire marketing strategy.

Organisation objectives. The organisation' marketing objectives must fit with the gaols of the new channel. It is also important to ensure that the channel has the capability to deliver the required orders to secure the organisation's objectives. The required length of the relationship with the channel partners must also be considered.

Cost of distribution. This is a significant proportion of an organisation's marketing costs. It is imperative to ensure that the selection process produces the most efficient and effective solution for our company to deliver and meet the customer's expectations. Identifying newer and lower cost for distribution can significantly improve profitability but this will need to be traded off, ensuring that customer service levels are maintained or improved.

Size and power of channel member. A new channel member may appear attractive initially as a result of its newness. This needs to be evaluated against the negotiating power of channel members. We could end up being squeezed on price with a consequential impact on profitability, even though it may secure larger order quantities.

Competitor's channel choice. The strength of the competitor in the channel needs to be considered. Presence in the channel may still be critical for us, but alternative routes to market may offer more attractive long term prospects if direct competition is avoided.

Expertise of channel member. It is vital to our organisation that the new channel member has the necessary technical expertise to satisfactorily distribute the electrical components. This is a key consideration if the channel member is to effectively sell and service our children's clothing product range.

Ability to handle tasks. It is necessary for the distributor to be able to provide adequate sales force coverage and activity, the required service level, stock handling and administrative expertise. In effectiveness in these areas will result in dissatisfied customers and poor performance levels.

4.0 Measurement of distribution channel performance

Having arrived at a strategic channel choice, we must act to implement, evaluate and control this strategy. The important element of this activity is to ensure that we can readily measure performance compared to the planned target, which should also be related to the company's objectives. We would use a number of metrics that relate to customer service levels regarding order fulfilment and availability, and distribution channel performance. These would also include sales value and volume, margin and profitability, brand awareness, returns and mark downs, new product trail and repeat purchase at the garment item level and within each clothing range. The management information would enable us to control and react in a timely manner to changes in the customers' requirements.

5.0 Conclusion

I have reviewed the prospects that new channels of distribution would offer us in response to our planned growth of the business and would welcome the opportunity to discuss this matter further.

Question 3

REPORT

The extended marketing mix to be adopted by a hotel
and
ICT added value provision

To: Mr Tony Lap, Hotel Managing Director

From: Miss Rachael Thomas, Group Marketing Director

(a) The extended marketing mix to be adopted by a hotel

In marketing its services a hotel group with 75 locations within England and Wales will need to consider the extended marketing mix which relates to product, place, price, promotion, people, process and physical evidence. The hotel will need to consider the following points when making their decisions about the marketing mix.

Product

What is the core customer need and determine what is the basic service that is required to meet this? The augmented service should meet or preferably exceed customer expectations. Continual monitoring of the services in relation to changing customer needs is necessary to ensure relevance of the product offering. For instance, is satellite (as well as terrestrial) TV required in all the bedrooms?

Price

How much should the service cost the customer and what pricing strategy the hotel should use are important considerations. An understanding of the pricing policy of the competition is crucial to evaluate how the price would affect market share and the volumes of customers using the hotel. An assessment of supplementing additional features to the base offering that would justify different prices for different segments of the market. This could be as a result of the hotel differentiating its pricing strategy between business and leisure customers.

BPP
PUBLISHING

Promotion

Determining what is the most effective means of promoting the hotel's services to its customers is important here. Nationwide above the line advertising or localised, more personalise promotions could be considered. One possibility is for the hotel to use advertising only and rely on word of mouth from existing customers to promote a quality service.

Place

The hotel needs to consider the location and additional facilities such as car parking capacity.

People (Staff)

Staff must be polite, friendly, attentive and helpful. For a hotel the impression that customers receive from the staff significantly contributes to the perception of a quality service. This is particularly important where the front of house staff deal with queries from customers that are out of the norm but receive a satisfactory response. Staff must be able to handle complaints and deal efficiently with customer concerns, must be trained to work the administrative systems and must embrace the marketing orientated philosophy. All staff are ambassadors of the hotel, from the Reception area to Catering to Housekeeping, and it is vital that they satisfy the customer in every way. It is the level of service from the staff that the customer will remember.

Processes

All systems supporting the front line staff must be efficient to avoid errors and time delays. This includes accessing the reservation system through the Internet or through direct telephone contact and final billing. Any process that causes the customer to wait for any amount of time is likely to have an adverse effect on perceived customer service.

Physical Evidence

The hotel's infrastructure should continue to remain modern and should be professional to convey the image of a quality service to the customer. The brand needs to be supported and communicated through the brand values. Front line staff should have uniforms with the corporate logo to communicate a quality service. Business cards, customer bills, invoices should include the brand name and portray the values of the organisation – contributing to the brand values. The hotels corporate colours and logos should be present on all forms of communication.

(b) **Examine the part played by new information and communications technology in providing additional value for the customers of your chosen organisation.**

The effective use of ICT would come into two main areas, which are firstly to help facilitate market research for the hotel and secondly to offer an enhanced customer friendly services whilst at the hotel.

ICT and Marketing Research; This could include monitoring user frequencies, sales data, conducting surveys via the Internet, researching competitors by viewing their websites, conducting telephone surveys to establish both business customer and private customer satisfaction levels. In addition a database could be set up to make best use of the customer information that is already available to the hotel. This would help to achieve their objective and retaining customers by employing relationship marketing techniques. Data could be collected for instance via Internet registration forms and used to establish preferences that would subsequently be used for specific targeting and planning new products. An effective marketing information system could be set up within the hotel to gain a greater understanding of customer expectations and needs.

ICT and Customer Services; The hotel could improve Internet services for customers by offering them good levels of information about new products and current and future promotional offers, such as special weekend rates for loyal customers or discounted regular user rates. Text messaging in relation to customer information could be used for those customers who have access to mobile technology. The key element to becoming marketing orientated is the recognition that identifying, anticipating and satisfying customer requirements is vital. Information technology should be utilised effectively to support this, such as implementing a central call-handling reservation system linked to each hotel location. This would help to ensure that calls are placed in the appropriate queues so that response times and quantity of telephone traffic can be monitored to ensure adequate resources are in place to meet customer demand.

Question 4

REPORT

The advantages of marketing
and
ethical and social responsibility
for
a global car manufacturer

To: Mr Stephen Barrow, CEO

From: Miss Marie Ann Neary, Global Marketing Director

(a) **Explain what you understand to be the advantages of marketing to both consumers and business organisations.**

The term marketing is generally understood to mean satisfying customer demand, which by implication suggests satisfying human needs. It is from that premise that we start to understand how marketing can be related to consumer and business organisations. The core concepts are described below:

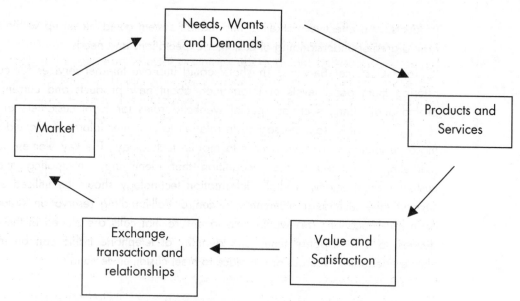

Needs, Wants and Demands; People and organisations have many complex needs that include basic needs such as security, comfort and food, social needs such as belonging and affection and individual needs such as knowledge. Wants are shaped by culture and individual personality. The ability to access these needs by people and organisations is determined by buying capability. Consumers view products as bundles of benefits and choose according to value. A mass produced family saloon represents a basic level of transportation, low price and fuel economy whilst a luxury saloon means comfort, status and exclusivity.

Products; These are a combination of goods and services that provide the augmented offering for the customer. There is the potential to capture a wide array of needs, wants and demands from across different regions of the world through a carefully and skilfully targeted car design brief that offer choice, value and innovation. Common component producers are selected for their ability to supply specialised global car assembly plants.

Value and satisfaction; This is determined by the capacity of each product to satisfy the customer's total demands from wherever the requirement is generated across the globe.

Exchange, transactions and relationships; As a means of satisfying needs of the customer the cost of the car must be able to deliver those perceived values. The ultimate measure of satisfaction is not only to capture the sale of a customer, but retain the customer with repeat sales over time. Building long-term relationships with valued customers, distributors, dealers and suppliers is vital to sustaining a successful business. The global car business must build strong economic and social ties by promising and consistently delivering high quality products, good after sales service and fair prices.

Market; These include actual and potential buyers. In order to maintain and develop a presence in the global market and to fulfil our organisation's objectives of profit, sales growth and improved market share we will need to provide benefits through features to meet customer requirements. Examples would be incorporating safety standards such a protection zone, air bags and safety belts as a minimum requirement for all markets.

(b) **Identify some of the ethical and social responsibility issues that face modern marketers**

Responsible marketers discover what consumers want and respond with the right products priced to give good value to buyers and profit to the producer. The economical argument is that the forces of supply and demand, with the overriding requirement of profit determine a market's performance. However in more recent times consumers of products such as cars are much more interested in the ethical and social responsibility stance of businesses concerned. For a global car manufacturer operating and supplying markets with a wide variety of cultural and moral values it is important to take these considerations seriously. For instance what is seen as acceptable in Europe may not be seen as acceptable in the Asian sub continent. For marketers this translates into communicating the positive impact on society at large and minimising any adverse comment. As an example the behaviour of the organisation impacting on the exploitation of third world resources to minimise costs of production has to be managed by marketers in the global economy.

Products and services are now designed to reflect a growing consciousness and concern with the damage that is being done to the natural environment through pollution and resource depletion. Evidence of the growth of ethical and social responsibility can be given utilising a communications mix to demonstrate good practice, such as with lower emission vehicles and the high use of recyclable materials in producing cars. Marketers have also to manage influential pressure groups and the green movement as a whole in order to maintain awareness of the positive ethical stance of a global car manufacturer to society at large. World events can easily overtake a large multinational organisation with a reputation of an uncaring capitalist business driven only by profit.

Question 5

REPORT

MEMORANDUM

TO:	Marketing Manager
FROM:	Gary Davis, Marketing Partner
DATE:	4th June 2002
SUBJECT:	The Market Planning Approach

1.0 The steps involved in the marketing planning process

In order to plan the marketing mix effectively, a systematic marketing planning process must be undertaken on a regular basis. The seven steps involved are as follows:

1.1 Corporate objectives

These decide on a mission statement and set the corporate objectives. In the case of the TV and Hi-Fi business the corporate objectives would describe the strategy to be adopted and the measures for the corporate objectives.

1.2 **Marketing audit analysis:**

1.2.1 **PEST** stands for Political, Economic, Social/cultural and Technological factors.

Political factors such as changes in government and the ramifications of their strategies such as tax levels, pollution policies, education issues, increased regulation, etc.

Economic factors such as the impact of the trade cycle, disposable income distribution and changes in purchasing power, inflation, changing consumer spending, etc

Social/cultural issues such as the ageing consumer, increases in one parent families, changing values, attitudes and beliefs to smoking for example, the changing family sizes, role of women, education of people etc.

Technological factors such as the increased rate of computer capability, production methods, etc. that may have an impact on the way customers shop.

1.2.2 **SWOT analysis**

This analysis helps the marketer understand the environment in which the organisation is operating and thus the marketing plan can be devised taking account of the issues identified.

Internal to business	**STRENGTHS**	**WEAKNESSES**
External business environment	**OPPORTUNITIES**	**THREATS**

Strengths and weaknesses are internal factors and form part of the internal marketing audit. We should look at all departments here such as finance, sales, research and development.

Opportunities and threats are external factors over which we have no control.

■ Strengths of the product/ service/ organisation

■ Weaknesses of the organisation

■ Opportunities available to the organisation (external factors)

■ Threats that may come from the competitions or other external factors.

It is also important that a SWOT analysis is undertaken to help plan the marketing mix.

1.3 **Marketing objectives set.** These determine what the business wants to achieve and should have SMART objectives – specific, measurable, achievable, real and timed.

1.4 **Marketing strategy.** This needs to identify the broad target customer perspective and consider the following.

A vital part of this activity is the process of target marketing involving segmentation – what are the key variables, targeting – who are the targets and positioning for the selected brand or the product.

The Ansoff matrix helps to identify the most appropriate strategy to be adopted based on product and market requirements. The matrix is:

Product

		Present	New
Market	Present	Market penetration	Product development
	New	Market development	Diversification

1.5 **Tactics** – this step plans the more detailed marketing mix tactics

Pricing policy, these can be through skimming the market with a high price or through selecting a lower price to gain the greatest market penetration within the segment.

Product policy and brand determines the quality levels, features required for the Hi-Fi and TV equipment together with the available options and potential new product development.

Place or distribution (logistics and channel management). This includes selecting the most suitable channel configuration, type of intermediaries and order processing systems.

Promotion includes the mix of advertising, sales promotion, public relations, direct marketing, personal selling, sponsorship etc

People –staff development, motivation, etc

Processes – customer friendly systems, customer care, etc

Physical evidence – uniforms, corporate logo, etc

1.6 **Implementation** of the plan. The required organisational resources need to be committed to the programme together with sufficient staff training to allow for a well managed activity.

1.7 **Monitoring and Control**

The methods to monitor via achievement of objectives on a regular basis need to be established and maintained to ensure a successful conclusion. The measures need to be responsive such that alterations to the marketing mix can be implemented. Any shortfall can be corrected in order that achievement of the objectives can occur.

2.0 **Marketing budget considerations**

The Marketing Budget is the planned allocation of costs within each of the product types for all the resources to be consumed in delivering the planned sales. It is important that the marketing budget relates directly to the business objectives and in particular is dovetailed into the overall business plan. Budgets should be flexible to allow for changing conditions or unforeseen circumstances. It can then be quickly changed to cover for such contingencies.

The budget should include a number elements listed below

2.1 **Schedule of financial requirements**

These will include all staff, materials including raw materials and consumables, and equipment needed to sustain the marketing activity. The equipment could include company cars, office equipment, mobile phones and laptop computers. There will be budgets for both the purchase of the capital equipment and for its use as revenue expenditure. The budgets will need to planned over the period of time of the marketing plan. A proportion of the budgets will cover the fixed costs for each period and the remainder of the budget will be phased over the predicted sales using the product life cycle as a guide. This will take into account the increased activity in the introduction and growth stages but will act as a constraining mechanism for expenditure during the maturity and decline stages as profit is planned to reduce.

2.2 Other resources

There are other non-personal considerations that are not directly related to sales but would be part of the communications strategy. This would include advertising, public relations, sales promotions and direct mailing. The promotional activity would be planned with contingency budgets to be used if required to raise awareness if there is a shortfall in planned sales or to sustain better than expected results during the middle and latter stages of the product life cycle. With the Hi-Fi and TV business, sales are often dependant on the general economic climate and skewed with year end sales prior to Christmas. Together with new product introductions all these influences will also need to be considered when the marketing budgets are constructed.

The marketing budget also applies to other marketing expenditures such as intermediary and dealer support within the channels of distribution. Where there extended third party channels a significant amount of management time will be directed to ensuring targeted customer service performance levels are achieved. Also other areas such as the market research activity, possibly utilising specialist companies will need to be considered in the budgeting process.

2.3 Measures

The normal assessment will relate to actual versus planned performance shown as variance reporting for each of the listed budgeted activities. These will indicate performance to date and predicted alterations if required to achieve year-end plans. There will also be some financial ratio analysis such as % sales and gross margin for the product ranges. The reporting system will normally highlight where there are highly and poorly performing product lines as a separate report so that further analysis can be undertaken

This memo has covered the requirements of a marketing plan and examined the factors to be considered in setting a marketing budget.

Question 6

REPORT

To: Managing Director

From: Arfon Jones, Marketing Manager

Date: 4th June 2002

Subject: The Product Life Cycle

1.0   Contents

2.0   Introduction

3.0   Marketing mix and PLC

4.0   Pricing decisions

5.0 Conclusion

1.0   Introduction

The Product Life Cycle describes the stages that a good or service follows in their growth and development. This concept is useful in many ways as we can decide on variables of a marketing mix, it allows us to predict sales and profit over the life of the goods or service and it also allows us to adapt different strategies during the different phases.

Sales

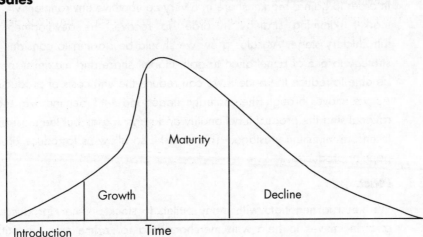

1.1   Introduction stage

When the product is introduced to the market, prices are high, demand is low, there are few competitors, promotional costs are high and the product is not widely available. Profits are usually negative at this stage.

1.2   Growth stage

Here, sales begin to pick up, prices fall, more competitors enter the marketing, promotional costs focus on the brand identify, the product is more widely available and profits begin to be make early in this stage and maximise towards the end of this stage.

1.3   Maturity stage

The level of demand peaks and even begins to fall, there are many competitors and prices are generally low. Distribution is wide and promotion is focused on retaining existing customers.

1.4   Decline stage

The rate of decrease in sales begins to increase. Prices will tend to change – either increase or decrease as unit costs increase. Competitors pull out of the marketing as the profits become low (if there are any). Distribution becomes more difficult as retailers stop stocking the product as new products are more popular with customers.

BPP
PUBLISHING

2.0 **Marketing mix and PLC**

The marketing mix for our computing software house needs to be adapted as it appears to be moving through to the decline stage of the product life cycle.

2.1 **Product**

The product has been tested and is launched into the market in the introduction phase. In the growth stage the product has gain market acceptance and is satisfying customer requirements. Sales reach peak in maturity and the product is no longer as much in demand as similar ranges of competitors offering. We could consider changing the offering slightly at this stage, but we do not want to spend too much of enhancing this product though – it may be more effective to leave it as it is, giving the customers the choice, but introducing a new line of an alternative range.

2.2 **Price**

In order to gain a market share in a very competitive environment we may look at a market skimming strategy in order to recover the development costs in the introductory stage. As sales grow we should be starting to consider modifying the strategy to one of penetration to gain market share and maximise profits. We may be able to reduce the price if we can reduce the unit costs of producing this range. As we move through the maturity stage and into decline we should consider rationalising the product functionality and removing all but the most popular ranges to ensure minimum wastage. This would also allow us to reduce production to the popular products.

2.3 **Place**

We need to negotiate with many outlets to stock our new products and perhaps offer incentives to help with merchandising for prime spots in outlets. As sales continue to grow we need to review the more costly channels of distribution and consider some rationalisation of existing outlets and also alternative routes to market. At maturity we need to be more efficient in our distribution and consider only supplying product through a limited number of cost effective outlets.

2.4 **Promotion**

At the introduction stage we will need to invest heavily in advertising to both the trade and consumer customers. Targeting trade journals, use of the Internet and appropriate newspapers are important. Promotion levels in the growth and maturity will depend on the level of promotion by the competition, although awareness of product developments will need to be communicated to the targeted publics. As the decline phase is reached it is too late in the PLC to consider large-scale promotion of this product to the customer. It may be possible to try and shift some of the existing outlets of the less popular ranges to retailers who are likely to sell at a discounted price. This also ties in with cutting distribution costs.

3.0 **Pricing decisions**

It is through pricing that a company covers the costs of separate elements of its various activities: research and development, raw materials, labour and equipment and overhead charges. The price charged for the product is required to generate additional funds in excess of these costs to meet company profit objectives. The pricing decisions should be related to and be consistent with the other elements of the marketing mix.

3.1 Internal considerations

There are a number of internal organisation factors that influence pricing decisions.

3.1.1 Cost; Prices are sets to generate sufficient profit over production and marketing costs. These are determined by economic considerations that provides ease of accounting control

3.1.2 Profit Margin; Normally mark-up pricing but can be related to contribution of fixed cost overhead pricing. The relationship between changes in profit margin and impact on volume of sales necessary to maintain profit levels is a critical consideration.

3.1.3 Market forces; Price set against prevailing supply and demand market conditions. Distorted, controlled or monopoly power will enable higher prices to be adopted.

3.1.4 Customer; Segment the market and price by what the market will bear. This relies on a close understanding of market and customer.

3.1.5 Objectives; Pricing strategy designed to support organisation's overall marketing and business objectives.

3.2 External considerations

These relate to the external influences of pricing decisions

3.2.1 Income; The level of disposable income will influence a consumer's purchase behaviour in terms of attitude towards products at different price points

3.2.2 Value; Whilst cost is an important consideration, value for money can be a more appropriate factor to consider. Consumers utilise non-rational reasoning for value such as status and image.

3.2.3 Promotions; These should be consistent with the customer's perception of brand values and positioning considerations.

4.0 Conclusion

This report will give us a better understanding of the issues involved in the product life cycle and pricing considerations. Please do not hesitate to contact me for further information.

Question 7

REPORT

Importance of Branding for a financial services company

and

relationship Marketing

To: Mr John Furnell, Managing Director

From: Miss Fran Hinderer, Marketing Assistant

Report Contents

1.0   Importance of Branding

2.0   Relationship Marketing

3.0   Conclusion

1.0 Importance of branding

A brand is a name, term, sign, symbol, design or combination of these that is used to identify the goods or services of one seller to differentiate them from those of the competition. Thus the brand identifies the maker or supplier of a product. A brand conveys a specific set of features, benefits and services to buyers. These can be:

1.1   **Attributes**; a brand first brings to mind certain product attributes. For a financial services company it relates to the ease of access to funds at competitive rates

1.2   **Benefits**; Customers do not buy attributes, they buy benefits. Hence attributes must be translated into functional and emotional benefits. This may relate to access of a better lifestyle through buying a better car or a recreational purchase such as a boat or holiday-of-a-lifetime.

1.3   **Values**; A brand also says something about the buyer's values. Thus purchasing a desirable lifestyle accessory must be managed through a responsible approach to repayment related to the desired benefits of the purchase.

1.4   **Personality**; A brand also projects a personality. The brand will attract potential customers whose actual or desired self-images match the brand's images.

A powerful brand has strong brand loyalty, name awareness, perceived quality, and strong brand associations. Marketers need to manage their brands carefully in order to preserve its equity. This requires continuous investment to provide a constant flow of improved and innovative products to satisfy customer's ever-changing needs. This must be supplement with skilful advertising, and excellent trade and consumer service.

Branding helps buyers in a number of ways. Brand names tell the buyer something about product quality. Buyers who always buy the same brand know that they will get the same quality each time they buy. Brand names also increase the shopper's efficiency for selecting differentiated products and they also help draw customer's attention to new products that might benefit them. The brand name becomes the basis upon which a consumer evaluates their decision making process about the new product's special properties.

Branding increases innovation by giving producers an incentive to look for new features that can be protected against imitating competitors. Branding results in more product variety and choice for consumers. For a financial services provider such as a bank it vitally important that they embrace the attributes of their brand to maximise their offering and protect their customer base. Differentiating their provision will protect and strengthen the loyalty to the brand by customers.

2.0 Relationship Marketing

For any organisation it is more efficient to keep customers rather than finding new ones, thus relationship marketing is important. A happy customer will come back for more. Over two thirds of people will go elsewhere if they received an indifferent service. This clearly indicates that there is room for improvement in this area for most companies.

Relationship marketing is a long-term approach to creating, maintaining and enhancing strong relationships with customers and other stakeholders. Organisations need to view any transaction as part of a long-term goal since if the customer is satisfied with the product/service they have received for the price they have paid they are more likely to return. A short-term outlook will consider a quick profit but not consider repeat purchases.

There are five different distinguishable levels or relationships that can be formed with customers who have purchased a company's product. They are:

(i)   **Basic** – Selling a product without any follow up

(ii)   **Reactive** – Selling a product with follow up encouraged on the part of the customer

(iii)   **Accountable** – Having sold a product the follow up occurs a short afterwards to confirm the customer's expectations have been met

(iv)   **Proactive** – The sales person contact the customer from time to time with suggestions regarding improved products

(v)   **Partnership** – The Company work continuously with the customer to deliver improved levels of value

For a bank to develop a relationship marketing orientation there is a five step approach that can be adopted.

1.   Identify the customers meriting this relationship. These could on a rotating annual review schedule

2.   Assign a skilled Relationship Manager to each customer who can tailor the needs and requirements of each customer to the banks offering

3.   Develop a clear job description for Relationship Managers. Describe there reporting relationships, objectives, responsibilities and evaluation criteria.

4.   Have each Relationship Manager develop annual and long range customer relationship plans

5.   Appoint an overall manager to supervise the RM Team

3.0 **Conclusion**

If a customer trusts an organisation they will have been treated well and are more likely to return. But trust is a two-way process. The business can trust its customers; they may offer a better deal. Loyal customers will spread the good news about a company and may even champion it. Loyalty is part of the long term, win-win trusting relationship an organisation should seek. Effective relationship marketing (RM) will give your product a clear and distinctive voice thus maintaining loyalty.

Topic Index

BPP
PUBLISHING

BPP PUBLISHING

Mr/Mrs/Ms (Full name)

Daytime delivery address

Postcode

Date of exam (month/year)

Daytime Tel

	8/02 Texts	9/02 Kits	Success Tapes (old syllabus)
STAGE 1 NEW SYLLABUS			
1 Marketing Fundamentals	£18.95 ☐	£9.95 ☐	£12.95 ☐
2 Marketing Environment	£18.95 ☐	£9.95 ☐	£12.95 ☐
3 Customer Communications	£18.95 ☐	£9.95 ☐	£12.95 ☐
4 Marketing in Practice	£18.95 ☐	£9.95 ☐	£12.95 ☐
ADVANCED CERTIFICATE OLD SYLLABUS *			
5 The Marketing Customer Interface	£18.95 ☐	£9.95 ☐	£12.95 ☐
6 Management Information for Marketing Decisions	£18.95 ☐	£9.95 ☐	£12.95 ☐
7 Effective Management for Marketing	£18.95 ☐	£9.95 ☐	£12.95 ☐
8 Marketing Operations	£18.95 ☐	£9.95 ☐	£12.95 ☐
DIPLOMA OLD SYLLABUS *			
9 Integrated Marketing Communications	£18.95 ☐	£9.95 ☐	£12.95 ☐
10 International Marketing Strategy	£18.95 ☐	£9.95 ☐	£12.95 ☐
11 Strategic Marketing Management: Planning and Control	£18.95 ☐	£9.95 ☐	£12.95 ☐
12 Strategic Marketing Management: Analysis and Decision (9/02)	£25.95 ☐	N/A	N/A

* Texts and kits for remaining new syllabus items will be available in the spring and summer of 2003.

SUBTOTAL £ ☐

POSTAGE & PACKING

Study Texts

	First	Each extra	
UK	£3.00	£2.00	£ ☐
Europe*	£5.00	£4.00	£ ☐
Rest of world	£20.00	£10.00	£ ☐

Kits/Success Tapes

	First	Each extra	
UK	£2.00	£1.00	£ ☐
Europe*	£2.50	£1.00	£ ☐
Rest of world	£15.00	£8.00	£ ☐

Grand Total (Cheques to *BPP Publishing*) I enclose
a cheque for (incl. Postage)   £ ☐

Or charge to Access/Visa/Switch

Card Number ☐☐☐☐☐☐☐☐☐☐

Expiry date ☐☐☐☐   Start Date ☐☐☐☐

Issue Number (Switch Only) ☐☐

Signature

We aim to deliver to all UK addresses inside 5 working days. A signature will be required. Orders to all EU addresses should be delivered within 6 working days.

All other orders to overseas addresses should be delivered within 8 working days.

* Europe includes the Republic of Ireland and the Channel Islands.

REVIEW FORM & FREE PRIZE DRAW

All original review forms from the entire BPP range, completed with genuine comments, will be entered into one of two draws on 31 January 2003 and 31 July 2003. The names on the first four forms picked out on each occasion will be sent a cheque for £50.

Name: _____   Address: _____

_____

_____

How have you used this Kit?
(Tick one box only)

☐ Home study (book only)

☐ On a course: college _____

☐ With 'correspondence' package

☐ Other _____

Why did you decide to purchase this Kit?
(Tick one box only)

☐ Have used complementary Study Text

☐ Have used BPP Kits in the past

☐ Recommendation by friend/colleague

☐ Recommendation by a lecturer at college

☐ Saw advertising

☐ Other _____

During the past six months do you recall seeing/receiving any of the following?
(Tick as many boxes as are relevant)

☐ Our advertisement in *Marketing Success*

☐ Our advertisement in *Marketing Business*

☐ Our brochure with a letter through the post

☐ Our brochure with *Marketing Business*

Which (if any) aspects of our advertising do you find useful?
(Tick as many boxes as are relevant)

☐ Prices and publication dates of new editions

☐ Information on Kit content

☐ Facility to order books off-the-page

☐ None of the above

Have you used the companion Study Text for this subject?   ☐ Yes   ☐ No

Your ratings, comments and suggestions would be appreciated on the following areas

	Very useful	Useful	Not useful
Introductory section (Study advice, key questions checklist, etc)	☐	☐	☐
'Do you know' checklists	☐	☐	☐
Tutorial questions	☐	☐	☐
Examination-standard questions	☐	☐	☐
Content of suggested answers	☐	☐	☐
Quiz	☐	☐	☐
Test paper	☐	☐	☐
Structure and presentation	☐	☐	☐

	Excellent	Good	Adequate	Poor
Overall opinion of this Kit	☐	☐	☐	☐

Do you intend to continue using BPP Study Texts/Kits?   ☐ Yes   ☐ No

Please note any further comments and suggestions/errors on the reverse of this page.

Please return to: Kate Machattie, BPP Publishing Ltd, FREEPOST, London, W12 8BR

REVIEW FORM & FREE PRIZE DRAW (continued)

Please note any further comments and suggestions/errors below

FREE PRIZE DRAW RULES

1   Closing date for 31 January 2003 draw is 31 December 2002. Closing date for 31 July 2003 draw is 30 June 2003.

2   Restricted to entries with UK and Eire addresses only. BPP employees, their families and business associates are excluded.

3   No purchase necessary. Entry forms are available upon request from BPP Publishing. No more than one entry per title, per person. Draw restricted to persons aged 16 and over.

4   Winners will be notified by post and receive their cheques not later than 6 weeks after the relevant draw date.

5   The decision of the promoter in all matters is final and binding. No correspondence will be entered into.